A Heart of Wisdom

CONTRIBUTORS

MarthaJoy Aft
Phyllis Ocean Berman
Susan Berrin
Paul Citrin
Thomas R. Cole
Ruth Daigon
Eliezer Diamond
Maggie Dwyer
Ben Engelman
Linda H. Feinberg
Linda Knaster Feldman
Dayle A. Friedman
Everett Gendler
Mary Gendler
Muriel E. Ginsberg
Hillel Goelman
Lynn Greenhough
Suzanne Hodes
Barbara D. Holender

Judith Magyar Isaacson
Norma Baumel Joseph
Marc Kaminsky
Cary Kozberg
Gloria Levi
Sheva Medjuck
Kerry M. Olitzky
Victor Hillel Reinstein
Carol Rose
Joel Rosenberg
Rosie Rosenzweig
Zalman Schachter-Shalomi
Jonathan Segol
Alice Shalvi
Danny Siegel
Rachel Josefowitz Siegel
Elizabeth Anne Sussman Socolow
Marcia Cohn Spiegel
Savina J. Teubal
Mickey Teicher
Anne Tolbert

A Heart of Wisdom

Making the Jewish Journey
from Midlife Through the Elder Years

Edited and with Introductions by
Susan Berrin

Foreword by
Harold Kushner

JEWISH LIGHTS PUBLISHING

A Heart of Wisdom: Making the Jewish Journey from Midlife through the Elder Years

2000 First Quality Paperback Edition

Permission credit information appears on p. 322.

Library of Congress Cataloging-in-Publication Data
A heart of wisdom : making the Jewish journey from midlife through the elder years / edited and with introductions by Susan Berrin ; foreword by Harold Kushner.
p.   cm.
Includes bibliographical references and index.
ISBN 1-879045-73-7 (hc)
ISBN 1-58023-051-2 (pb)
1. Aging—Religious aspects—Judaism. 2. Respect for persons. 3. Jewish aged—Religious life. I. Berrin, Susan.
BM540.A35H43   1997
296.7'084'6—dc21   97-25581
                                                                    CIP

Manufactured in the United States of America
Cover design: Karen Savary
Text design: Sans Serif Inc.

www.jewishlights.com

For my mother and father, Vera and Harry Berrin,
who have given me the ageless gifts of patience,
compassion,and love.

CONTENTS

ACKNOWLEDGMENTS

When I first began soliciting material for *A Heart of Wisdom*, several people wondered why I had asked them to contribute to a book about growing older. This rebuff provided me with an opportunity to launch into a discourse about aging as a lifelong experience, not just as a phenomenon of our latter years. Growing older is a process that must be acknowledged because we spend more of our lives being "old" than we do being infants, toddlers, or adolescents. I hope that this anthology—which includes Jewish texts and thought on aging as well as personal, reflective essays, stories, and poetry—will encourage everyone, regardless of where they are along the continuum of aging, to engage consciously in this experience. While we are always growing older, our first awareness and acknowledgment of aging often comes at midlife. I have chosen, therefore, to include in this volume material from midlife onward.

With gratitude to those who have helped make this anthology possible, I welcome you along the path.

I want to thank Harold Reinstein for his photographic assistance and Nathan Ehrlich, who walked me patiently through computer crises.

Estelle Latchman acted as my extra set of eyes for pertinent aging resources, and Sam Seicol, Chaplain at the Hebrew Rehabilitation Center for Aged in Boston, provided support and assistance.

I am grateful to friends and colleagues whose suggestions have enriched this book: Mona Fishbane, Peninnah Schram, Suzanne Kort, Maxine Lyons, Barbara Moscowitz, Rosie Rosenzweig, and Victor Reinstein.

I would also like to thank Jewish Lights Publishing, especially Sandra Korinchak, whose friendly voice on the other end of the telephone has been a constant source of willing assistance, and my editor, Arthur Magida, whose insights have helped clarify and distill the meaning of this work.

I am sincerely indebted to each contributor to this volume, who so willingly joined me in exploring this uncharted terrain—a landscape of peril and promise.

My thanks also to:

My grandparents, who, although they died before I reached adulthood, and thus, before I could know and appreciate them fully, introduced me to the varied lives of Jewish elderly: Ida and Nathan Latchman, and Faigel and Israel Berrin. Rebecca Rabinovitz, who became my *bubbe* through marriage, died recently at age 95. Her indomitable spirit and sense of self challenged my earlier assumptions about aging. We often talked and cooked together during my weekly visits to Boston while commuting to graduate school from my home in Maine.

My children, Noa Chana, Yosef Chaim and Tzvia Raizel, who with patience, understanding and a great deal of pride have learned one of aging's most important lessons: adaptability.

My husband, Victor Reinstein; may we grow old together. In "Rabbi Ben Ezra," Robert Browning wrote, "Grow old along with me! The best is yet to be." So be it.

Susan Berrin

FOREWORD

Harold Kushner

As a rabbi, I come out of a tradition that venerates age and is sometimes uneasy with the immaturity and impetuousness of youth. (I recently ran across these lines in a poem: "I look at the young in all their grace and beauty/And all I can think of is brown-and-serve rolls/Before they are cooked.") So I was not at all troubled by the thought that youth was slipping away from me when I turned thirty. I also didn't feel I was getting old when I turned forty. On the contrary, I felt I was finally leaving an extended "childhood" behind. As a thirty-something rabbi, I had always felt uncomfortable being looked up to as a moral guide and surrogate parent figure by people many years older than I was.

But halfway between my fortieth and fiftieth birthdays, something happened. I calculated that, for the first time in my life, the years behind almost certainly outnumbered the years ahead. I began to write books instead of giving sermons, perhaps out of an unconscious need to be assured that something of me would survive in a permanent state. I not only had to confront my own mortality, I had to confront (somewhat belatedly) the American notion that life peaks between age twenty-five and thirty and begins to decline after that.

Do you doubt that? Try this little experiment. Go into a store where greeting cards are sold, and look at birthday cards for middle-aged men and women. They will almost all be about loss, about life slipping away, about the fact that we are losing our figures and our vigor.

There is perhaps no issue on which Jewish values diverge from American values more sharply than on this one: as we grow older, as we lose physical grace and gain wisdom, as our bodies sag and our souls ripen, does that represent a net gain or a net loss?

There is a story, probably apocryphal, of a reporter interviewing the mystery writer Agatha Christie, whose second husband was a prominent archaeologist, and asking her what it was like to be married to an archaeologist. Ms. Christie is supposed to have replied, "Oh, it's wonderful. The older I get, the more interested he is in me." Even if the exchange never took place, the story is true. It is true because it says something valid about the human condition: Once we get past superficial physical impressions, older people are more interesting than younger ones. Of course we are. We have experienced more, we have met more people and learned from them, the fires of competitiveness have been quenched.

There may have been a time, ages ago, when growing old was less of a challenge than it is today. Sheer survival and living to an old age was a challenge, but those who did were assured of an honored place in society. Life remained essentially the same from generation to generation, and those who had already traveled that road were listened to with reverence and respect as they told us about what lay ahead of us. But in a world such as ours that changes so rapidly, knowledge of the past becomes a useless anachronism. Our grandchildren's world is so different from the one in which we were raised that they see our experience as quaint and exotic but not terribly useful. We are equivalent to generals who concentrate on fighting the last war instead of the next one.

Additionally, in a world that rewards people for being attractive and/or productive, older people past their attractive and productive years, like teenagers who have not yet reached them, are seen as having little value.

We embarrass younger people. We frighten them by foreshadowing what will happen to them as they age, as they leave behind their most desirable years. So they keep their distance from us, impatient with our complaints of physical ailments and our recollection of the "good old days."

And yet growing old will be the lot of virtually all of us (except for those who will die young) and there is perhaps no greater gift that we, the pioneers into the land of the elderly, can give those who will come after us than setting an example of how to grow old thoughtfully, usefully, and gratifyingly. Let us show others how to do it right and let them, for our sakes and for theirs, honor us for it.

The fifth of the Ten Commandments instructs us to "honor your father and your mother that your days may be long upon the land." But there is no evidence that people who are good to their elderly parents live longer than people who aren't. (This commandment, by the way, like the other nine, is addressed to adults with aging parents, not to children.) I would suggest that we understand the commandment to mean that, if we show honor and respect to our parents when they are old, we will be fashioning a world in which we will not have to be afraid of growing old, a world in which length of days will indeed be a reward and not a burden. There can be no greater blasphemy against God's gift to us of life than to see a long life as punishment to be endured or released from.

If society teaches us to see life as an expendable resource, something that gets used up as we live it, then we will be dismayed at the prospect of growing old. Each birthday will send us the message that we have less life remaining than we did a year ago. But suppose we could learn to see life not as something that gets used up but as the accumulation of treasure. Then with every passing year, we would see ourselves as having *more* life than we had the year before, because of all the new insights and experiences that the year had brought us.

Your life is not a bottle of wine that gets used up little

by little with every sip. Your life is like a book. If it is a good book, we enjoy every chapter, but we enjoy the last few chapters most of all, because only then do we realize what the book was really about. And when we have finished it, we say, "I enjoyed it so much, I wish it had gone on longer, but I'm glad to have shared in the story."

A Heart of Wisdom is one book whose stories we all share, for it helps put the latter "chapters" of our lives— the latter half of our lives—in a context that is meaningful and purposeful. It shows that, throughout our lives, we are connected to God, to community, to family, and to ourselves in ways that can surprise and delight, as well as frustrate and annoy. It shows that a good life is a life in which we have learned from what we have experienced and in which others can learn from our wisdom—and in which we are all valued as essential members of our world, from the beginning of our days to the end of our days.

INTRODUCTION

Just as the spiritual journey of the patriarch Abraham and the matriarch Sarah took them into unfamiliar, uncharted territory, growing older takes us into lands that are new and novel. Each of us discovers anew the phenomenon of being old, of having more years behind us than ahead of us, of dealing with frailties and the imminence of death while also taking pride in the accomplishments and legacies of younger generations.

While the experience of growing older varies from person to person and sometimes from generation to generation, how we perceive aging and how we approach it depends, in part, on the prism through which we have viewed the rest of our lives: who we are as we age and who we have been, our passions and goals and how we have satisfied them, the obstacles we have faced and how we have overcome them.

The path from birth to death is as diverse as it is complex. Often, we do not even realize we are aging. We do not wake up one morning to find ourselves "old." It is a gradual, subtle, and continuous process of growth and development, of gains and losses, of surprises and disappointments.

I have often heard of an older person ambling down a shop-lined street. Suddenly, she sees reflected in a store window an elderly person staring back at her. In disbelief, she asks herself, "Who is that old woman? Surely not I!" Our inner structure—our intellect, emotions, and internal frame of reference—may lag ten or twenty years behind our physical aging, since our inner and outer selves do not necessarily age simultaneously. But at every age, we are the full measure of our experiences, the composite of our emotional, physical, spiritual, and intellectual travels since our birth.

As we age we often focus our attention on the deterioration of the body and the mind and on the losses that we have experienced. But growing older also brings infrequently proclaimed gains: developing inner strengths, wisdom, clarity, and often new freedoms. As Rachel Kessler told me at the age of 96, "It takes a lifetime to know oneself." After decades of harvesting and distilling life experiences, we can develop an ability to understand and forgive ourselves and others. Only after acknowledging the inevitable end of life can we understand its full significance. Only as elders can we recognize some of our internal changes, which often simultaneously include a greater sense of dependence (primarily physical) and independence (spiritual).

After years of nurturing love and friendship, of being present for children and grandchildren, friends and lovers, we can discard the unessential and distill the most enduring moments and experiences. This can result in a deeper understanding of love as a sustaining factor in our lives and in new wisdom. As sociologist Monika Ardelt says, "Wisdom-related knowledge is the rediscovery of the significance of old truths through a deeper and more profound understanding."[1] Their growing capacity for reflective thinking allows elders to accept imperfection, which often produces greater empathy and compassion for others.

For many elders, wisdom grows not only through their experiences with others but also through self-reflection. It develops, as they age, through refinement and clarity, minus the distortions of ego. As psychiatrist Allan B. Chinin wrote in *In the Ever After*, "Wisdom develops from self-confrontation and self-mastery."[2] And as the Psalmist wrote, "Number our days that we may attain a heart of wisdom."

A Heart of Wisdom provides an opportunity for the reader to engage with textual sources and analyses, personal voice narratives, poetry, stories, and ceremonies in an effort to understand—from a Jewish perspective—the process of growing older. I hope it will help frame aging in a Jewish context so that as individuals, we can base our own aging and the care we give the elderly on Jewish values, and as a community, we can let our attitudes toward the elderly be informed by Jewish teachings.

HONORING WHAT IS BROKEN

Jewish texts abound with comments on aging. The guide to Jewish textual sources in Appendix I lists text sources about aging from the Torah, Psalms, Proverbs, Talmud, and Midrash. While extensive, it is by no means exhaustive. As the Psalmist proclaims to God, "Cast me not off in my old age." Although deferential treatment toward the elderly originates with the commandment to honor one's parents, Jewish tradition broadens this to include *all* elderly. This reverence is articulated often in Jewish texts, most notably in Leviticus 19:32, "Rise before the gray headed . . . show deference to the old." And it is age, not status, that entitles the individual to respect. In Judaism, even what is "broken" is honored: The first set of tablets that Moses received from God and subsequently smashed was, according to *midrash,* placed in the Ark alongside the whole tablets.[3] The tablets were holy and had not lost their holiness by being broken. And so the elderly, who may be ill or needy, are still whole and holy and deserve our attention and respect.

Jewish tradition teaches that all elders, regardless of their formal learning, have acquired wisdom, simply through the experience of living. Age, then, becomes a metaphor for learning. The word *zaken,* or "elder," is so associated with wisdom that the term has come to refer to anyone who has acquired wisdom, regardless of their age. When Moses felt overwhelmed by his role as leader and beseeched God for help,[4] he was told to gather seventy elders of Israel. Commenting on this instruction, the *Torah Temimah* (Rabbi Baruch HaLevi Epstein), cites a Talmudic teaching: *"Ayn zaken eleh hachacham,"* "There is no elder but one who is wise."[5] In the same Talmudic passage, Rabbi Yossi expands this teaching with a play on words by saying, *"Ayn zaken, eleh mi'shekanah chochmah,"* "There is no elder except one who has acquired wisdom."

Wisdom is hopefully acquired through life experiences. Commenting on Genesis 24:1, "Abraham had become old, he had come through the days," the *Torah Temimah* states, "An ordinary elder, each one according to their values, gathers wisdom and knowledge according to their trials and the events of their many days."[6] Wisdom is developed by distilling ordinary experiences. From the Talmudic teaching that the *zaken* is one who has *acquired* wisdom, Rebbe Nachman of Breslov taught that one should strive to increase wisdom in every stage of living and aging.[7] We are never too old to enrich ourselves or be enriched by a deeper understanding of who we are.

In a teaching on aging as the acquisition of wisdom, Rebbe Nachman poignantly interprets the verse "Let me see your face" as the wrinkled face of age. Boldly twisting the text and understanding, he playfully recasts "Let me see your face" as *haderet panim,* honoring the face of the elder. Obviously, beauty is not limited to the smooth, unlined faces of youth.

NUMBER OUR DAYS

Much of Jewish life revolves around the sanctification of time: marking the sacred passage of each day, week, month, and year. As we age we are neither discharged from the commandment to sanctify time nor dismissed from our partnership with God, one of Whose mystical names is *Atik Yamim*, the "Ancient of Days." Neither the daily, weekly, monthly, or yearly cycles of Jewish living nor the rituals of Jewish life are age-specific. The commandments that give structure to our lives and the rituals that give breath to our encounters do not cease as we age. While the obligation to perform *mitzvot* begins at bar and bat mitzvah, it has no endpoint. Whether we are young, middle-aged, or old, we continue to be engaged in a covenant with God, responsible for sustaining and being sustained by our fragile universe. While our relationship with God certainly changes and matures as we get older, we need not feel that we have ever been abandoned, since God promises, "Even unto your old age I shall endure, for I created you and I shall bear you."[8]

Hopefully, we use the experience of aging to engage with, not distance ourselves, from the world. When she was in her eighties, psychoanalyst and writer Florida Scott Maxwell wrote about her passion and intensity increasing as she grew older: "Age puzzles me. I thought it was a quiet time. . . . Only a few years ago, I enjoyed my tranquillity. Now I am so disturbed by the outer world and by human quality in general that I want to put things right as though I still owed a debt to life."[9]

How we live an individual day often indicates how we live our entire lives. By midlife, by our forties and fifties, of which Victor Hugo wrote, "Forty is the old age of youth; fifty the youth of old age," we begin to focus on and invest for not only our financial and physical security but also, as Rabbi Abraham Joshua Heschel noted in his essay "To Grow in Wisdom," our spiritual, emotional, and intellectual well-being as elders. In his commentary on *Pirkei Avot*, the sixteenth-century mystic Moshe ibn Yehudah HaMachiri also suggests a framework of spiritual investment, portraying the week as a time of preparation and the Shabbat, which corresponds to old age, as a time of harvest. As we age we begin to face the tasks of learning and doing as elders within a world of negotiated choices. In some measure, how we age reflects the nature of our personality: We age as we have lived. Adaptability is essential for positive aging, since change is inherent in the aging process. As elders we learn about increased limits and decreased capabilities, about loss and about the richness of each day.[10] We also face the questions posed by the certain presence of death ahead of us.

"Natural monastery," rather than referring to seclusion in a wooded grove, represents the life state in which physical diminishment and the loss of loved ones have, as clinical gerontologist Jane Thibault has written, "cleared away the obstacles to experiencing and appreciating each moment with its own beauty and/or pain. It was as if life had been stripped down to its barest essentials, so that the real could shine through and be appreciated, even if the real involved pain and suffering."[11] As a life is filled with days, so the day is filled with minutes. How that time is structured and how it takes shape is of critical importance. For religious Jews, each day is punctuated by prayer. For all the elderly, each day is hopefully centered on some task or encounter that enhances a sense of self and connects them with family, friends, personal interests, community, or the larger issues of society.

CARE, COMPANIONSHIP AND COMMUNITY

Women in their sixties and seventies now face a task unparalleled in the history of families. With increased longevity, it is becoming more common for older women, having emptied their nests, to find themselves becoming primary caregivers once again—now to an elderly parent. It is not always an easy role to carry out. There is little formal training for caregivers and even less acknowledgment of the remarkable tasks they perform.

The parent-child relationship grows more complex as the players grow older. Some adult children, while trying to provide a mooring and lifeline for their elderly parents, encounter abusive harassment from them, while others find fulfillment and a resolution to earlier child-parent issues.

During caregiving, adult children may grieve the lost role as "child" and a spouse may grieve the imminent loss of a partner. Caregivers may remember how family members cared for their aged parents or spouses, although this model may be problematic or impossible to replicate. While caregiving may exacerbate painful dynamics in a parent-child relationship, it may also provide new opportunities for closeness, intimacy, and understanding.

We rarely understand just what it means to get older. When she was three, my daughter Tzvia said, "When I get older, I'm going to touch the sky." She wasn't imagining "older" as being eighty, but more likely being like her brother and sister, who are respectively six and nine years older than she is. In our youth-oriented culture, even older people may have distorted ideas about what it means to age. In part, this has been engendered by the often inconsequential contact between youth and elders. The more we segregate people by age, the greater is the glorification of youth and the denigration of the elderly. This creates the illusion of "them" and "us."[12] But by integrating the generations, we can learn from and respect each other. As neighbors, as members of synagogues and communities, and as friends we must move out of our age-segregated spheres so we can influence and fulfill one another.

The Biblical story of Ruth and Naomi portrays Naomi as old, widowed, and helpless. For Biblical scholar Rachel Dulin, Naomi "represents the cause of every old woman in Israel who was widowed, childless and lonely. . . . She represents the widows for whom the prophets cried out and sought justice . . . and the elderly women of ancient

Israel: those women, who, even more so than their male counterparts, felt the painful imprint of their aging years."[13] What redeems Naomi in her old age is love, companionship, and family.

Friendship and community are two of the most significant factors in human contentment. In many essays in this volume, we hear a longing for and an appreciation of friendship, for a sense of belonging, which can be enhanced only by community. One of the most difficult transitions for an older person is to think, speak, and act as an "I" instead of as part of a "we" because of losses incurred while aging.

As an elder becomes increasingly frail, being alone can become more disquieting. Aging, particularly if it is accompanied by illness, can create emotional isolation and depression. Being committed to help the elderly compels us to create a sense of community for them. We must also adapt religious ritual so it resonates with the experiences of the aged. Ethical wills, new prayers for healing, and modifications of the *m'shberach* prayer for illness provide soulful prayer and a cultural-spiritual acknowledgment of change. While some rituals are performed privately, more public ceremonies cement a familial or communal connection, which negates the virtual social invisibility of many elderly.

Long ago, Rebbe Nachman of Breslov concluded that a society is judged by the way it treats its elderly. As the aging population continues to grow, it will be our collective, Jewish responsibility to *imagine* and design innovative prayers, programs, structures, living facilities, and communities that foster continued growth and vital living for and with the elderly. It will be our task to create alternative living facilities in which the elderly are cared for but are not segregated; centers where they continue to grow, teach, and mentor and where the generations are integrated so they sustain and nourish each other.

THE JOURNEY TO WISDOM

As the life span has increased we have begun to define aging in new ways. What we once considered "old" is today "midlife." Although aging is a lifelong process, often we do not contemplate growing old until we are at least in our forties or fifties, when we begin to ask such questions as "Who am I? What have I done with my life? What do I want to do with my remaining years?" Often a milestone, a career change, the children leaving the family nucleus, a health concern, a retirement, or the death of a friend or a family member will spark questions about life's ultimate meaning. With possibly less life ahead of us than behind us, how do we now prioritize our goals, our dreams, and our passions?

Midlife sometimes provokes a crisis because we cannot relinquish the destructive patterns of our childhood and young adulthood, or because we do not approach older adulthood with a willingness to embark on the journey still ahead of us. Aging is a circuitous road that rambles through many stages between birth and death, between creation and eternity. This "journey," in some ways resembling that faith-full journey taken by our ancestors Abraham and Sarah,[14] takes us from a life of knowledge and experience toward a heart of wisdom.

Elderly in many faiths around the globe have raised crucial spiritual and religious questions as they try to understand the meaning of life and death. "Adulthood" for Confucius was both a noun and a verb that marked a process of becoming and moving toward sagehood. Old age was counted in the length of days of self-reflection and self-improvement rather than as a chronology of years. Confucius' approach to sagehood—a graduated set of tasks that leads to wisdom and harmony[15]—resembles in form, and, to a lesser degree, in content, the life stages enumerated in *Pirkei Avot*.

New terms such as "young-old" (generally referring to

those who are sixty-five to eighty years old) and "old-old" (eighty years old and older) may punctuate geronto-logical discussions, but if we live longer, what is the purpose and meaning of all these years? What specific tasks give meaning to elderly Jews? What new roles do the aged and the not-so-aged play? We know that all of life's stages pose specific challenges and offer unique rewards. Midlife and the aging years are no exception.

As we grow older we need to break old routines and let new ideas and activities emerge. We may engage in a life review, which lets us revisit earlier parts of our lives so we can better understand the issues of our life and enjoy the pleasures of our memories. During a life review, we honestly appraise our lives, reliving our joys, making amends for our transgressions if possible, validating our experiences, and consciously altering our legacies. As we confront the values and goals of our youth we also hopefully transcend youth's egocentricity and adopt new goals for our remaining years. But ultimately, we will assess our life against the backdrop of death. Only after acknowledging the inevitability of death can we accept the limits of our lives with integrity.

AGING IN A COMMUNAL CONTEXT

Our aging population is growing older and larger. Since 1971, there has been a 6 percent increase of Jews in the United States who are over 65 years old. Currently, Jews sixty-five years and older make up about 18 percent of the total Jewish population. This is expected to increase to about 22 percent by the year 2010. As this percentage of Jewish elderly increases, it also represents an increasingly older, "aged" population.[16] Healthier lifestyles and medical advancements have contributed to this increased life span.

Recent studies have pointed out that the image of the

Jewish elderly in the United States is based more on stereotype than reality. In fact, fewer elderly are European born: Close to 80 percent of Jewish Americans sixty-five years and older were born and raised in the United States.[17] Today's elderly represent a wider variance of place of origin and ethnic identity. They practice varying levels of religious observance and reflect diverse political and social views. They are also distinguished by what they have contributed to society and their expectations of aging.

Compounding the experience of aging is the trauma of aging in a society that devalues the elderly—a trend that goes against the grain of Jewish tradition. The Jewish prophetic tradition requires that we address "need" communally rather than leave this task to individual benevolence. There are two avenues to address the needs of the Jewish aged: educational and practical. A curriculum on intergenerational issues and the relationship between children and elders, between the young and old, should be developed and implemented in all schools of Jewish learning. We need to help young people realize that the elderly are not to be feared. Shared experiences and visits between youth and elderly can help cement that understanding and create intergenerational links. A recent study by the Association of American Retired Persons (AARP) found that "children who drew [pictures of] older persons they knew, such as a grandparent, were more likely to portray the older person in positive ways. Children with generalized drawings of older persons they did not know were more likely to portray older adults in negative stereotypes."[18] School curricula that include Jewish texts and teachings about aging, stories, games, activities, and *tsedakah* projects will demystify aging and help children understand their place in the cycle of life while also creating meaningful connections to their elders. When he beseeched Pharaoh to let the Israelites leave Egypt, Moses said, "With our young and with our old, we will go."[19] Moses recognized the community as one single entity and acknowledged the community's future in its youth and its history in its elders.

While learning about aging should begin in the elementary school years, it can be addressed appropriately in many educational settings. Schools for Jewish communal service professionals and for rabbis can offer programs that explore Jewish thought about the elderly and Jewish filial and communal responsibility as related to the contemporary Jewish family.

Policy, set by Jewish communal organizations and agencies, should reflect the fact that "family" includes the elderly. Policy and communal programs should be consistent with Jewish values and address the breadth of the experience of aging.

Caring for the elderly and creating a society whose members have much less fear of growing old; a society in which the elderly are revered, in which all regard time as sacrosanct; in which we believe, as Abraham Joshua Heschel did, that "to be is a blessing" is a task for all of us. We need to be able to design our lives so that the meaning and understanding of growing old and of being old are integral to our constant development as individuals. Such tasks are monumental. But, if they are shared between individuals, families, communities, and society, it might be possible to provide for a fuller, more meaningful life throughout the span of one's years. May we all go from "strength to strength" as we journey through all of our ages and our stages.

I. TEXT STUDIES

They who learn from the young, are like what? Like those who eat unripe grapes and drink wine fresh from the winepress. But they who learn from elders, what are they like? Like those who eat ripe grapes and drink aged wine.

—Pirkei Avot 4:26

TEXT STUDIES

How we relate to elderly parents—and to elders, in general—is influenced by Jewish texts and teachings and by the popular culture in which we live. When these two come into conflict, as is often the case, we must be aware and conscious of the teachings of Jewish tradition.

In this section, Dayle Friedman's chapter, "Crown Me with Wrinkles and Gray Hair," provides a solid basis for understanding these textual sources on aging. Friedman not only cites and interprets traditional references to aging but also offers guidelines for shaping our relationships with the elderly. Eliezer Diamond's chapter, "Do Not Cast Us Away in Our Old Age," provides a scholarly grounding for understanding the complex issues surrounding children's responsibilities towards their aged parents. Honoring our fathers and mothers, *kibud av v'em,* is a commandment, a *mitzvah* motivated by *tsedakah,* righteousness. For children providing care to elderly parents, that *mitzvah* often unfolds as an exceptional human drama. Not only are we beholden to our parents for what they have done for us, but we support and care for them out of a sense of *rightness.* In addition to the Fifth Commandment, Leviticus 19:3 teaches us to revere our parents, *Ish imo v'aviv tira'u:* "Every person shall revere his mother and his father." These two commandments—to revere and to honor—represent the dual aspects of our responsibility to our parents: attitudinal and behavioral.

Together, they maintain the dignity of elders while providing for their concrete needs.

Danny Siegel's illuminating "The Mitzvah of Bringing out the Beauty in Our Elders' Faces" builds upon the textual base established in Dayle Friedman's chapter. Siegel's poetic and creative interpretations of these passages are to be read in the genre of our oral tradition, the spoken word. His commentaries on reverence for the elderly show us how to weave this *mitzvah* into our daily lives. Joel Rosenberg's portrayal in "Alternate Paths to Integrity" of Biblical characters who are elderly—King David, Jacob, and Abraham and Sarah—offers moving observations about the Bible's view of old age and what these specific figures teach us about growing old.

Hillel Goelman's chapter, "Passages: The Commentary of Moshe ibn Yehudah HaMachiri on *Pirkei Avot*," elaborates on the developmental stages of life recorded in *Pirkei Avot*. Ibn haMachiri's commentary elucidates aging as a process of *tshuvah*, or repentance; of drawing closer to God; and of devotion to Torah. These essays offer a Jewish framework for developing communal programs and personal relationships with Jewish elders.

Crown Me with Wrinkles and Gray Hair: Examining Traditional Jewish Views of Aging

Dayle A. Friedman

When I was a child, I was fascinated by a television commercial for a well-known hand lotion. In the scene, a mother is mistaken for her teenage daughter. The two are then seen together holding their hands up for inspection: The mother's hands now look "younger looking," almost like her daughter's—a miracle allegedly due to the hand lotion.

What a different scene is presented by a classic Jewish text. In Genesis Rabbah, the *midrash* on humanity's beginnings, the rabbis explain that until Abraham, the elderly had no distinctive physical appearance. But the elderly patriarch was distressed that people who saw him with his son, Isaac, could not discern who was the elder and thus could not offer him the honor and deference due the aged. He pleaded before God to "crown him" with signs of old age. Hence, wrinkles and gray hair entered the world.[1]

Dayle A. Friedman, a rabbi with a master's degree in social work, is director of chaplaincy services at Philadelphia Geriatric Center. She is also an adjunct faculty member of the Reconstructionist Rabbinical College and trains students from all Jewish denominational movements in the Rabbinic Education on Aging Project's clinical internship program.

These contrasting scenarios—the TV commercial and the *midrash*—encapsulate, to a certain extent, the vast rift between contemporary attitudes toward aging and those in Biblical and rabbinic traditions. In late twentieth-century North America, aging is seen as a plague to be avoided—or, at least, to be concealed. In Jewish tradition, bearing the mark of many years is considered a reward to be coveted. Why this gap in perception? In secular culture, the worth of the individual is ordinarily measured by what he or she does, by the material contribution that he or she makes to society. Beauty and desirability are equated with youth, and dependency and frailty are dreaded. But in Jewish tradition, the individual has an intrinsic worth, since we are all created in the divine image. One's value is not connected to productivity, strength, or physical beauty.

In this time of a graying Jewish community, when more of us are living to ever more advanced ages, it behooves us to search in the Jewish tradition for perspective and guidance on how to face the period of life that has been called the third age. Although Jewish tradition is broad and deep, and has developed in varied ways over the centuries and around the globe, one can discern some prominent themes and values. An examination of traditional Jewish sources on aging reflects an apparent paradox: On one hand, the sources realistically depict the impairments and losses of aging; on the other hand, they treat old age as a positive and worthy stage of life.

DO NOT CAST OFF THE AGED

In some Biblical and rabbinic sources, growing older can be a frightening prospect. This is reflected in Psalm 71:9: "Cast me not off in the time of my old age; when my strength fails, forsake me not," and when Rabbi Jose ben Kisma laments the loss of his youth: "Woe for the one thing that goes and does not return."[2] In the same passage, Rav Dimi similarly describes youth as a crown of roses, and old age as a crown of thorns.

Of the physical and mental impairments of the aged, a *midrash* baldly states, "In old age, all powers fail."[3] Isaac became blind in his old age,[4] and the elderly David was so frail that his body was constantly cold.[5] The physical losses of aging are poignantly described by the eighty-year-old Barzillai the Gileadite: "I am this day fourscore years old; can I discern between good and bad? Can thy servant taste what I eat or what I drink? Can I hear any more the voice of singing men and singing women?"[6] An exhaustive catalogue of the sorrows and sensory losses of aging is metaphorically described in Ecclesiastes 12:1–7:

> *So appreciate your vigor in the days of your youth, before those*
> *days of sorrow come and those years arrive of which you will say,*
> *I have no pleasure in them; before sun and light and moon and*
> *stars grow dark, and the clouds come back again after the rain:*
> *When the guards of the house become shaky,*
> *And the men of valor are bent,*
> *And the maids that grind, grown few, are idle,*
> *And the ladies that peer through the windows grow dim,*
> *And the doors to the street are shut—*
> *And the noise of the hand mill growing fainter,*
> *And the song of the bird growing feebler,*
> *And all the strains of music dying down;*
> *When one is afraid of heights*
> *And there is terror on the road . . .*
> *Before the silver cord snaps*
> *And the golden bowl crashes,*
> *The jar is shattered at the spring,*
> *And the jug is smashed at the cistern.*
> *And the dust returns to the ground*
> *As it was,*
> *And the lifebreath returns to God*
> *Who bestowed it.*

The Babylonian Talmud[7] interprets this woeful passage as a catalogue of all the physical changes and disabilities brought on by aging. The rabbis who cite this passage vie with one another to describe the most horrific visions of old age. Though several authorities apologetically demur, explaining the daunting descriptions as applying only to the wicked, the rabbis generally see physical debilitation and impairment as a fact of life of old age.

OUR LIVES NEED PURPOSE

Some rabbinic sources also view mental deterioration as an inevitable feature of aging. In depicting an individual who today would probably be diagnosed as demented, one text quotes an old man: "I look for what I have not lost."[8] Another old man misinterprets the sound of twittering birds: "Robbers have come to overpower me."[9] Despite the dominant view that the old are wise, some sources dispute this: "There is no reason in old men and no counsel in children."[10] Even Moses, who is physically as strong as ever at age 120, is described in one *midrash* as having lost his capacity to teach, or even to follow a presentation given by his disciple, Joshua.[11] This loss of power is so devastating that Moses, who has consistently and passionately pleaded to live, now begs God to let him die.

Although these texts describe aging as it was experienced hundreds, even thousands of years ago, the essential reality they depict remains unchanged today. Despite medical and scientific advances that have lengthened the life span from under fifty years at the turn of the twentieth century to close to seventy-five today, we have not succeeded in evading frailty and finitude. Our society is loath to acknowledge—and accept—the seeming inevitability of physical and mental deterioration for most older people. This has serious consequences, such as the isolation of the elderly, the denial of aging, and a loss of self-respect among elders.

Aging is also a time of losing loved ones. This can be devastating to one's sense of meaning. In a Talmudic tale, Honi the Circle Maker, a kind of Jewish Rip van Winkle, goes to sleep for seventy years, only to awaken to a world in which no one knows him and in which everyone he loves has died. In utter despair, he cries out, "Either fellowship or death!"[12] The tradition recognizes that for some frail older people, there can come a time when living itself can become a burden. The midrashic work *Yalkut Shimoni Parashat Ekev* portrays a fascinating encounter between an old woman and Rabbi Yosi ben Halafta. The woman, who had "aged greatly," says, "Rabbi, I have aged too much and now my life is worthless, for I cannot taste food or drink, and I want to die." The rabbi asks what mitzvah has been part of her daily practice. She answers that she goes to the synagogue early each morning. The rabbi advises her to refrain from attending the synagogue for three consecutive days. She follows his counsel, and, on the third day, she becomes ill and dies.

To the old woman, the fact that she no longer gets pleasure from living makes her life seem worthless. The amazing response of the rabbi is to help her to stop doing the very things that seem to be spiritually prolonging her life. This startling text seems to suggest that one's evaluation of the quality of his or her life is a legitimate element in decisions about life and death, and that prolonging a life experienced as burdensome is not obligatory. To contemporary Jews struggling with wrenching decisions about life-extending medical treatments, this *midrash* may provide useful guidance. Although it has no halachic authority, it does provide support for basing decisions on elderly patient's wishes as well as for forgoing life-extending treatments when living has become burdensome to the person.

AGING CAN BE A POSITIVE EXPERIENCE

Along with, or perhaps in spite of, these realistic and rather dire depictions of the hardships of aging comes a fundamentally positive view of aging. Long life is considered a reward for righteous living. While complying with most of the *mitzvot,* or commandments, in the Torah implies no assurance of reward, in a few cases long life is promised. Length of days is assured for those who honor their parents,[13] for those who do not remove a mother bird's young in her presence,[14] and for those who use accurate measures in commerce.[15] In addition, those who observe "all of the laws and ordinances" are promised "length of days."[16] Finally, according to Proverbs 16:31, one attains old age through *tsedakah,* or righteous living.

Many *midrashim* describe old age as a reward for virtuous living, such as faithful attendance at the *beit midrash,* or house of religious study,[17] and for a life marked by righteousness and Torah. An entire page of the Talmud is filled with various rabbis' accounts of the particular worthy deeds that explain their longevity.[18] Another example of this reasoning is given by Rav Addah bar Ahaba:

> The disciples of Rav Addah bar Ahaba asked him: "To what do you attribute your longevity?" He replied: "I have never displayed any impatience in my house, and I have never walked in front of any man greater than myself, nor have I ever meditated [over the words of the Torah] in any dirty alleys, nor have I ever walked four cubits without [musing over] the Torah or without [wearing] phylacteries, nor have I ever fallen asleep in the House of Study for any length of time or even momentarily, nor have I rejoiced at the disgrace of my friends, nor have I ever called my neighbor by a nickname given to him by myself, or some say, by the nickname given to him by others."[19]

REVERING THE AGED

Old age is seen as reward and blessing, and the elderly are to be treated with deference and respect. In addition to the obligation to honor one's parents, the Holiness code (Leviticus 19) outlines our responsibilities to older adults in general, "You shall rise before the aged [gray-haired] and show deference [*hiddur*] in the presence of the old [*zaken*]; you shall fear your God: I am the Eternal."[20]

This *mitzvah* is understood to dictate deferential treatment toward scholars as well as older adults. *Zaken,* or "old," is taken to refer to people of wisdom, not just to those who have attained wisdom through life experience.

The rabbis mandate that we display reverence toward everyone over a certain age.[21] "What is the deference [*hiddur*] demanded by the Torah? That you not stand in his [the older person's] place, nor contradict his words, but behave toward him with reverence and fear."[22] Included among those meriting this deferential treatment are elderly non-Jews and Jews who are neither learned nor particularly righteous, since they are assumed to have acquired understanding of God's ways in the world through life experience.[23]

Hence, revering the elderly means recognizing the value of their experience. Even if they have forgotten their learning through dementia or some other frailty, one still owes them respect: "Take care to honor the old man who has forgotten his learning for reasons beyond his control, as it is said, 'both the [second, unbroken] tablets and the broken tablets [of the Law] were kept in the Ark [of the sanctuary]."[24] Respect for the elderly is not predicated on their capacity to contribute socially or to benefit those younger than they. They are inherently worthy, even when they are "broken," and are to be cherished and nurtured, just as Israel treasured the first set of tablets of the Law, which were broken by Moses.

One must not merely give honor to the older person;

one must do this in such a way that the older person knows that the honor is meant specifically for him or her. For example, one must rise in the presence of an older person but should wait to do so until the older person is within four cubits, so that he or she will recognize that this honor is being accorded to him or her.[25] In addition, one must reach out to older persons where they are: If older persons are standing, even if one is sitting and engaged in work, one must rise to meet them. Clearly, by obliging Jews to revere the dignity of every older person, tradition recognizes the value of that person's experience and perspective.

WISDOM IN THE ELDER YEARS

What is it about old age that makes it desirable and deserving of respect? First and foremost, Jewish tradition associates old age with wisdom. The old are viewed as leaders with wisdom to impart. As the people of Israel are enjoined, "Ask your father and he will tell you, your elders and they shall instruct you."[26] Or, in the words of the Book of Job, "For wisdom is with the old, and understanding with length of days."[27] Among the generation in the wilderness, it is the elders, the *zakenim,* who were Israel's leaders. While many sources understand *zaken* to be a generic term for a leader of any age, using a term that also denotes old age surely reflects an association of wisdom with age. The guidance of elders is critical to the survival of the people of Israel: "When is Israel able to stand? When it has elders. . . . For one who takes advice from elders never stumbles."[28]

Rabbinic doctrine urges accepting elders' opinions when there is a dispute between generations. Even if the elders seem to be arguing for destruction and the youth for construction, the elders should be heeded, for "the tearing down of the old is building, and the building of the young is tearing down."[29] Thus, the elders' perspective is exemplified as uniquely valuable for the guidance of the community. So inexorable is the link between old age and wisdom that the sage Bar Kappara exclaimed, "If wisdom is not here, can old age be here?"[30]

Old age is not merely a time for savoring the lessons gleaned from a lifetime of experience and learning. On the contrary, Jewish tradition teaches that in old age one is called to continue to learn and grow. A person who has been a student of Torah in his or her youth should continue that learning.[31] Studying Torah, in fact, can sustain a person in old age, for it can be done even when that person is unable to work or produce a livelihood: "[The Torah] . . . guards him from all evil in his youth and gives him a future and hope in his old age."[32] An aged person not only can continue to follow paths that have been spiritually fruitful throughout a long life but can transform his or her life up until the very last day. In explaining the verse "Better is the end of a thing than the beginning thereof,"[33] Ruth Rabbah states, "A man may act wickedly in his youth, yet in his old age he may perform good deeds."[34]

Old age can be a time of broadening one's involvement with others and the world to create a better life for future generations. One example of this is reflected in the talmudic understanding of the obligation to teach a child Torah. According to the rabbis, not only is a parent obligated to teach a child, but a grandparent is obligated as well.[35] Older persons have unique contributions to make to the young. One beautiful example of this is the story of Naomi the old woman whose sons have died childless and whose daughter-in-law, Ruth, stays with her rather than return to her own people. When Ruth has a child, he is nursed by Naomi, and is considered by all to be her son, too. The women of the village say, "he shall be to you a restorer of your life, and is a nourisher of your old age."[36] Naomi is simultaneously nourished by—and a nourisher of—the younger generation. She represents a powerful model of generativity in old age.

Another example of concern for the future is seen in two stories about old men who plant trees, though skeptics tell them that they will not live to see the fruits of their labors. In one story, a 100-year-old man is challenged by Emperor Hadrian about why he wastes his time planting shrubs. The man answers, "If I am worthy, I shall eat; if not, just as my forefathers toiled for me, so I toil for my children." The emperor promised the man a reward should he live to see the trees produce figs. Indeed, the man lived, and was rewarded with riches, for the emperor said, "His Creator has honored him, so shall not I?"[37] In a parallel tale, Honi the Circle-Maker gives a similar rationale for planting a tree at age seventy.[38] In both cases, the older adult is depicted as caring about the welfare of those yet to be born. It is apparent that being engaged with the future also sustains older persons, for it gives meaning to their life.

THE *MITZVAH* MODEL: A JEWISH VISION FOR AGING

In Jewish tradition, old age is still a time of quest for a life of meaning. This message is embodied in the concept of *mitzvah*. Through *mitzvah,* or religious obligation, the older Jew can achieve a profound sense of self-worth and social value. This can empower the physically or mentally incapacitated so that they, too, experience personal significance. This *Mitzvah* Model provides Jews today with a framework for approaching our relationship to aging, both as individuals and as a community.

From birth, the Jew is part of a community that extends through time and space. Membership in this community involves inclusion in the *brit*—the covenant with God established at Sinai—which binds each Jew to *mitzvot* and the commandments, both ritual and ethical. One's fate beyond this world is traditionally seen as dependent on a lifetime of observing *mitzvot*. On a broader scale, redeeming the Jewish people and, indeed, the whole world rests on the collective fulfillment of this ancient covenant.

In this traditional worldview, each Jew's relationship to the *mitzvot* has cosmic significance. How—and whether—one observes *mitzvot* affects one's social and religious status. One can gain *kavod*, or "honor," by an exemplary performance of *mitzvot*; by being faithful, for example, to *mitzvot* under difficult or dangerous conditions, or by imbuing observance with a particular fervor and intentionality called *kavanah*. Within the social world of the covenantal community, one achieves the highest honor by facilitating others' observance of *mitzvot*. Thus, it is a special honor to lead others in reciting prayers and to be counted in the quorum for prayer, the *minyan*, or *birkat ha-mazon*, the grace after meals. Thus, any Jew can gain merit and honor through performing *mitzvot*.

It is easy to see how valuable this concept and experience can be for older adults. Being conscious of obligation gives the elderly precisely what they may lack: the opportunity to experience life as meaningful. By performing *mitzvot*, older Jews can participate in valuable activities, have a meaningful social role in the covenantal community, and structure their time.

Abraham Joshua Heschel suggested that it is through being obligated that one truly exists. Older adults who believe that they are still obligated see themselves engaged in the central human task of *tikkun olam:* repairing and redeeming the world through observing the *mitzvot*. According to Heschel, "What a person lives by is not only a sense of belonging, but a sense of indebtedness. The need to be needed corresponds to a fact: something is asked of a man, of every man. Advancing in years must not be taken to mean a process of suspending the requirements and commitments under which a person lives. To be is to obey. A person must not cease to be."[39]

For older adults to know that they are as bound to *mitzvot* as any other Jew tells them that something is expected of them, that their actions matter, that they can transcend the narrow confines of their current lives, which may have been influenced by the debilitating messages from the culture around them.

Halachah, or Jewish law, specifies no special category of obligation for the old. While there is a very clear beginning point of obligation—bar mitzvah—there is no end-point. There is also no automatic assumption that an older person is any less competent to perform a *mitzvah* than anyone else.

Yet, the experience of aging may present formidable barriers to observing the *mitzvot,* such as the inability to get about without assistance, sensory deficits, cognitive impairment, and memory loss. The question then arises: How does the *Mitzvah* Model apply to those thus hindered? The tradition understands that observing *mitzvot* should be accessible and attainable for Jews. The Torah itself states: "Surely, this *mitzvah* which I enjoin upon you this day is not too baffling for you, nor is it beyond reach. . . . It is very close to you, in your mouth and in your heart, to observe it."[40]

THE "SLIDING SCALE" OF ELDERS' OBLIGATIONS

Models for understanding the obligations of impaired older adults are found in the halachic literature regarding the obligations of those who are ill or physically incapacitated. According to this model, *mitzvot* are assumed in principle to apply to each individual, but rabbinic authorities use sensitivity and creativity in defining *mitzvot* so that impaired individuals can fulfill their obligations by doing only what they are capable of doing.

For example, the obligation of daily prayer is considerably altered for someone who is physically or mentally incapable of performing it in its entirety. One who is old or weak and unable to stand may recite the *amidah,* the "standing" prayers, while sitting down.[41] One who cannot speak may discharge the obligation by mentally reciting the prayers or by meditating upon them.[42] One who does not have the endurance to complete the entire liturgy may abbreviate the *amidah.*[43] Even the *Sh'ma* can be abridged to include just the first line if a person cannot concentrate longer than that.[44]

What is most significant about this "sliding scale" model of obligation for the old one is that once obligated, one remains obligated, even if his or her capacity is diminished. All the social and personal benefits of being *metzuveh,* or "commanded," continue to accrue. And, as long as one performs the *mitzvah* to the extent of one's ability, one is considered to have fully discharged the obligation.

The *Mitzvah* Model has important implications for today's Jewish elderly, not just for those who are religiously observant. Based on the teaching in *Pirkei Avot* that "the world stands on three things: on Torah, on worship, and on deeds of lovingkindness," the obligations of a Jew can be understood to include study, ritual observance, and social action. If older adults are still to be obligated to perform *mitzvot,* then the community is responsible to facilitate their participation as fully as possible. The aged must be given access to study, prayer, *tsedakah, gemilut hassadim,* acts of kindness, and all facets of communal life. They must not be segregated into "Golden Age" clubs whose primary focus is recreation. The elderly are valuable resources, not just recipients of service. Their experiences can be used in synagogues, communal organizations, and Jewish education, where there is a shortage of skilled teachers.

The continued obligation of older Jews to worship may require that synagogues be more accessible to those in wheelchairs or who use walkers, that synagogues provide large-print prayer books and assure that sound is amplified in sanctuaries. Carpools or vans can facilitate the participation of older Jews in communal activities. Such efforts can enrich life for the older Jews—and for the community—since they affirm that old age is a time of meaning and possibility. As we face our personal journeys through aging, as well as the momentous impact of the "age wave" on our community, this fundamentally positive view can help us to fulfill the ancient vision of the Psalmist:[45]

> The righteous will flourish like the palm tree:
> They will grow like a cedar in Lebanon.
> Planted in the house of the Eternal,
> They shall flourish in the courts of our God.
> They shall yet yield fruit even in old age;
> Vigorous and fresh they shall be,
> To proclaim that the Eternal is just!
> [God is] my Rock, in whom there is no injustice.

"Do Not Cast Us Away in Our Old Age": Adult Children and Their Aging Parents

Eliezer Diamond

As parents and children grow older, mothers and fathers who once seemed all but omnipotent may be weak and ailing, and children who were carried in their parents' arms are now the ones who do the carrying—physically, emotionally, and financially. This difficult shift in roles is further complicated by practical and psychological factors. Adult children generally have families of their own, and the responsibilities one has towards one's spouse and children generally makes it difficult to attend to parents as well.[1] Furthermore, one tends to put the needs of one's children before those of one's parents. In the words of a maxim cited by the rabbis, "The love of a father is for his son; the love of a son is for *his* son."[2] Yet, certain rabbinic attitudes can help resolve these tensions between the adult children and their parents.

When a spouse and a parent compete for one's energy and attentions, Jewish law and tradition generally grant priority to one's spouse. Indeed, Genesis dictates that "a man leave his father and mother and cleave to his wife; and they shall be as one flesh."[3] Therefore, one is usually

---

Rabbi Eliezer Diamond, assistant professor of Talmud and Rabbinics at The Jewish Theological Seminary of America, lectures widely on issues affecting the Jewish family.

obligated to defer to one's spouse. Maimonides ruled, for example, that both husband and wife have the right to bar one's in-laws from entering one's home.[4] If a man is living near his parents and his wife is feuding with her in-laws, halachic authorities generally require the husband to move his family farther away from his parents.[5] But Maimonides also specifies that a woman whose husband has banned her parents from their home may (and, presumably, should) periodically visit her parents at their home, especially when they require her presence.[6] Moreover, a husband who prevents his wife from visiting her parents is obligated to divorce her and pay her the full divorce settlement stipulated in their *ketubah*.[7]

These are instances of blatant conflict. Often, however, there is good will on all sides, but the time, money, and energy available to the adult child are limited. What do the rabbis say about how these precious resources should be allotted?

HONORING OUR PARENTS

In the area of finances, one is primarily obligated to the spouse and children. But this is not exclusive. Financial obligation to parents is certainly no less than one's responsibility to the community at large:[8] If necessary, up to 10 percent of one's income, the minimum percentage one must normally dedicate to *tsedakah*,[9] must be reserved for parental needs.[10] Moreover, adult children should be mindful that their material well-being is often partially due to their parents' generosity. Yet, children who have benefited from parental largesse are sometimes tight-fisted when their father and mother ask them for help. For this reason, the rabbis decreed that parents who have given their property to their children may draw from it whatever is necessary for their own sustenance.[11]

Generally, for halachic and practical reasons, the

obligation to honor one's parents expresses itself not so much in expenditure as in personal service. Early rabbinic sources require an adult child to feed, clothe, transport, and provide whatever other services are necessary[12] for their parents. Rabbinic authorities in *Eretz Yisrael* of both the Tannaitic (20–200 C.E.) and Rabbinic (200 B.C.E. to 500 C.E.) periods assumed that these obligations were monetary as well as instrumental. That is, one is required to buy food for one's parents as well as to feed them. The Amoraim of Babylonia (Talmudic scholars from 220 to 500 C.E.), however, concluded that the child's obligation is one of service only. While Babylonian rabbis give no reason for the ruling,[13] which certainly disputes the plain meaning of earlier texts, possibly they wished to assure that the adult child has sufficient funds to support his own family before assuming the financial support of his parents.

How can responsibilities of sustenance and service be divided if there are several children? In thirteenth-century Germany, Rabbi Meir of Rothenburg[14] ruled that if some siblings are wealthy and others are not, the financial burden falls solely on the shoulders of the wealthy siblings, to be shared by them in proportion to their wealth.

What remains unanswered is how to distribute the responsibilities of service. If a parent who is partially dependent is living with a child, for example, the child's responsibility is physical as well as monetary. In nineteenth-century Russia, Rabbi Yehiel Michel Epstein[15] argued that the wealthy children bear sole responsibility in this area as well. His reasoning may be related to the Babylonian Talmud's observation[16] that attending to one's parents causes financial loss through work or opportunities missed.[17] Because commitment of time and monetary loss may be closely related, Rabbi Epstein placed the burden of service on those siblings who are better able to absorb the possibly negative financial consequences of helping their parents.

DIVIDING RESPONSIBILITIES

But what if one sibling is more capable physically and emotionally to attend to a parent than are the other siblings? What if the family life of one child will be affected more negatively than that of the others as a result of the parent's constant presence in his or her home? While Rabbi Epstein did not raise these issues explicitly, the strong implication of his view is that we avoid rigidly dividing responsibility among siblings, and balance the needs of the parents against the resources and needs of their children.

A crucial aspect of service is the attitude with which it is provided. As the rabbis observe, "One may feed one's parent pheasant and yet this will result in [the son's] banishment from the world."[18] They give the following example: "There was a man who fed his father fatted fowl. Once his father asked him, 'My son, where do you get these?' His son replied, 'Old man, eat and be quiet, just as dogs eat and are silent.'[19] The words and gestures that accompany acts of service are certainly a vital component of honor. When a parent visits or is living in a child's home, the child should make every effort to honor the parent. Here, for example, is a contemporary rabbinic view of how a parent should be treated at a child's table: "When the father is aged, and the son takes him to his house, the son remains seated at his normal place at the head of the table as previously, but . . . the father nonetheless is to perform the ritual washing of the hands first, and to receive the first portion of food, as well as other designations of honor at the table. This is our practice, and there should be no deviation from it."[20]

DEALING WITH MENTAL FRAILTIES

What are the parameters of a child's obligation to a parent who is mentally disturbed or even severely mentally handicapped (for example, a parent with Alzheimer's disease)? The medieval midrashic work *Seder Eliyahu Rabbah* states:[21] "Even if one's father's spittle is running down his beard [in other words, if he is mentally disturbed],[22] his child should obey him."[23]

On the other hand, certain Talmudic sources imply that one may leave his or her parents in certain instances, such as parental abuse. When Rabbi Kahana, a third-century Babylonian émigré to Palestine, was thinking about leaving Palestine after being reviled by fellow students there, he obliquely asked Rabbi Johanan's advice: "If a man's mother insults him, his wife's father honors him, to which should he go?" Rabbi Johanan replied, "Let him go where he is honored."[24] This latter source, as well as another in the Babylonian Talmud concerning Rabbi Assi and his mother,[25] may be the basis for the following ruling by Maimonides: "If one's father or mother should become mentally disordered, he should try to treat them as their mental state demands, until God shows compassion towards them. If he finds, however, that he cannot endure the situation because of their extreme madness, let him leave and go away, asking others to care for them properly."[26]

Rabbi Abraham ben David (known as RaBaD) of twelfth-century Provence, an older contemporary of Maimonides, vigorously challenged this position: "This is an incorrect teaching. If he leaves, whom will he charge to supervise the well-being of his parents?"[27]

Both views have merit. Just as limits are placed on a child's financial filial obligations, one's physical and emotional responsibilities presumably stop short of being self-destructively involved with one's parents. In some cases, though, such as severe illness, moreover, it may be in the parents' best interests to receive their primary care from professionals rather than from their emotionally involved children.[28] At the same time, one certainly cannot expect a stranger to show the same concern as a child for a parent. Thus, while Maimonides' view is the one generally accepted,[29] a child should never treat the care given by doctors and nurses to his parents as a substitute for filial love, involvement, and concern. Within one's abilities, one should visit sick parents regularly and reassure them through speech and action that they are still on the minds and in the hearts of their children.

THE DILEMMA OF TRUTH-TELLING

When a parent reaches the terminal stage of an illness, a child must often decide on the proper treatment when the parent is incapable of making such a decision. The child must also decide what to say outright, what to mask, and what to withhold from an elderly, infirm parent. This problem is intensified when a parent demands full disclosure from the child as part of the child's obligation to honor the parent's wishes. The most complete treatment of this question is by twentieth-century Rabbi Bezalel Stern, who was asked about someone who has terminal cancer but whose doctors have decided not to disclose the full gravity of his condition to him. The patient has demanded that his son, as a matter of honoring his wishes, tell him whatever he knows about the diagnosis. What shall the son do?

Rabbi Stern argued that the child is exempt from obeying his father for two reasons. First, most halachists do not require a child to obey a parent if such obedience would not directly benefit the parent.[30] Thus, informing the parent of his or her condition would probably create much anguish, and there is no filial imperative to share the medical information. Second, Rabbi Aha of Shabha in

Babylonia in the eighth century,[31] at least according to one tradition,[32] qualified the Talmud's ruling that a parent may forego filial honor by allowing only the non performance of service. On the other hand, even if a parent is indifferent a child may not behave in a hurtful manner toward his mother or father. And since the rabbi assumed that the son would cause his father pain by informing him of his illness, he forbid him to do so.

Of course, Rabbi Stern's ruling assumed that such disclosure has a uniformly negative effect on a patient's well-being. This view, once widely accepted in the medical community, has now been rejected by many health care practitioners.[33] It seems, therefore, that a child needs to decide how much a parent should be told, always remembering that the primary filial responsibility is the physical and mental health of the parent, not blind obedience to a parent's stated wishes.

HONORING PARENTS WHILE COPING WITH THEIR SINS

Finally, how can a son or daughter honor and serve a parent who has emotionally, physically, or sexually assaulted them? While sexual abuse is only alluded to and not addressed directly in rabbinic sources,[34] and while rabbinic notions of acceptable physical behavior of parents toward children differ from those of contemporary Western society,[35] the rabbis *were* aware that some parents are not worthy of the filial honor and respect prescribed by the Torah.[36] What are a child's obligations, if any, toward such parents? The authoritative text for this issue is the following *mishnah*: "If one has any kind of son, that son exempts his father's wife from the levirate marriage [the Biblical injunction that a childless widow marry her deceased husband's brother] [Deuteronomy 25:5–11], is liable to punishment for striking or cursing his father [Exodus 21:15,17], and is deemed to be his son in every respect."[37]

The Babylonian Talmud asks: "What does 'any kind [of son]' include? Rabbi Judah says: It includes a bastard."[38] As a result of this interpretation, the Babylonian Talmud raises the following problem: Elsewhere, the rabbis exempt from punishment one who curses someone not living a life of Torah. Someone who has fathered a bastard has clearly not followed the Torah's dictate. Why then, should his son be punished for cursing him? The Talmud replies that indeed, a bastard is punished for cursing his father, but only if his father has repented of his sin.[39]

A similar discussion concerns the Tannaitic dictum that children are obligated to return any objects in their father's estate they know were stolen, even if the owners have despaired of recovering their goods and thereby relinquished ownership. This is done to honor their father. The Talmud limits this obligation to the children of a repentant parent.[40]

Medieval rabbis disagreed over what conclusion to draw from these Talmudic discussions.[41] To the eleventh- and twelfth-century French rabbis Rashi and Rabbenu Tam, the Talmud exempts a child from all obligations of honor and service if a parent has sinned and is unrepentant.[42] But Rabbi Isaac Alfasi, who lived in North Africa and Spain in the eleventh century, and Maimonides read the Talmud more narrowly: Even if one's parent is unremittingly sinful, the prohibition against striking or cursing one's parent still applies.[43] The Talmud states only that because the parent is sinful the usual capital punishment for striking and cursing a parent is not administered to the offending child. Moreover, Maimonides specifically obligates a child to honor a sinful parent.[44]

Some halachists have attributed to Rabbi Moses Isserles yet a third view: One may refrain from honoring a sinful parent but is forbidden from actively causing that parent pain.[45] This balances the outrage and hurt of the child with the Torah's compassion for all individuals. Perhaps, too, we should note how the seventeenth-century rabbi David ibn Zimra resolved the apparent contradiction between Maimonides' ruling that children honor even sinful parents and the Talmud's conclusion that children of a deceased, unrepentant father are not required to uphold his honor by returning stolen goods found in his estate. Rabbi Zimra pointed out that the Talmud was discussing a case of a father who had died unrepentant. In the case of a living parent, however, there is always a chance that a moment of contrition and reconciliation may arrive. While we do not require a child to honor such a parent, he or she can keep alive the opportunity for healing by not engaging in gratuitously hurtful behavior.

Most important to remember is that by providing care and hospitality for our aging parents, we mirror the act of making a place for the Creator of every living thing in our hearts and homes. According to a *midrash*, God explains the importance of the Sanctuary by saying:

> "You are my sons, and I am your father. . . . It is an honor for sons to dwell with their father, and it is an honor for the father to dwell with his sons. . . . Make, therefore, a house for the father in which he can dwell with his sons."[46]

Passages: The Commentary of Moshe ibn Yehuda haMachiri on Pirkei Avot

Hillel Goelman

Rabbi Judah used to say, "At five years old, one begins the study of Torah; at 10, the study of Mishna; and at 13, he is ready to obey the commandments. At 15, he begins the study of Gemara; at 18, he marries; at 20, he enters the chase; and at 30, he is at full strength. At 40, he gains the power of understanding and at 50 he can begin to give advice to others. At 60, he enters old age; at 70, he turns gray; at 80, he becomes full of vigor; and at 90, he is broken down. At 100, he is like a dead person who has passed away and faded from the world."

—Pirkei Avot 5:24

This concise, schematic view of human development is in the section of *mishna* known as "Ethics of the Fathers," or *Pirkei Avot*. Although this is one of the most widely quoted Jewish teachings on the human life span, its underlying meaning is puzzling. On the level of *pshat,*

Hillel Goelman received smicha *from Rabbis Zalman Schachter-Shalomi, Shlomo Carlbach, and Akiva Mann. A member of the Or Shalom community in Vancouver, he is on the faculty of education at the University of British Columbia. The major teachers in his life are his wife, Sheryl Sorokin, and his two sons, Zachary Lev and Chaim Nadav.*

the literal meaning of the text, it appears to be a combination of an early child development textbook and Gail Sheehy's *Passages*, the popular guide to the stages of an adult's life. But at a deeper level, what is the passage's underlying intent? Are these stages to be taken as milestones of the normal, expected stages of a person's life? Or is this a prescriptive statement that provides guidance and recommendations for how people conduct their lives? As a central piece of ethical and religious instruction, what fundamental spiritual lessons does this text reflect? What instruction does one derive from it regarding how Jews are to live their lives?

REVEALING GOD'S PRESENCE IN EACH MOMENT OF LIFE

Perhaps the dearth of rabbinic commentary on this passage—rare in a tradition characterized by extensive and intensive textual analysis—is what draws attention to an essay that focuses exclusively on the passage written by a sixteenth-century mystic near Safed in northern Israel. Moshe ibn Yehuda haMachiri lived in the village Ein Zeitim, a Galilee settlement, which dates back to at least the eleventh century.[1]

While the *yeshiva* of Moshe ibn Yehuda haMachiri is cited by contemporaries in Safed as a respected center of Jewish learning, little is known of ibn Machiri himself, except that he wrote a fascinating text, *Sefer Seder Hayom*, or the *Order of the Day.*

First published in 1598, *Sefer Seder Hayom* attempts to unveil the mystical intentions of daily religious rituals and to draw attention to the manifestation of God's presence in each moment and in every action done by each person. This volume includes ibn Machiri's commentary on the above-cited section of *Pirkei Avot*. Though a separate and distinct text, the commentary on *Pirkei Avot* is linked thematically to the *Sefer Seder Hayom*. The commentary draws its name from the opening words of the opening verse: *"Ben hamesh l'mikrah,"* "At five years old one begins to study the Torah." Just as each period of the day and each phase of the Jewish year is characterized by a specific manifestation of the Divine presence, each period of a person's life is also characterized by a specific way in which one becomes aware of the Divine presence. In this way, ibn Machiri is extending the classic kabbalistic teaching of *kol ha neshama tihalel Yah,* the idea that every breath of every living creature is imbued with God's presence.

The most dominant motif in ibn Machiri's commentary is the sense of awe, wonder, and gratitude one should feel simply for being alive. Each person's appearance on life's "stage" is fleeting and occurs only because of the graciousness of a loving and benevolent God. It is incumbent upon us, ibn Machiri teaches, to be constantly aware of the preciousness and impermanence of this life, the purpose of which is to be a partner with God and to bring an awareness of divine energy to the world.

While I am now summarizing some of the key points in ibn Machiri's text, do not consider this to be a substitute for the original Hebrew text which is full of nuances, word plays, gendered language, and references to a wide range of Jewish sources. Hopefully, they provide insight into how a medieval kabbalist living in the Galilee understood and expressed his own personal and spiritual journey through the life span.

FOCUSING OUR ENERGIES

The early, formative years are marked by being introduced to the world of literacy, specifically Jewish text. By learning to read the Torah at age 5, the Mishna at age 10, and the Gemara at age 15, one proceeds through adolescence and into early adulthood equipped to negotiate through the sea of Jewish religious law. The text, and the ability to probe it, provide a guiding compass through the turbulence and potential chaos of one's life journey.

Ibn Machiri is not alone in his interpretation that it is important for a boy to begin to master the study of Gemara—a key tool in the religious and psychological development of a Jewish man—before the sexual drive begins to strongly assert itself. The injunction to a father to ensure that his son is married by the age of 18 is not intended so much to encourage the son to begin to fulfill the religious commandment to "be fruitful and multiply" but rather to prevent the young man from finding other, inappropriate, possibly destructive outlets for his sexual energy.

When a young man reaches the age of 20, he begins *lirdof*, "to chase," which some interpret as "chasing the study of Torah" and others as "chasing the demands of an occupation." Ibn Machiri implies that "chasing" energy is applied to the initial phases of building a family and a household, the physical structures and contents of family life. By age 30, the man enters the age of "full strength," when his physical strength is used to create a stable world consisting of material goods and shelter for his family and, as the product of his own sexual strength, children to provide for him in his old age. At the age of 40, a turning point is passed, and reflection and contemplation become a major focus.

"AT 40, HE GAINS THE POWER OF UNDERSTANDING"

Ibn Machiri sees the age of 40 as the midpoint of life. He bases this on verses from the Psalms that characterize the normal life span of a person as seventy to eighty years. Although the temptations for bodily pleasures still exist, they begin to decline in intensity and frequency as physical strength weakens. At the same time, "the strengths of the spirit and intellect are just awakening." This awakening forms the major focus for this phase of life.

Having accomplished material acquisition, the individual begins to ask, "Is this all that life is about"? At this stage, we become more aware of our own mortality. Ibn Machiri urges us to prepare for the final day of judgment, when we will be asked to account for our lives, not in terms of material growth and physical pleasure but rather in terms of spiritual knowledge and understanding.

"AT 50, HE BEGINS TO GIVE ADVICE TO OTHERS"

The enlightenment process continues in our fifties. The self-reflection that began in the previous decade now leads to two activities: one focused within one's self and the other directed toward others. An honest accounting of one's mistakes must include a sincere expression of *teshuvah,* or repentance.

The person reviews the times when the challenges and temptations of the material world led him to make poor decisions or to commit "sins" against himself and others. Ibn Machiri calls for an honest acknowledgment of those misdeeds and asks that we correct any damage and develop a vision and a commitment to overcoming similar temptations in the future.

Teshuvah, ibn Machiri writes, is the first task to be done when we reach fifty years of age. The second task, one that is equally important, is using the wisdom and understanding one has gained through repentance and learning as a basis for teaching others. Although learning begins as a child, the texts only provide points of orientation in the stormy, unpredictable sea of life. The skills we develop as we wrestle with these texts are the same skills we will need to navigate through life's experiences and challenges.

Beginning at the age of fifty, ibn Machiri writes, one's insight and intellect are "more settled." At this stage, a person "does not get caught up in frivolity and can control the urges to chase after emptiness. . . . He knows what must be done to avoid destruction." Ibn Machiri urges the individual to act and instruct others to act, in ways which will prevent moral and spiritual destruction. Recognizing the truth within us and offering truth to others as instruction are the challenges beginning at age 50.

"AT 60, HE ENTERS OLD AGE"

At age sixty, we realize that physical death can come at any time. Entering *zikna*, or old age, the individual becomes aware of the whiteness of his hair and beard (*zakan*). Our lives are merely shadows, Ibn Machiri writes, and only God knows the precise moment when this life will end.

Ibn Machiri tells a story of a king who advises his servants to treat each day as if it were their last. They are instructed to dress in their finest, most festive white clothing. The white clothes, representing their repentance for their sins, prepares them to enter the palace of the King. This teaching is neither a fatalistic nor a depressing view of the life journey. Ibn Machiri claims that at age 60, although we have finished much of our life's work, we maintain sufficient strength to examine, fix, and improve what is left of our lives.

"AT 70, HE TURNS GRAY"

Ibn Machiri turns to the riddles and alliteration of the Hebrew text to explain the age of 70. The Hebrew word for "gray" is *sayvah*, which ibn Machiri links etymologically to the word *teshuvah*, which means "repentance." "One's eyebrows turning from black to white," is an outward sign that one must turn away from one's bad deeds (*lashuv m'ma'asav*).

Ibn Machiri notes that this age carries a deeper sense of urgency than earlier passages. The enormous task of reflection and repentance seems disproportionate to the little time remaining in one's life. He likens the situation to preparation for Shabbat: Those who spend time and spiritual effort readying themselves for Shabbat will have a Shabbat of rest and happiness. Beginning at age 70, we realize the imminent approach of Shabbat. What preparations have we made? What preparations are still unfinished? Ibn Machiri writes, "How will I renew myself with holy, beautiful work which will be seen as good in the eyes of God? And when will this great adventure of life end?"

"AT 80, HE IS FULL OF VIGOR"

While ibn Machiri's writing about age 70 danced with alliteration, his section on age 80 dances with numerology and time. The number seven represents completion and wholeness. Once one transcends the "normal" cycle of seven to the level above, signified by the number eight, one has taken a meaningful step toward spiritual fulfillment.

Ibn Machiri points out that the seventh day of the week is Shabbat and that the seventh month of the Hebrew calendar, Tishrei, hosts the holidays of Rosh HaShanah, Yom Kippur, Sukkot, and Shemini Atzeret. "In each instance," he writes, "the seventh unit of time is precious and special. It is a time of quiet and peace. So it is also in the lifetime of a person." One who lives to age 80, ibn Machiri observes, has done so by merit of intense preparation and deep spiritual work in the first seven decades of life.

Ibn Machiri gives two reasons why age 80 is called the age of vigor. First, he traces the reference to a biblical statement that in the eightieth year a person develops *gevurot*, or "vigor." He then argues that the person has reached the eightieth year "because he overcame adversity" (*ki gavrah yado*). Obtaining eighty years can happen only with spiritual fortitude and discipline. Material accomplishment does not add years to life.

"AT 90, HE IS BROKEN DOWN"

Despite being bent over by the weakening of the body, a person of 90 years has "surpassed the number of years which he is allotted. He is asked, therefore, to tell the great story of his life and how he achieved this miraculous accomplishment. He reflects on the good deeds which lengthened his days on earth and enabled him to continue his work of Torah."

Living to this age is seen as miraculous, a testimony to the righteousness of the individual. The great *mitzvah* at this age is to use one's life as a basis for teaching others how such a long life can be lived. Ibn Machiri instructs us to seek out people who have reached their ninetieth birthdays and ask them how to merit long lives, how to avoid doing evil, and how to replace the soiled clothes of one who sins with the pure white garb of one who has repented sincerely.

"AT 100, HE IS LIKE A DEAD PERSON"

In what way is a person 100 years old "like a dead person"? The intellectual capacity of one who reaches 100 years of age is so diminished that it is not possible to recall with any accuracy the specific sins one has committed. If a 100-year-old no longer has understanding or self-awareness, he is unable to consciously address his transgressions and repent. Even the purest of individuals needs to continue to atone and make repentance.

Ibn Machiri adds, almost rhetorically: "The person is so old and faded from this world that he could not sin even if he wanted to. What kind of *teshuvah* can be done by someone who cannot even sin?"

THE MEANING OF OUR LIVES BRINGS US CLOSER TO GOD

Just as *Sefer Seder Hayom* guides us on a journey to God "every day, every night, every Shabbat, every holy day, in our homes, on our journeys, when we lay down and when we rise up," the text *Ben Hamesh L'mikrah* provides a map through the decades of one's life. The text gives voice to the mystical view that time is not linear and sequential but a richly textured, ultimately mysterious phenomenon.[2]

Although ibn Machiri writes of pain and loss, sin and redemption, it would be an exaggeration and distortion to conclude that he presents a profoundly negative attitude toward living, aging, and dying. In his book *The Middle Passage,* psychoanalyst James Hollis articulates a Jungian perspective, which complements ibn Machiri's view that life can be a hard, sometimes painful, journey. Hollis quotes Jung's observation that neurotic pain "must be understood ultimately as the suffering of a soul which has not discovered its meaning."[3] It is in this discovery, ibn Machiri would tell Jung, that one addresses the challenges of living, aging, and dying. And we use the discovery of that meaning to bring us closer to the Source of all Creation and to provide a joyful, uplifting, affirming life as a Jew. That we live, age, and die is a clear expression of the existence, patience, and benevolence of the Source of all Creation. Each moment, day, week, year, or decade in which we participate in this fantastic drama is a most amazing gift. Know and love the gift, ibn Machiri taught. Do not waste this incredibly mysterious and wonderful opportunity.

Surprisingly, in the closing lines of his text, ibn Machiri abruptly changes his direction, tone, and substance. We hear no more of sin, desire, and lust. In fact, he appears to question the assumptions upon which his text had been based, and he suggests another teaching of the Mishna: that a person should continue to seek a most "suitable" friend, or *chaver*, who will teach and accompany him through the stages of his life. For example, if one is dealing with the energies of young adulthood, he can find a *chaver* who knows and understands the rhythms and challenges of that period, while a *chaver* in his 80s or 90s would be asked about the meaning of life.

This final turn and twist in the text is quite amazing. Until then, the primary focus had been on how individuals should address their own personal problems, issues, sins, and repentance. This spiritual work was to be a matter of individual effort, performed alone with God. In these closing lines, though, ibn Machiri urges us to do our most important spiritual work with others, and even suggests that it cannot be done otherwise.

Aging does not necessarily bring a lonely burden of sinning and repenting. Indeed, Judaism teaches, *"ain ha Torah niknet elah b' chavurah,"* "the Torah can only be acquired through community." From the small village of Ein Zeitim at the end of the sixteenth century, Moshe ben Yehuda ibn Machiri brought us a similar message about bringing our individual souls into loving and meaningful contact with the *neshamah klalit,* the all-inclusive soul of Creation.[4]

Joel Rosenberg teaches Judaic Studies and World Literature at Tufts University. His commentary on Genesis was published recently as part of The HarperCollins Study Bible, and he also translated Kol Haneshamah: The Reconstructionist Sabbath and Festival Prayer Book. *He is writing a book of essays about the Jewish experience on film.*

Alternate Paths to Integrity:
On Old Age in the Hebrew Bible

Joel Rosenberg

One doesn't hear much about the old age of Adam, Seth, Enosh, or Methusaleh, all of whom are said to have lived more than 900 years. Their titanic life spans should naturally make us wonder when our ancestors could properly be said to have become "old" and what the quality of life was like for those most senior of citizens. But since Scripture tells us only what it wants us to know, the only meaningful fact we can glean from its chronology of humanity's early generations is that the life span grew progressively shorter (or so it seemed to the Biblical writer) as time and history progressed.[1]

Perhaps this was the ancient historian's way of saying that the earliest humans needed more time to propagate the species or that the descent from immortality was not immediate (as the Garden story invites us to assume) but gradual, and that human beings were most responsible for their own wear and tear. At any rate, not until Genesis 6:3 does God decide to make official the diminished life span, affixing for the typical human life the more manageable sum of 120 years. That's close enough to the "70 or, by reason of strength, 80 years" mentioned by the Psalmist[2] for the human life cycle to begin to appear to us in its more familiar contours, and only at that point do we begin to find in Scripture a more focused view of old age. Of this, the Hebrew Bible has much to say, but three moments particularly stand out most vividly to me, perhaps because of the contradiction they encompass.

THE LAST DAYS OF KING DAVID

The first is the Bible's brief description of the old age of King David.[3] The text tells us that the aged king had trouble keeping warm, even though his servants covered him amply with bedclothes. So they found for him a beautiful young virgin named Abishag, who would lie with him and attend to his needs. In its typically oblique and laconic way, Scripture doesn't tell us anything else about Abishag or about her reactions to this odd form of service, or what she and the king might have talked about, or even if she actually kept him warm. We are only told that "the King was not intimate with her."

There is infinite sadness in this short account. It tells in a remarkably condensed way how the body's death begins before death: The warmth of the life force flees, and its few remaining embers can only be fleetingly kept alive, if at all, by the warmth of others, especially the young. I'm not speaking here of sexual warmth, although the text has no qualms about mentioning the king's failed sexuality. This was, after all, a man famous for his sexual prowess, and so there was no better barometer of his condition at that moment than the sexual. It is that moment, more than any other, that the tradition chose as the premise for the drama of succession that occupies the following narrative. Somehow, David's sexual senescence and his political obsolescence are made synonymous.

Nonetheless, we can be sure that whatever blessings Abishag willingly (or unwillingly) brought to the king, more than sex was at issue here. Abishag, after all, is brought in when garments and blankets have failed. Although it might dishonor Abishag to speak of her as a garment, there is a useful metaphor here for relations between the aged and the young. The king, in a sense, is naked without her, just as some of the aged might be naked without the presence of the young. Their warmth, their conversation and laughter, their life force, their hopes and dreams are capable of warming, if only temporarily, a body and spirit from which warmth has fled. It is almost as if an unwritten commandment lay at the core of this scene: "Thou shalt not uncover the nakedness of old age."

Scripture, again in its typical way, leaves a lot unwritten in this scene, and we must write the rest of it from our imaginations. In the best-case scenario of this event, I'd like to imagine that Abishag and King David did much talking in those late-night hours, and much peaceful sleeping, and that a certain warmth, albeit a nonsexual one, passed between them. I'd like to think that King David asked her about her brothers and sisters in the town of Shunem, about her boyfriend with whom she would soon be reunited, about shepherding and farming in her village, about the smell of the dew-studded grass in the early morning, about the sound of the owl. I'd like to think they told each other their dreams, the ones they had when they were asleep, and the ones they had when they were awake. I'd like to think that David sang to her some of his more serene, upbeat psalms, and that whenever he awoke trembling from a bad dream, she stroked his face and ears until sleep returned. I'd like to think she found him wise and learned, honorable and kind.

But that is the best-case scenario. And as blankets cannot recover warmth that has fled, even such a benign reimagining cannot cover up the immense pathos that the story conveys. It seems to tell us that the grave is a place of infinite coldness and infinite aloneness.

King David's mental capacity, we should note, is in no way diminished at this advanced stage of life. So senility doesn't shield him from full awareness of his bodily incapacity. He must face it as a daily, almost minute-by-minute reproach and remember at every step who he once was and who he is no longer. This, too, is a form of nakedness.

Is there a psalm for this condition? Will the old psalms

serve? Is it similar to being helpless before one's foes in battle? Is this a battle in which the opportune help of the Eternal in a moment of need can make a difference? Is there a psalm for sadness? Or for opportunities missed? Or for some wrong turn at a crossroad that one took years earlier that made all the difference in the world?

Prayer can cover any variety of moments in the present, but is it adequate to rewriting the past? The richer the life, the more numerous the opportunities for regret, but is there a psalm for regret? Is there a psalm for conversations we wish we had had with a loved one who is long gone? Is there music that can soften or make more bearable an emptiness in the heart? Surely, even a best-case scenario of old age cannot cover that kind of nakedness.

JACOB'S YEARS OF SOJOURNING

Another scriptural moment reflecting old age comes at a time of great triumph and happiness for the House of Israel: Jacob is reunited in Egypt with his son, Joseph, whom he had long believed was dead. Joseph then takes him to meet Pharaoh.[4] It is an archetypal moment—the head of the House of Israel meets the head of the Egyptian nation—but the scene is almost comic in its brevity. Jacob greets—or blesses—Pharaoh, and Pharaoh, not knowing what to talk about, asks him, "How many are the years of your life?" And Jacob answers, "The years of my sojournings are one hundred and thirty. Few and hard have been the years of my life, and they have not measured up to the years of my fathers' sojournings."

This is an uncommonly candid glimpse into the inner life of Jacob. Pharaoh's question had presumably dealt only with a quantity of years, but Jacob feels motivated to comment on their quality. (The Hebrew word *kammah* means both "how many?" and "how?") This man, who in the end will have been both dispenser and recipient of the bounty of God, both giver and receiver of blessing, now dwells on the dearth of blessing in his life. The Hebrew is more revealing than the English. Our translations usually say simply "years," but both Pharaoh and Jacob speak of the "days of the years," requiring us to focus not just on a span of time but on the *experience that fills it.* And English translations usually say "hard," although Jacob actually says "evil."

It is only at that moment that the full significance of Jacob's life compared with the lives of his parents and grandparents becomes clear. All the years of hard labor, debt, servitude, household strife, fear and trembling, famine, exile, and bereavement now speak louder than the few moments of blessing, promise, and redemption. Jacob, the inveterate competitor, is here moved to compare his attainments with those of his generational predecessors, and his years do not measure up, in quantity or in quality, to theirs. This is a moment of profound despair. In his famous essay "The Eight Ages of Man," Erik Erikson spoke of the final stage of life, which is characterized as a struggle between "ego integrity and despair." Erikson's reproach seems merciless:

> [Integrity] is [the] accrued assurance of [one's] proclivity for order and meaning . . . an experience which conveys some world order and spiritual sense, no matter how dearly paid for. It is the acceptance of one's one and only life cycle as something that had to be, and that, by necessity, permitted of no substitutions: it thus means a new, a different love of one's parents. It is a comradeship with the ordering ways of distant times and different pursuits . . . [T]he possessor of integrity is ready to defend the dignity of his own life style against all physical and economic threats. For he knows that an individual life is the accidental coincidence of but one

life cycle with but one segment of history; and that for
him, all human integrity stands or falls with the one
style of integrity of which he partakes. . . .

The lack or loss of this accrued ego integration is
signified by fear of death: the one and only life cycle is
not accepted as the ultimate of life. Despair expresses
the feeling that the time is now short, too short for the
attempt to start another life and to try out alternate
roads to integrity.[5]

To Erikson, each stage of life encompasses a polarity
(such as trust/mistrust, autonomy/shame and doubt, ini-
tiative/guilt), as if one party to the struggle would be van-
quished while the other stands in triumph. But Jacob, the
archetypal wrestler, would surely tell us that no stage of
life carries unqualified victory or defeat. The angel of
doubt, after all, retreats without disappearing, and the
victorious ego limps away with the wounds of battle
etched on its loins. We would misread Jacob's words to
Pharaoh if we were not to see them as part of a moment
in flux. Jacob, in a sense, is still grappling with the angel
he left behind at the river Yabbok. Despair attacks him
momentarily, but there is still enough blessing (albeit
stolen and wrested from others) left in him to mete out,
in varying degrees, to his children and grandchildren.
And indeed, just prior to his meeting with Pharaoh, at his
reunion with the long-lost Joseph, Jacob had indicated
his readiness for death: "Now I can die, now that I have
seen your face, and seen that you are still alive!"[6]

In fact, if we omit everything from the text that is *not*
the speech of Jacob, those two contradictory utterances of
his, one of joy and one of despair, are adjacent moments.
They confirm the impression that Jacob is, indeed, still
wrestling in the same battle he has been waging since the
womb, where he battled with Esau. And that, too, tells us
something important about old age: The issues of our
youth never wholly disappear, but remain within us to

the end. All too often, others confuse this clinging to the past with a failure to confront the change around us. But only by being who we are can we reinterpret our obsessions in light of what we see now. For most of us, a lifetime is too short a time to resolve our internal quarrels. To say, as Erikson does, that the one and only life cycle is not accepted as the ultimate of life is not a gesture of despair but an insistence that the time we spend in our bodies is too small and too pitiful to contain us. Jacob, surely, would have found a kindred spirit in the poet Dylan Thomas (who died young), who wrote about raging against the dying of the light, the fading of youth.

Perhaps for this reason, what Pharaoh calls "life" Jacob calls "sojournings." He is relentlessly a stranger to his biological life, a resident alien in the land of bodily time. Jacob is used to being on the lam. And Pharaoh, with his question about Jacob's age, is, from Jacob's perspective, simply one more immigration officer in search of vital statistics.

Jacob, for his part, turns Pharaoh's question on its head by taking it so seriously and answering it so personally. But the conversation seems to fall apart before it has barely begun. One can only imagine that Pharaoh, who was accustomed to being viewed as a god, was brought uncomfortably close to being reminded that he, too, was of flesh. Surely, Jacob would have been able to read on Pharaoh's face the desire for him to quickly exit from this audience, and so he lets Pharaoh off the hook by blessing him and leaving. Thus ends Israel's first and only meeting with Egypt on an equal footing. From then on, the House of Israel would look upon Egypt only from a high station or from a low station—or glancing backward from the road as it flees toward its own Land.

The archetypal dimension of Jacob's encounter is, in effect, the very reverse of its plain sense. Jacob, who is old, is the embodiment of a young civilization, while Pharaoh, who seems at this juncture immune from aging, embodies an ancient civilization. It therefore might seem strange that Jacob is the one who is more openly pained by the weight of the past, by the puniness of his achievements measured against those of earlier generations. And this, in its way, is prophetic of the nation he has engendered, of its destined vocation of ceaseless study, struggle, and remembrance, of its relentless conviction that things used to be better than they are, but might someday be better again. Pharaoh, by contrast, represents stasis, lack of memory, and the self-proclaimed eternity of a culture that sees nothing new under the sun. In such an Egypt, it will be all too easy for a new Pharaoh to arise "who knew not Joseph."

As it turns out, Jacob was to live another seventeen years beyond his meeting with Pharaoh. He died at the age of 147—long enough, surely, to soften somewhat his despair over lost "alternate roads to integrity." Even so, down to the very end, his right hand battled with his left, and the angel of the Yabbok continued to whisper in his ear. The Book of Genesis devotes two whole chapters to Jacob's distribution of blessing and inheritance; nowhere are the issues of one's life better played out than in the hard choices over who gets what—and why. Of all the rites of passage, perhaps the making of a will is the most difficult, the most painful, and the most self-defining. Jacob's deathbed blessings are a perfect register of the turmoils that shaped him; even as he tries to vindicate subversion, they are a scandalous validation of the system he had once subverted, for they affirm once again the entrenchments of unequal love.

If only we fully understood what the words really mean as part of our tradition and as part of our personal history. All we have is the text, which, by maddeningly withholding so much of its riches from us, requires us to decipher it the way that grown-up orphaned children try to unravel clues about the inner life of their departed parents from snapshots of the parents' youth, from half-remembered snatches of conversation, from the cracked record of neurotic scenarios that repeat endlessly in life without shedding much light.

Jacob's first deathbed blessings go not to his children but to his grandchildren, Menasseh and Ephraim. Even before this, he *adopts* them as his children, stating, "They are mine, like Reuben and Simeon." As we eventually see, they are to be considered a great deal more his than Reuben and Simeon. It is also easy, perhaps, to understand the unspoken part of his explanation for this action: "For when I was coming from Paddan-Aram, Rachel died in my company in the land of Canaan, when still a short distance from Ephrath, and I buried her there on the road to Ephrath, which is Bethlehem."[7] There's a curious skewing in the Hebrew version of this sentence, which properly reads: "And I, . . . Rachel died in my company . . . " as if it were he who had undergone Rachel's birth-pangs and death who was the subject of the sentence. And yet Jacob, like Rachel, experienced a type of birthing travail—the one caused by him and Esau—a travail that still rages like "a ravenous wolf."[8]

THE DELIGHT OF SARAH'S LAUGHTER

The final scriptural moment is the first chronologically. Starting with Genesis 18:1, Abraham and Sarah regale three mysterious guests with Bedouin hospitality. Abraham stands before them as they eat beneath a tree, and Sarah stands at the opening of the tent that stands behind him. And the guest—for these three, who in the desert heat begin to grow luminous and indistinct, have now become one—now says, "Where is Sarah, your wife?" Abraham replies, "There, in the tent," and the visitor says, "I shall surely return to you in the ripening of time, and you shall behold then a child for Sarah, your wife." And Sarah, who long ago stopped having her menstrual flow, laughs!

The text says that Sarah laughed—*bekirbah*—which we normally translate as "to herself" or literally "within herself." Tanhuma and Rashi render this "at her innards," as if to say (comments Rashi), "these inner parts carrying a child? These shrunken breasts bearing milk?" And the biblical Sarah adds, "After I have worn out, shall I have *ednah*?" This, too, is a word whose meaning is unclear: Pleasure? delight? Eden? Rashi's explanation is no clearer. He says, "*tzihtzuah basar,*" which means literally, "the polishing of flesh" (the friction of sexual contact?), or, depending on how the first word is translated, "clarity of flesh" or "purity of flesh" or even, "glistening fluid of flesh." I like the last one, because it carries the suggestion of the fluids of sexual excitement, of placental nourishment, of a life growing within a life—all senses that merge in meaning with pleasure, delight, and Eden. Shall this dried-up flesh find its fluids returning? Moses, too, when he died at 120, was said to be one "whose eyes had not dimmed, whose moisture had not departed."[9]

But then, maybe it simply means "within herself." Maybe there's a peculiar nuance to that inward laughter that even the divine ear seems to momentarily misconstrue. This isn't a laughter of embarrassment or scorn, or one that disparages her insides or her body, or that expresses disbelief or questions the divine design. It is a quiet laughter of wonderment and awe, of amazement and bemusement, a laughter of . . . well, of *ednah*, pleasure and delight, of the womb widening, of fluids returning, of life reawakening, of hope kindled and fed.

This laughter has no recipient and no target. It is a laughter aimed somewhat at oneself, but it is also gentle and liberating—a laughter that realizes we can never be fully certain of who we are, even long after we thought we knew for sure. It is the sudden discovery of what Erikson called "alternate roads to integrity," the startling awareness late in life that hundreds of such roads are accessible around us no matter how advanced we are in age, if only the veil about our eyes can be lifted, if only the angel who brings the message can be heard. This kind of laughter is how we discover not to take ourselves too seriously. It confirms our humanity. It is the lifeblood of a society's health. It is the life force itself.

But *does* the divine ear misconstrue it? For the same reasons that we can easily misunderstand Sarah's laughter, we can also misunderstand God's reply: "Why does Sarah laugh, and say, 'Truly shall I bear a child now that I am old?' Is anything too wondrous for *The Fount of Life?*" And then, further on, we have the following troublesome exchange:

> And Sarah denied it, saying, "I did not laugh," for she was afraid.

> And [YHWH] said, "No, but you did laugh."

With just a slight alteration in punctuation and emphasis, this exchange can be construed quite differently:

> And Sarah protested it, saying, "No, I laughed because I was in awe."

> And [YHWH] said, "Ah, but you did laugh."

In the first version, Sarah denies her own laughter. In the second she protests YHWH's interpretation of her laughter. In the first, she is terrified to find a human visitor suddenly become a divine presence. In the second, she is an intimate of that presence, able to converse with it as with a friend. In the first, YHWH seems to be accusatory; in the second, YHWH is teasing. In the first, the laughter seems inappropriate; in the second, it is accepted and celebrated.

Maybe both versions are true. Maybe some parts of each are true. Maybe Sarah's awe turned to fear, and then the Divinity broke the tension by replying in a teasing way that turns her fear back into awe. Maybe, at that moment, they all laughed, including Abraham, and that laughter rang from one end of the universe to the other.

Danny Siegel is an author, lecturer, and poet. He has spoken in more than 200 North American Jewish communities on tsedakah *and Jewish values. His twenty books address such topics as* mitzvah heroes *and practical, personalized* tsedakah. *Ziv Tsedakah Fund, the nonprofit* mitzvah *organization he founded in 1981, has distributed nearly $2,000,000 to individuals and projects.*

The Mitzvah *of Bringing Out the Beauty in Our Elders' Faces*

Danny Siegel

We need to know the name of the *mitzvah.* Just as *Shabbat* is most certainly not the same as "Saturday," *tsedakah* is not the mere equivalent of "charity," and Torah is so much more than "law." So, too, the Jewish term for relating to elders is much more than simply "respect."

The name of the *mitzvah* concerning elders is הידור פני זקן *Hiddur pnai zaken.* The first word in this phrase, *hiddur,* is one of those Hebrew words that one struggles to translate and retranslate over many years. As life's experiences enrich our understanding of Judaism's grasp of what old age is all about, and as we meet more and more elders and ourselves approach old age, we continually redefine this concept. Right now, when I am 52, my translation of *hiddur* and its root, *hadar,* would be something like "beauty, grandeur, awesomeness," and my current translation of *hiddur pnai zaken* would, rather lyrically, be "allowing the beauty, light, glory, and majesty of our elders' faces to emerge, reemerge, and shine forth (as we, in turn, benefit from their light)."

The term *hiddur* comes from the verse in Leviticus 19:32:

מפני שיבה תקום והדרת פני זקן

Mipnei sayvah takum v'haderet p'nai zaken.

"You shall rise before an elder and allow the beauty, glory, and majesty of their faces to emerge."

Reverence for older people is most assuredly a *mitz-*

vah, and whatever it takes to make it happen, Jews are required to do no less than Jews are required to fast on Yom Kippur. A few ways to do this include giving elders access to computers (and specific networks for elders on the Internet); providing them with cats, dogs, birds, fish, butterflies, plants, and gardens; having them make *tsedakah* boxes and challah covers for us or with us; providing them with meaningful jobs; adapting automobiles to let them continue to drive despite individual impairments they may have; driving them, if they can no longer drive, to cemeteries before Rosh Hashana to pray at the graves of family members and friends; arranging for regular visits with infants and children; installing handrails, ramps, and curb cuts outside synagogues and other Jewish communal buildings; taking photographs with them; reviewing old photographs and writing oral histories with them; providing them with catalogs from Elderhostel and providing scholarships to Elderhostel programs for those living on limited incomes.

Which is all to say: Jews are required to provide whatever is best suited to the personal needs and desires of the elderly.

And which is also to say: Provide whatever will rid our elders of possible loneliness and give them happiness.

Of course, there is no *them* and there is no *us*. God willing, we will all reach old age. Maimonides said it best when he defined the *mitzvah* of loving others as we love ourselves:

כל מה שארצה לעצמי ארצה לו כמוהו

Kol mah sh'ertze l'atzmi ertze lo k'mohu.

"Whatever I want for myself, I want the same for others; whatever I do not want for myself, I do not want for others." (*Sefer HaMitzvot*, Positive *Mitzvah* 206)

Just as we are required to figure out ways to get

wheelchairs on to the beach and to invent beepers with Braille numbers, so too are we required to use all our talents, intelligence, and creativity to perform the *mitzvah* of *hiddur pnai zaken*.

Following are Jewish texts that provide further insight into the great, even cosmic, importance of this particular *mitzvah*. They are primarily from the Talmud. For clarity, I have put translations of the texts within quotation marks and my brief commentaries into italics.

TEXTS OF LAMENT

דאמרי אינשי כד הוינן זוטרי
לגברי השתא דקשישנא לדרדקי

"When we were young, they told us to act like adults.
Now that we are old, they treat us like babies." (Talmud Bava Kamma 92b)

Only babies should be babied. By avoiding a patronizing tone of voice, we avoid humiliating our elders. Losing our sense that a human being is still there, amid the disorientation and peculiar behavior of some elders, benefits neither the elder nor those caring for the elder. A New York Times *article described the work of a woman who takes her electronic keyboard to the homes of Alzheimer's-plagued elders and sings for them (and sometimes with them). We may not be capable of that degree of humanity, but we must strive for it.*

תניא רבי יוסי בר קיסמא אומר
טבא תרי מתלת
ווי לה לחדא דאזלא ולא אתיא
מאי היא
אמר רב חסדא ינקותא
כי אתא רב דימי אמר
ינקותא כלילא דוורדא סבותא כלילא דחילפא

"Rabbi Yossi ben Kisma says: 'Two are better than three. Woe for the one that leaves us and does not return.'
What is that?
Rav Chisda said: 'Youth.'
When Rav Dimi arrived [from Israel], he said: 'Youth is a crown of roses. Old age is a crown of thorns.'" (Talmud Shabbat 152a)

Our sages were not naïve. They observed life as keenly as does the modern geneticist who maps genes. The natural acceleration of an elder's aches and pains and slowing down is disappointing and discouraging to all. A sense of betrayal may set in: All is not well. Things were better long ago—or even not so long ago.

TEXTS ABOUT HEALTH AND LONGEVITY

איתיביה אביי
המביא גט והניחו זקן אפילו בן מאה שנה
נותן לה בחזקת שהוא קיים
...כיון דאיפליג איפליג

"Abayye made the following point:
'One who is delivering a *get* [a divorce document] on behalf of someone who was an old person—even a hundred years old—should assume that the old person is still alive . . . since, if the man has lived so long, he is bound to continue living even longer.'" (Talmud Gittin 28a)

This text refutes the universal Law of the Degeneration-with-Age Curve. A student sent me an article stating if an old person lives into his or her seventies, living into his or her eighties and beyond is more probable. I would have believed the text even without the article, but it is comforting to know that social scientists have reached the same conclusions as the Talmud.

אמרו עליו על רבי חנינא בן דוסא שהיה בן שמונים
שנה והיה עומד על רגלו אחת וחולץ מנעלו

וְנוֹעֵל מִנְעָלוֹ
אָמַר רַבִּי חֲנִינָא חַמִּין וְשֶׁמֶן שֶׁסָּכַתְנִי אִמִּי בְּיַלְדוּתִי
הֵן עָמְדוּ לִי בְּעֵת זִקְנוּתִי

"It was said of Rabbi Chanina that at the age of 80 he could still stand on one foot and remove and replace the shoe on the other foot.

Rabbi Chanina said, 'The warm baths and oil with which my mother rubbed me have served me well in my old age.'" (Talmud Chulin 24b)

When I speak about Maimonides' text "Whatever I want for myself, I want for other people," my audiences almost always react first with "Most of all, I want good health." So, they especially enjoy hearing that Rabbi Chanina was healthy in old age as a result of his mother's special care when he was a child.

But what the people in the audience really mean (but may not even suspect) is "Good health and meaning in my life," as the following selections from Maimonides indicate:

כָּל אִישׁ מִיִּשְׂרָאֵל חַיָּב בְּתַלְמוּד תּוֹרָה
בֵּין עָנִי בֵּין עָשִׁיר בֵּין שָׁלֵם בְּגוּפוֹ בֵּין בַּעַל יִסּוּרִין
בֵּין בָּחוּר בֵּין שֶׁהָיָה זָקֵן גָּדוֹל שֶׁתָּשַׁשׁ כֹּחוֹ

אֲפִילוּ הָיָה עָנִי הַמִּתְפַּרְנֵס מִן הַצְּדָקָה
וּמְחַזֵּר עַל הַפְּתָחִים...
חַיָּב לִקְבּוֹעַ לוֹ זְמַן לְתַלְמוּד תּוֹרָה בַּיּוֹם וּבַלַּיְלָה
שֶׁנֶּאֱמַר וְהָגִיתָ בּוֹ יוֹמָם וָלַיְלָה

"Everyone is required to study Torah.
Whether rich or poor, of sound body or suffering from infirmities,
young or very old and weak—
even so poor that the person survives by receiving *tsedakah*
and by begging from door to door—

all are required to fix a time for Torah study daytime and
night time,
as the verse says, 'Recite it [Torah] day and night.'
[Joshua 1:8]"
(Maimonides, Hilchot Talmud Torah 1:6)
    Only one thing needs to be said in commenting on this verse:
Retiring from Torah study is an oxymoron.

כשם שחייב אדם ללמד את בנו
כך הוא חייב ללמד את בן בנו
שנאמר והודעתם לבניך ולבני בניך

"Just as a person is required to teach his or her child, so,
too, is the person required to teach his or her grandchild,
as the verse [Deuteronomy 4:9] states, 'And make these
things known to your children and to your grandchildren.'" (Maimonides, Hilchot Talmud Torah 1:2)
    And, if I may add, also to one's great-grandchildren.

A TEXT ABOUT THE GENERATIONS

אמר רב פפא היינו דאמרי אינשי
נפישי גמלי סבי דטעיני משכי דהוגני

"Rav Pappa said: 'There are many old camels bearing the
hides of young camels on their backs.'" (Talmud Sanhedrin 52a)
    The context of Rav Pappa's words is this: Nadav and
Avihu—the aspiring sons of Aaron—expressed their hope that
Moses and Aaron would die soon so they could take over the
leadership of the Jewish people. But Nadav and Avihu died be-
fore Moses and Aaron, and Jewish sages blamed the young men
for their own early deaths.
    I hesitate to write this, but sometimes we hear similar opin-
ions, though not as blatantly expressed. If you listen carefully to
analyses of data about the increasing segment of the American

population that is old—beyond the numbers, statistics, and charts about limited resources—one hears a little bit (and it is only a little bit, and only on occasion) of this thought: "Were we not responsible for the elders, we would have more resources for ourselves." But, as I stated before, there is no them *and* us.

TEXTS ON OLD AGE

מי שהוא זקן מופלג בזקנה
אע"פ שאינו חכם עומדין לפניו

"One stands in the presence of a very old person,
even if that person is not a sage."
(Maimonides, Mishneh Torah, Hilchot Talmud Torah 6:9)

Elders have a certain glory about them, which is why we are expected to rise in their presence. Rising has nothing to do with the elders' achievements. This text encourages us to consider each elder as an individual.

וסדר הישיבה כך היא
הזקנים יושבים פניהם כלפי
העם ושאר העם כולם יושבים שורות שורות
פניהם כלפי הקודש ופני הזקנים (טור)

"The seating arrangement in synagogue is as follows:
The Elders sit facing the people, and the rest of the congregation sits in rows facing the Holy Ark and the faces of the elders." (Rabbi Moshe Isserles [quoting the Tur] on Shulchan Aruch, Orach Chaim 150:5)

In addition to learning from the Torah which is in the Ark, we can also learn from considering the faces of the elders.

TEXTS ON DYING

כמישחל בניתא מחלבא

[Rav Nachman said to Rav, "Dying was as gentle as] lifting a hair out of milk." (Talmud Mo'ed Katan 28a)

Dying should be gentle. People should live as long as God believes they should live and they should not die for the wrong reasons: from loneliness, boredom, or uselessness; for lack of food because the money of their youth will not suffice for the needs of their old age; because of reliance on medications when love and care will suffice; for lack of heat in the winter and lack of cool air in summer; for lack of good teeth because of inaccessible dental care; because no one asked them to dance or to play with their babies or to advise them on their troubled love lives; because someone did not hug them or kiss them or touch them enough; because no one asked them, "What are you good at doing?"; because young people did not rise in their presence; because the Jewish community built them gorgeous old-age homes but mistook their emotional needs for medical needs; because no one asked them to share their life stories; because no one said, "Explain this verse in the Torah for me"; because they were told too many times, "Let me do this for you"; because no one asked them for tsedakah *money when everyone else was being asked, or suggested they help prepare meals for other elders in need; because not enough people adopted* mitzvahs *that would contribute to elders' longevity and well-being.*

רב ששת איתחזי ליה בשוקא
אמר ליה בשוקא כבהמה איתא לגבי ביתא

"The Angel of Death appeared to Rav Sheshet out in the street.
Rav Sheshet screamed at him, 'In the street, like an animal? Come home with me [so I can die like a mentsh in my own bed].'"
(Talmud Mo'ed Katan 28a)

And, if some elders are dying for the wrong reasons, we must teach them to do as Rav Sheshet did, to scream and demand a better end. As Myriam Mendilow, z"l, the genius who founded Life Line for the Old in Jerusalem, said, "Here they forget to die." They are so busy living.

"Dying for the right reasons" is apparent at any good nursing home where there is a clear distinction between treatment and care. One of the better approaches to nursing care for the elderly, which has been proposed by Dr. William Thomas's Eden Alternative, proposes that elders enjoy the sounds of birds and the silence of cat feet stalking the birds, and the not-so-silent sounds of the paws of dogs chasing cats, and the sounds of children chasing dogs; fresh, sweet air from thousands of plants . . . and, of course, longer and happier lives.

A TEXT ON SARAH'S LIFE AND DEATH

ויהיו חיי שרה מאה שנה
ועשרים שנה ושבע שנים שני חיי שרה
ותמת שרה בקרית ארבע...
ויבא אברהם לספד לשרה ולבכתה

"Sarah lived a hundred years and twenty years and seven years.
Those were the years of Sarah's Life.
And Sarah died in Kiryat Arba . . .
Abraham mourned for her and wept for her." (Genesis 23:1–2)

Throughout the centuries, Torah commentators have been struck by the juxtaposition of "Sarah lived" with the following verse, which says, "Sarah died." Innumerable sermons have been written on these verses, but the message is clear: Until her dying day, Sarah lived fully. To be sure, she suffered dislocation and sadness. Still, she lived a full and meaningful life, experienced "adventures and troubles," and witnessed "miracles and marvelous things."

The commentators say that at the age of 100, Sarah was as beautiful as she had been at the age of twenty. "Beautiful" in the sense of "gorgeous"? I doubt it. No one can say. But of this we may be certain: At the age of 100, she was radiant and her face was majestic. By this radiance, the generations who followed her have benefited in infinite ways. This is old age as it ought to be.

II. Midlife Passages

*You shall be like a tree planted by the water,
bringing forth fruit in its season; its leaf will not
wither.*

—Psalm 1:3

MIDLIFE PASSAGES

In midlife, we enter Dante's "dark wood, where the straight way [is lost]" and we begin to wonder about—and to acknowledge—the challenges of our own aging. Midlife is a time when we look at our lives as more than a succession of years. It is a time to ask: Who am I? How shall I use my remaining years?

As we grow older and closer to death, living becomes ever more precious. In this section, Letty Cottin Pogrebin's essay, "Time Is All There Is," speaks of her concern for her "shrinking future" and her new, deepening commitment to sanctify time. In "Empty Pockets," Linda Knaster Feldman writes about reconnecting with Judaism in her mid-fifties and shares with us her joy at the gift of "starting over" in a new home and a new city. In "Cycling and Recycling," Mary Gendler describes midlife as a time to recognize and affirm "the seeds nestled in the spiritual womb." She envisions aging as a form of continued motion, acknowledging the way the details of her life have taken on a cyclical pattern.

Kerry M. Olitzky in "Redigging the Wells" and Thomas R. Cole in "You Never Knew What Powers Lay Within You" both write about themselves as they try to understand and integrate in midlife the legacies they've inherited from their parents.

At midlife, we learn that we must finally seize permission to be essentially ourselves. As we "take stock" of our lives, as we begin to understand the collapse of previously held assumptions, as we assess the first half of our lives and plan for the second half, we irrefutably acknowledge our finitude. This gives a new urgency and authenticity to our search for meaning.

Time Is All There Is

Letty Cottin Pogrebin

Time is experienced differently in different cultures. The Japanese, for instance, known for their painstaking attention to detail, pride themselves on the precision of their vocabulary for closely observed segments of time. Words such as *ma*, "the time of silence between two words or two sentences," or *nemawashi*, "the time it takes a group of people to agree on something," simply have no counterparts in other tongues.

For the Jewish people, time is schizophrenic. Marked and sanctified in religious contexts, time is then loosely squandered in social settings. In fact, "Jewish time" is famously up to thirty minutes beyond the hour for which an event was called. (The Zionist leader Nahum Goldmann once said, "I tried my whole life to come late to a Jewish meeting and never succeeded.") Commenting on Jews' congenital tardiness, Rabbi David Wolpe speculates, "Perhaps the clock moves too swiftly for our people, whose span is measured not in minutes, but millennia. So we are leisurely about beginnings." In social situations,

Letty Cottin Pogrebin, a founding editor of Ms. *magazine and nationally known lecturer and social critic, is the author of eight books, including* Deborah, Golda and Me: Being Female and Jewish in America *and* Getting Over Getting Older: An Intimate Journey.

we are also leisurely about endings. "Christians leave and never say good-bye," goes the old wisecrack, "while Jews say good-bye and never leave." Or as my friend J.J. puts it, "How long did you stay after you left?"

Yet, in the spiritual sphere, Jewish time is never casual, never flabby or undisciplined. On the contrary, it is measured to the nanosecond: Starting and ending times are observed "religiously," and time itself is separated into two dimensions: the ordinary and the sacred. Judaism's preoccupation with time is evident throughout Jewish texts and traditions. The Torah opens with "In the Beginning" and the Talmud with "From when?" Both are designations of time which, according to Debbie Weissman, the director of the Institute for Humanistic Jewish Education in Jerusalem, suggest that "the main thrust of Torah is to teach us how to spend our limited time on earth wisely." In *Jewish Days: A Book of Jewish Life and Culture Around the Year,* Francine Klagsbrun writes, "Jews as a people have been more connected to time than to places or things." Given Jews' peripatetic history, we haven't had the luxury of attachment to place (except for our eternal attachment to Jerusalem) or to things that might be wrenched from our possession by the next oppressor. Our connection to time, however, is woven so much into the very fabric of Jewish life and Jewish death that one could say we are not just the people of the book, but of the clock and the calendar.

THE NUMBERS OF OUR LIVES

The Jewish day is delineated by a set of prayers and time-bound obligations. The night, according to the Talmud, is divided into three watches: In the first, dogs bark; in the second, donkeys bray; and in the third, mothers nurse babies and husbands and wives speak in whispers. (Each watch is symbolic of a stage of civilization leading to the Messianic era). On Friday evening, the Sabbath candles must be kindled no later than eighteen minutes before sundown. On Saturday, the end of the Sabbath is calibrated in time (forty-two minutes after sunset) and in stars (a minimum of three), and the final blessing of the *havdalah* service demarcates the separation between sacred and profane time. The Jewish month is divided precisely into twenty-nine days, twelve hours, and 793 *halakim*—a measurement of three and a third seconds. Each new moon is celebrated with the rituals and study sessions of Rosh Chodesh ("head of the month"), a special day that has become associated with women. The Jewish lunar year is 354 days long with a leap month every three years or so to catch up with the solar calendar. Jews observe a sabbatical year every seven years and a jubilee year every fiftieth year.

The human life cycle is similarly time-tethered. The *brit milah* (ritual circumcision) takes place on the eighth day of a male infant's life. The bar or bat mitzvah occurs at age 13. The traditional Jewish mourning period is divided into fixed time segments: The first seven days (*shiva*) makes different demands than the rest of the first month (*shloshim*), which makes different demands than does the next eleven months.

Likewise, the holiday cycle is freighted with enumerated time: Six traditional fast days; eight days to eat unleavened bread; eight days to light Chanukah candles; ten days of repentance; seven weeks in which we "count the *omer,*" which compute the days between Passover, the Israelites' liberation from slavery, and Shavuot, the giving of the law on Mount Sinai. Counting is the Jewish way of noticing: It is a reminder that a day counts—or that it doesn't. Counting imputes meaning; one does not count what one does not value.

MAKING SENSE OF OUR
SHRINKING FUTURE

"To live as Jews, we must experience time distinctively," writes Rabbi Irving Greenberg. Which is not to say that Jews are better than other peoples, only that they are heirs to a unique means of recording, sensing, and ordering time—a legacy I absorbed through ethnic osmosis and religious praxis.

Since turning 50 a few years ago (*anno horribilus,* to quote Britain's Queen), I have become even more time-obsessed. For most women of my generation, growing older raises concerns about appearance, a reasonable focus given the culture's pathological equation of beauty with youth. For me, however, the core issue is not age, but time; not my lost looks, but my lost years. I'm not saying I relish each new sign of physical deterioration, but depression over one's ever-expanding waistline cannot compare with the existential angst brought on by contemplating one's incredible shrinking future.

The questions seem cosmic and overwhelming. Why does time seem to speed up the older we get? How can I slow life down and experience it more mindfully? How much time do I have left in which to enjoy my loved ones, do my work, be an active part of my community? How long will my senses let me read the newspaper, taste a peach, listen to Mozart? Actuarial tables say that the average woman in her fifties will live at least three more decades, but how many of those years will be healthy, sentient, and productive? Why is it that the people who most seem to cherish life are those who are facing death? Can I reorder my priorities without the diagnosis of a life-threatening illness? Can I use the knowledge of my mortality to savor time more fully right now?

Since turning 50, I've become not only more obsessed with time but more mindful of it. Aware of the glory of the ordinary—of "the miracle of a boring evening at home" as one Holocaust survivor, Gerda Weissman Klein, put it when she accepted an Academy Award for the film based on her life in the name of all those who never lived to see that miracle. I also see how often we take the ordinary for granted, how most of us live in T.S. Eliot's "unattended moment." I've taken to studying time. If I really concentrate, I can feel it racing by. Sometimes, I can even slow it down, though attentiveness to the moment is no more natural than good posture, and even the most dutiful consciousness tends to wander off, forgetting its mission.

The urgency of Thomas Mann's admonition speaks to my soul: "Hold fast the time! Guard it, watch over it, every hour, every minute! Disregarded it slips away, like a lizard, smooth, slippery, faithless. . . . Hold every moment sacred. Give each clarity and meaning, each the weight of thine awareness, each its true and due fulfillment." But how? The only moments I know that are measured so exactly and lived so watchfully are musical moments—that millisecond when the timpani must enter or the cymbals clash—or the attenuated ten-second count in a boxing match or the final seconds in a close basketball game when one feels time pass into a different dimension. If human destiny were to swing back and forth as precipitously as the score of a basketball game, we too might tune into every second with rapt attention. Otherwise, it's impossible (if not insane) to attempt such vigilance as would be required to heed Mann's words and give each moment equal weight. By the same token, it would be unrealistic to hope to live each day with the "unambiguous happiness" that the author Robert Hine felt when he emerged from years of blindness and beheld the world in all its glory—the same world the rest of us hardly notice when we wake up to it every morning. Short of returning from death or darkness, how can we see more clearly what we have while we have it?

THE GIFT OF SHABBAT

I find my answer in the Jewish view of time, whose concepts are eminently transportable to secular life. In his book *The Sabbath*, Abraham Joshua Heschel says that most people look at time as "a slick treacherous monster with a jaw like a furnace, incinerating every moment of our lives." Recoiling in fear from its fierce appetites and its foreshadowing of our mortality, we turn our backs on time and take refuge in space, or rather in what Heschel calls "thing-hood," substances that occupy space.

Reading this, I realize that I spend much of my life producing *things*—magazine articles, vegetable soup, political petitions—things I can see, touch, read; things I can measure as the product of my waking hours; things that take up space in my life. As long as I have something to show for my time, I tell myself that I know where the time went and what it was for. I feel I master time when I use it well, packing it to the fullest. But, insists Heschel, "One can only master time in time."

You don't have to be Jewish to see the paradox. While most of us try to control time by harnessing it to produce things that have a real presence in physical space, we miss experiencing time as a thing unto itself. Time *as* time can only be mastered in its own realm while we're inside it, attending to it, appreciating it, moving with and not against it. This, Heschel writes, is why we have the Sabbath—God's gift of time.

The novelist Mary Gordon once interviewed Alice Shalvi, a prominent Israeli feminist and founding chair of the Israel Women's Network, who also happens to be an Orthodox Jew, a professor of English literature, and the grandmother of fifteen.

"How do you do it all?" asked Gordon.

"The answer," said Shalvi, "is the Sabbath. How many women do you know who have twenty-four hours a week when they are not on call, [but are] forced to reflect and to be quiet?"

Though as fully engaged in worldly pursuits as anyone I know, Alice Shalvi has something in her life that most of us are missing. Heschel calls it, variously, "a palace in time . . . not a date but an atmosphere . . . a sanctuary in time . . . the opportunity to sanctify time, to raise the good to the level of the holy."

BECOMING MINDFUL OF EACH MOMENT

Such blissful certitude is beyond me, but with some effort—a leap of consciousness, if not faith—I've been able to construct a vastly scaled down version of the palace in time. I am learning to set aside moments of pure-time serenity, moments that allow me to cherish life despite, or because of, the ever-encroaching intimations of mortality that come with age, moments in which I can be intensely mindful of the present as it is unfolding, whether in stillness or in passion. I have not lost my need to produce "things," nor can I hold every moment sacred as Mann would have it, or even every Sabbath, as Heschel and my ancestors would wish. But I find that I can perform one small ritual that satisfies my need for mindfulness in the present. I can stop running long enough to honor those moments, ordinary or sublime, that seem to me deserving of elevation "to the level of the holy." I call these my *shehechiyanu* moments, and I acknowledge them as gifts of time.

Observant Jews say a blessing over dozens of everyday acts, from waking up to washing, breaking bread, drinking wine, studying Torah, doing a good deed, even going to the bathroom. The blessings help them acknowledge the wonders of creation and notice things that might otherwise be done mechanically and without inner meaning.

I have always been especially moved by one blessing in particular, the *shehechiyanu*, which is usually said at the start of a holiday, or at a *simchah*, a joyful event such as a wedding, or upon doing or seeing something for the first time, something that gives one inordinate happiness. It is a brief sentence that simply thanks God for having sustained us and enabled us to live long enough to reach this special moment. It is also known as the Blessing over Time.

I've taken to saying a *shehechiyanu* in situations that overwhelm me with awe and gratitude—moments of transcendent joy, love, humility, or peace, in which doing and being, an act and its meaning, are one and the same. Living in a *shehechiyanu* moment brings me as close as I have ever come in secular life to the realm of the sacred. The least I can do is to stop and say, "Thank you." The least any of us can do is to stop complaining about aging and start feeling grateful for the glorious gift of the time of our lives.

Empty Pockets:
Beginning Again in Midlife

Linda Knaster Feldman

Doors were closing. The *Los Angeles Times,* downsizing for the third time, dismissed 200 of us. Friends were drifting, taking Prozac, and unable to turn life styles into a life. My daughter was five hours away by car and my son two and a half hours by plane. I was divorced for the second time and could barely remember the days when I walked into a room and all heads turned in my direction.

A year before, broke and midway through my fifties, I was living in a room in my brother's house no larger than one in a nursing home. I was doing better now: a new car and computer, a book deal with a major publisher, and a one-bedroom apartment of my own.

Behind my desk was a photograph of Georgia O'Keeffe with that "don't mess with me—I know what I'm doing" expression on her face. I sat in my over-sized gray chair bought on Venice Boulevard for $12 and wanted my face to say what Georgia's did.

Linda Knaster Feldman, a native of Queens, New York, has worked in politics and written for Senator Alan Cranston, Barbra Streisand, McCall's, *and* Rolling Stone. *For several years, she wrote a weekly column about older people for the* Los Angeles Times. *She cowrote with gerontologist James Birren* Where To Go From Here: Discovering Your Own Life's Wisdom *(Simon & Schuster).*

I spent a few days whining after the *Times'* ax fell: "I just can't seem to get ahead. I have no life, and even if I did, I have no one to share it with." Then I spent a few days counting my blessings: "I have a book to write. I have wonderful children who love me. I'm a size eight. I have a granddaughter named Kaya Raven." But then I started asking myself, "How will I end up?" I only knew that I didn't want to be an old lady living in Los Angeles without money.

I drove up to Santa Cruz to see my daughter and granddaughter. Since my granddaughter's birth, I had visited once a month for a week. My daughter's husband had left her to be with his "authentic soul mate." Only now, a year later, did I realize that he had done them a favor and unwittingly set in motion the first ripple of what would become a crucial part of my new life.

On this trip, I thought about possibly moving there—a place where women never shave their legs or wear makeup, panty hose, or silk blouses—so I could live near my daughter and granddaughter. I dreamed of a yellow house with lace curtains, a sunporch, and a large back yard with fruit trees. As a writer, I needed a place where I would enjoy being indoors. On my way out of town, I stopped to look at the last possible house rental. The house was yellow. With lace curtains. And a lemon tree in the back yard. I dubbed it "Snow White's cottage." The owner and I hit it off, and three days later I wrote her a check for $3,600—first, last, and security.

My moving date was September 21, *erev Rosh Hashanah*, 1995. I vacillated between ecstasy and terror. For several days, I had no appetite, slept poorly, and couldn't work. My hands were icy cold and it was August in Los Angeles.

DAYS OF COURAGE

I flipped through my Rolodex, calling folks I hadn't spoken to in a very long time. "I've decided to move to Santa Cruz and wanted to say good-bye," was how I started off each call. I did this for ten days. I couldn't get over how people reacted—as though what I was doing took courage.

Three people gave me the name of the same person to look up as soon as I arrived: Murray Baumgarten, a professor at the University of California at Santa Cruz. I called him before I left Los Angeles. "What are you doing for Rosh Hashanah?" he asked. "Join the temple and have dinner with us. See you this weekend."

Join the temple? The last time I was a synagogue member, I was married, my children were attending Hebrew school, and I was demanding that the Hebrew school principal resign because of incompetency. The night before I left Los Angeles, I joined Santa Cruz's Temple Beth El by fax. By return fax, I was advised that my High Holiday tickets would be waiting for me.

As soon as I turned my rented moving truck northward onto Highway 101 toward Santa Cruz, I felt free. I left behind my misery, some good work, more people who cared about me than I had realized, two ex-husbands, and not one conflicting emotion. I had engineered an ending—a conscious disengagement that released me to my own future. I was dedicated to creating a new life and not being a victim of a life lived without awareness.

My daughter and I began our relationship again. My granddaughter and I began to know each other anew. My Jewishness took on a new relevance. That first weekend in Santa Cruz was no accident of timing. Murray Baumgarten taught me the concept of *kavanah:* Ordinary prayer or thought, given conscious intention, could be elevated to a higher level. Had I not been a Jew, would this relocation have been the same?

I was not afraid life would change. But I was afraid of surrendering my will so change could occur. I had never been one to go with the flow. Now, I had to learn to be patient in Santa Cruz while writing a book about a process to which I had only just awakened: becoming an adult. So I "became" the book. And I became a Jew again. And I started understanding that there was a higher power Whom I must trust—starting with myself.

PUTTING MY TRUST IN GOD

At my daughter Julia's prodding, we began to celebrate Shabbat together. My granddaughter included one extra *Amen* after every blessing, and we still laugh at this new tradition. Our ordinary life stopped on Friday night, and we rejoiced with each other. I learned how to make Julia's vegetarian tofu dishes taste a little "Jewish."

I don't remember when I started saying "Thank you, God" for a beautiful day, or for writing two pages that didn't end up in the trash, or for the sweet baby kisses, or for my son Jason, who passed the bar examination, or for fragrant roses, or for the smell of sunshine in the sheets on the laundry line. All this is now a part of my daily life.

My granddaughter calls me *Bubbe*. I tried to talk her out of this when she first spoke that word. I was hoping for "grandmere," something a little elegant that she could call out to me when we were at the ballet together. But *Bubbe?* Where did that come from? When she is impossibly sweet she calls me "my *Bubbe*." It's the "my" part that melts my heart. I belong to someone.

My granddaughter is the center from which all things balance in my life. Would I have found that had I not changed my life at 55? Am I happy? I do not own a house. I have no health insurance and no dependable source of income. I am several thousand dollars in debt, haven't shopped retail in three years, I have no serious romance, and I have no idea of what my next project will be. But the answer is, "Yes, I am definitely happy."

I submitted my book two months earlier than scheduled. During the week that I waited to hear from my editor, I took a walk in the redwoods by myself. I found a circle of trees and sat in their midst—the kid who lived behind a candy store in New York, a child of the working class, a woman who gave up her virginity in Holland to a Chilean diplomat, and a woman who had had six careers. I looked up at the treetops, wondering what would become of me. Whatever my fate, it was no longer entirely in my hands. What a thing to admit. I had done all that I could do.

On the first anniversary of my arrival on Rosh Hashanah, I heard Rabbi Litvak talk about how Jewish bodies are traditionally buried in clothing without pockets because we should leave this earth having completed our purpose here. I thought, "Why not retire at the end of every day with empty pockets, having 'spent' all your imagination and resources and not knowing whether tomorrow would provide another opportunity?"

My year in Santa Cruz had been a good one. Georgia O'Keeffe's picture still hangs behind my computer, but now we have some mutuality in our eyes. Life is good, but no less difficult. The horror of finally becoming an adult is that there is no one to blame. And the joy of finally becoming an adult is that I have, at last, realized what my friend gerontologist Robert Butler calls an appreciation of the importance of the elementals in life—nature, sensuality, relationships, and the creative spirit—which keep us vulnerable to the beauty around. My pockets are empty every night, but my spirit is ready to take on whatever might be next.

"You Never Knew What Powers Lay Within You"

Thomas R. Cole

One morning in September 1953, my father, Burton David Michel, went off to work and drove his car into a bridge abutment. He never came home. The Jewish New Year always coincides with the anniversary of my father's death. Saying *kaddish* for him, I have rarely been able to open my heart (as the prayer exhorts) to glorify, exalt, and honor the One who is beyond all praise. It has never been easy for me to taste the sweetness of a New Year, to celebrate the birthday of the world, or to feel the joy of creation.

Now, at the age of 47, I struggle to awaken from the long psychic numbing that followed my father's death. If only I could have learned about death more gently, like the six-year old in Chaim Potok's *My Name is Asher Lev*, whose father looked sadly at a dead bird lying on its side near their house. Asher could not bring himself to look at

Thomas R. Cole is professor and graduate program director at the Institute for Medical Humanities, University of Texas Medical Branch in Galveston. A graduate of Yale University, Wesleyan University, and the University of Rochester, he is the author of articles and books on gerontology including The Journey of Life: A Cultural History of Aging in America *and* The Handbook of Humanities and Aging.

the bird. His father quietly explained that every living being would someday be as still as the bird.

"Why?" Asher asked.

"That's the way the *Ribbono Shel Olom* made His world, Asher."

"Why?"

"So life would be precious. Something that is yours forever is never precious."

I wish that my father had lived so he could have guided me through life's harrowing shoals. It is too late for that. But now in midlife—squirming in that awfully thin neck of my life's hourglass—I am confronting many unwelcome feelings: continued yearning to have my father back, guilt at having outlived him, and rage at being left behind by him. Gradually and with much help, I realize that trying to deny or avoid these feelings is the primary source of my own suffering. As a scholar I have been writing about spirituality and aging for more than a decade. As a person, however, I know that the fullness of my own aging depends not only on intellectual insight and religious commitment but also on the continuous work of emotional healing.

Recently, I've been jolted out of my numbness by I.L. Peretz's 1894 story, "Bontshe Shvayg"[1] ("Bontshe the Silent"). Bontshe Shvayg lived in a nineteenth-century Polish *shtetl,* or market town, without leaving a trace—no accomplishments, no children, no relatives, no luck. Not once did he ever complain. After he died, Bontshe's wooden grave marker was blown out of the ground by the wind, and the grave digger's wife used it to boil potatoes. "He lived like a grain of gray sand at the edge of the sea," writes Peretz. "No one noticed when the wind whirled him off and carried him to the far shore . . . The death of a tram horse would have caused more excitement."

But in the next world, Bontshe's death was a great occasion. The "Messiah's horn sounded in all seven heavens." Father Abraham welcomed him cordially at the gates of heaven. Two angels presented him with a golden chair in which to sit. At the Heavenly Tribunal, no one doubted the outcome. Despite an obscure life of unremitting poverty and suffering, the defense told the judge, not once did Bontshe "feel a drop of anger or cast an accusing glance at heaven."

Throughout his brief trial, Bontshe the Silent stood trembling, his eyes closed, head slumping toward the ground. When the judge finally spoke to him in reassuring tones, Bontshe's tears sealed his eyes shut. "The Heavenly Tribunal can pass no judgment on you," said the judge gently. "It is not for us to determine your portion of paradise. Take what you want! It's yours, all yours!"

Bontshe opened his eyes and looked up for the first time to make sure he understood the judge's words. "*Taki?* [really]" he asked.

"*Taki*! *Taki*! *Taki*!" answered the entire court. "All heaven belongs to you. Ask for anything you wish."

"Well, then," answered Bontshe, "what I'd like most of all is a warm roll with fresh butter every morning."

The last two sentences of the story are devastating: "The judges and angels hung their heads in shame. The prosecutor laughed."

EACH PERSON'S FULL FLOWERING TAKES A LIFETIME

At first, this story seems to be about a heavenly reward for Bontshe's quiet and virtuous endurance on earth. The reader expects a conventional tale of redemptive suffering complete with a happy ending. But Peretz has something else in mind. "There in the world below, no one appreciated you," the judge tells Bontshe. "You yourself never knew that had you cried out but once, you could have brought down the walls of Jericho. You never knew what powers lay within you."

Why does the prosecutor laugh? Why do the judge and angels hang their heads, when Bontshe asks for only a warm, buttered roll as his portion of heaven? They are mocking Bontshe's timidity—his utter inability to resist, to cry out on his own behalf, to glimpse the divine spark in his soul.

My friend Marc Kaminsky recently pointed out to me that "Bontshe Shvayg" is both a socialist polemic and a religious fable. As polemic, the story condemns a social order that permits such complete erasure of a life, that fails to provide supportive structures of love and work necessary for individual flourishing. But it also condemns Bontshe for failing to act vigorously on his own behalf.

As religious fable, "Bontshe Shvayg" gives new meaning to my mother's old aphorism: "God helps those who help themselves." It challenges each of us to overcome our protective psychic armor and to harness the divine powers that lie within us. Don't expect a sudden infusion of divine empathy to yield instant redemption, Peretz seems to say. The full flowering of each human individual requires a lifetime of personal effort. Each of us must struggle here on earth for our own portion of paradise.

Who is Bontshe Shvayg? As a character in Jewish history, Bontshe Shvayg is an ancestral figure: the docile, *shtetl* Jew. He is the beloved father whose passivity makes us ashamed—the way Freud felt as a child when his father failed to challenge the anti-Semites who knocked his hat off in the streets of Vienna. Bontshe is the old world counterpart of Arthur Miller's Willie Loman.

Bontshe can also remind me of the homeless people I sometimes avoid on the streets of Houston. But more often, he represents my long-dead father.

"You never knew what powers lay within you," the judge told Bontshe before offering him all of paradise. By then it was too late for Bontshe, who had never set out on the long road of self-development toward spiritual maturity. When my father, Burton David Michel, died at age 27, he felt trapped, torn between his father and his father-in-law, each of whom wanted him to work in his business. On his tombstone are the words "A Man of Tender Conscience." Like Bontshe, my father never came into full possession of his own powers.

When the stunned six-year-old in *My Name is Asher Lev* asks if he, too, will die one day, his father answers, "Yes. But may it be only after you live a long and good life." Ever since my father died, I have wanted to know what it means to "live a long and good life," and I have yearned for guidance and the strength to live my own answer. The world's great religious traditions have always tried to answer this question, offering images of life as a spiritual journey and attempting to guide believers through the paradox of physical decline and spiritual growth in the second half of life.

"IF NOT NOW, WHEN?"

In Jewish tradition, I think we can learn much about aging and the stages of life from Rabbi Hillel's famous aphorism: "If I am not for myself, who will be for me? If I am only for myself, what am I? If not now, when?"

I first heard this passage as a child at Temple Mishkan Israel in North Haven, Connecticut, where Rabbi Robert E. Goldburg frequently used it to encourage generosity for the poor in our upper middle-class Reform congregation. At the time, it made me feel selfish. Rabbi Goldburg never made the point that ideally, self-development leads not to selfishness but to an awareness of one's finitude, to self-transcendence and a sense of the sacred. This is how I have come to view Hillel's three questions.

Hillel's aphorism can be seen as a kind of moral questionnaire for the stages of life, a spiritual supplement to the ancient Sphinx's riddle: "What goes on four legs in the morning, two legs at noon, and three legs in the late afternoon?"

In the morning of life, we need to receive the continuous supplies of love and nurturance that we need to stand on our own two feet and fend for ourselves in an imperfect world. At noon (or midlife), Hillel seems to say, we learn to fulfill our obligations to provide love and nurturance to others.

In the long, late afternoon of life—as the shadows lengthen and our personal time on earth grows short—we feel a new urgency: "If not now, when?"

We may already know that the scientific answer to the Sphinx's riddle is "man," but have we learned how to lead our own "long and good" life? Have we worked to blend the answers to Hillel's first two questions in our own unique way and arrive at what Thomas Mann called the "smiling knowledge of eternity?"

I have been blessed with many opportunities to come into my own as a father, husband, teacher, and writer. Yet only now am I acknowledging the shell-shocked, Bontshe-like little boy inside me who becomes withdrawn or depressed to avoid feeling guilty, angry, or abandoned again. Slowly, I am becoming strong enough to love this brief and rare gift of life; to enjoy my family, friends and students; to glorify the One who is beyond all praises.

I plan to keep growing into a strong Jewish elder who freely celebrates the gifts of life and helps future generations develop the powers that lie within them. But if I die tomorrow, and I plead my case before the Heavenly Tribunal, I will ask for a warm, buttered roll—and the time to share it with my father, my mother, my wife, and my children. Let the prosecutor laugh and the angels hang their heads!!

Redigging the Wells of Spirituality—Again

Kerry M. Olitzky

I have not written much about my parents or about their spirituality, and certainly not about their old age. Perhaps this is because I have been fearful that I might transgress the commandment to honor one's father and mother. Maybe I am just apprehensive about the many conflicting images that such writing might conjure up, having never publicly shared what would now acquire permanence in print for all to read—including my parents, may God permit them to continue the pleasures of old age.

But possibly the impending eightieth birthday of my father prompts me to collect my thoughts about their spirituality in old age. His bodily deterioration and decreasing mental acumen make the nagging routine of habits he has developed over a lifetime all the more obvious and annoying as we prepare for his birthday. Or

Kerry M. Olitzky is a rabbi and director of the school of education and graduate studies program at Hebrew Union College–Jewish Institute of Religion, New York. He has pioneered the areas of Jewish Twelve Step spirituality and Jewish gerontology. His most recent books include Preparing Your Heart for the High Holy Days: A Guided Journal *and* One Hundred Blessings Every Day.

perhaps this bit of prose is a statement of appreciation for my mother's obstinate resilience while recuperating from a fractured hip that occupied much of her recent seventy-fifth year. She still refuses to succumb to the pain of each morning's first steps, after nights of interrupted and fitful sleep.

The "spirituality" of my mother and father, however we may define it (and certainly they would definitely define it differently than I would) is elusive, yet it draws me closer to them as we all consider our finitude in the shadow of the Almighty. Their spirituality is my inheritance. It is what has pushed me to struggle with the questions of ultimate meaning that I face each day.

MY FATHER: REMEMBER THE BURDEN OF YOUR JEWISHNESS

While my father was recently visiting us, I encouraged him to join us in *shul*, a place that was never his favorite destination, even when he forced himself to take me during my childhood. And yet he had dragged me and coerced me into going along with my older brothers. He was not a typical carpool parent, dropping kids off and then continuing to other activities. His was not a religious pursuit, and he was surely not concerned about providing me with a context in which to connect with the holy. He just wanted me to remember the "burden of my Jewishness." That was the sole purpose of the synagogue and of my Jewish education. He had little use for religious education (except for its moral implications) because it couldn't help much in the "real world" where "people try to take advantage of others."

En route to the synagogue, he would criticize something about the sacred space we were about to occupy: the rabbi, an increase in dues, the synagogue board's inability to manage, even the custodian's failure to keep the building clean. It was in those moments that I learned most about him and his real religious essence.

Like the Hebrew prophets who guided the Jewish people when it seemed that God had failed to do so, my father constantly worried about the underprivileged, the working masses, about those he considered forsaken by society. My father never cared to accumulate many material things, nor was he interested in a large wardrobe, a fancy car, or a big house. A couple of clean shirts purchased as a bargain were all that he needed. And certainly, one pair of shoes was sufficient. Perhaps this was part of a post-Depression mentality (my mother continues to hoard canned goods in every available closet) or a legacy of the poor, immigrant home in which he was raised. We've never really discussed it. I just drew these conclusions on my own.

But he and my mother modeled the social values that drove me into the rabbinate and gave me the impetus to cling fiercely to my Jewish identity during a Southern childhood that was not kind to Jewish boys who preferred books over hunting and fishing and the local Friday night beer binges. This is the man who somehow taught me not to listen to the seductive message of secular society, preferring instead that I listen to the inner script of my own conscience.

On this particular Shabbat, in my home, after attributing his inability to accompany us to synagogue to being unable to sit for so long because his "arthritic bones can no longer take it," he added, "Why are you so insistent that I come? Are you afraid it's bad for business?" When I protested his comment, he said, "It is just a business, you know. Nothing more. Don't ever forget it." What was he trying to teach me with those acerbic words? Humility? Honesty? Was he encouraging me to be careful, always on my guard lest I allow my Jewish life to be turned into a business practice or to be seduced by institutional and community politics?

He knew that I hold the synagogue dear to me, that I work tirelessly for its survival and resurgence as a force in the Jewish community. Maybe he was expressing a freedom common among the elderly to finally do what they want regardless of what others think.

It seems strange that an adult has to wait eighty years to do what he or she really wants to do. And yet, it's certainly a position understandable to all of us who live in the complex web of family life. Perhaps my father was exhibiting *chutzpah clappei malah*, standing up to God in his own humble way, much like Rabbi Levi Yitzchak of Berditchev, the Hassidic master who argued with God on behalf of his people. Perhaps by not going to synagogue, my dad was protesting the life that God had given him: the monotonous work on an assembly line which produced guidance systems so missiles could deliver their destruction on target; the unending pain in his stenosis-ridden spine; his deteriorating vision; the deaths of his parents and a brother; the cancer of his wife—my mother. These are the familiar challenges of old age. Running like Jonah, he thought he was out from under God's scrutiny. Maybe he couldn't run away from God—a lesson that Jonah learned as well. But if he was forced to endure God's scrutiny as part of his Jewish inheritance, he wanted God to keep up God's part of the bargain. And like Abraham who was my father's namesake, my dad argues on behalf of today's residents of Sodom and Gomorrah. His is a painfully passionate spirituality: one that is not for the feeble of heart or of soul. All this I have inherited.

MY MOTHER: FAYGE TO FRANCIS, THEN BACK TO FAYGE

Although my mother tried, she could never recapture the Jewish essence that her parents had provided when we all lived together in Pittsburgh's Squirrel Hill, a mostly Jewish neighborhood. In the Florida sunshine, there was no fresh-baked challah, no homemade *gefilte* fish with horseradish—only an occasional chicken soup to heal our transplanted souls. I knew that I would have to discover Shabbat on my own.

My mother thrived on her Jewish ethnicity. She visited each new Jewish commercial enterprise (regardless of its product) that emerged in our Southern town. Slowly, she sloughed off layers of her Jewish religious practice.

In the Jewishly vacant environment of Pinellas County, Florida, everyone wanted to "fit in." She went from Fayge to Frances, from a strictly kosher kitchen to experimenting with the "lower *traife*" cuisine of the local South. We went from "making Shabbes" to "making Friday night Temple night." Nevertheless, her ingenuity and resourcefulness helped her beat breast cancer thirty years ago when few in our community talked about the power of prayer and the ability of the individual to direct her or his own healing. Of course, no one then talked about God, either. But she expressed her thanks every day for being alive. And she continues to do so.

It is this same peculiar mix of American-Jewish identity that has attracted my mother, finally in retirement, to many of the things that her exhausting days of work prevented her from engaging. She joined the synagogue sisterhood, regularly attends Saturday morning services, studies *Parashat Hashavuah* with her rabbi twice a week, and volunteers at the local Jewish home for the aged two mornings each week. She now models an active religious life, one that she had surrendered to the pressures of "making ends meet" some years ago. She even likes being called "Fayge" and tries to observe Shabbat regularly with my father in their new condominium apartment.

MY SPIRITUAL INHERITANCE

These are the genes I carry—sometimes begrudgingly, sometimes with a profound sense of indebtedness—as I confront the spirituality of the elderly, all the while doing what my graduate school instructors warned me not to do: understanding and applying aging theory through the lives of those I know and love. And yet, Judaism (as well as my aging parents) seems to have taught me just the opposite of my graduate education, for theory means nothing if we cannot consider the lives of people and the relationships we share with them. As Martin Buber taught: All life is in meeting.

According to one of the most instructive scenes about family life in the Torah, "Isaac dug anew the wells of water that had been dug in the days of his father Abraham which the Philistines had stopped up after Abraham's death. Isaac gave them the same names that his father had given them."[1] It was not enough for him to dig wells on his own in a new place, even if he knew where water would be found. As we all must do in our own way, Isaac had first to redig the wells that his father had once dug. Before Isaac could become himself (before he could develop his own spiritual life), he had to *become* his father and live through the spiritual life that his father had chosen. Abraham had done the same thing with his father, Terach. Many will recall the *midrash* (told so often that many believe it is a story in the Torah): Abraham is watching over the store of idols while his father tends to some other business. While his father is gone, Abraham smashes all the statues. Upon his return, Abraham's father is furious. Abraham claims that one idol had destroyed another. Terach doesn't believe this. Finally, Abraham is able to explain to his father his belief in one God. It takes the son to teach the father.

I have learned much from watching my parents confront the vagaries of life as they age. I hope they will find spiritual sustenance for their aging souls. And just as they have been forced into looking at their own spiritual lives, I know that I must likewise confront my own spirituality as I grow older. I have changed and evolved as they have—perhaps, to some extent, because they have—as I face the life that God has given me. When my wife confronted cancer five years ago, I had to face once again my mother's struggle, which I recalled from childhood: The wondering, the uncertainty, the questioning of God's role in the life of our family. It is a theme that continues to come back to me as I grow older, as my children grow and mature, and as my parents face the infirmities that accompany them along with the blessings of old age.

How shall I prepare spiritually, now that I am in middle age, to maintain my covenantal relationship with God into my older years? This is a lesson I must learn from my parents. I am now at the age they were in my earliest childhood memories. I know, as did Isaac, that I can't begin on my own. First, I have to redig and rename the wells my parents dug—the ones that they dug for themselves and for me—before I can attempt to claim any well as my own, however distant it might be from theirs. I know that I have to rehearse the spiritual struggle of my parents. Instead of rejecting it, I must hold it fiercely within my heart. It's the only way to make the journey. And there, just as I remember from my adolescence, will I find the light on the front porch patiently waiting, beckoning me home.

Cycling and Recycling

Mary Gendler

I am a 55-year old Jewish American woman. If I lived in Nepal, I would probably be dead by this age. If I lived in Malaysia, in five years I would no longer be permitted to drive a car. If I'd grown up in Eastern Europe, I would likely be feeling "old." But in America, 55 is still very much part of middle age, although in some circles I am already considered a "senior." I am fortunate in that I do not yet feel a diminishment of energy or health, but I have begun to feel a sense of limitation, which helps me focus and prioritize how I want to spend the years I have left.

Because my husband, who is twelve years older than I, has just retired, I am also thinking about my elder years. This is about a decade earlier than the time many people begin taking stock of their life and what is left of it. And yet, my timing makes sense. I am just coming to the end of menopause, a tumultuous, upsetting period, which has made my life hell for several years. Might this not be a natural time, especially for women, to stop and reevaluate—a preretirement mini-pause connected to our body rhythms, a built-in urge to reflect on direction/

Mary Gendler is a psychologist, photographer, artist, gardener, adventurer, and writer who lives in Andover, Massachusetts. She has written on Jewish feminism and is currently trying to figure out how to grow old usefully, gracefully, and wisely.

redirection, an opportunity to search for the seeds in our spiritual womb that have not yet fully germinated but that can still grow and bear fruit? Since this particular life passage has been so important in my maturing and aging process, I will pause for a moment to explore its meaning to me.

MENOPAUSE AS MINI-PAUSE

I live in cycles. My body, my emotions, and my interests all cycle and recycle. All humans cycle, I believe, but women especially are tied biologically to these ebbs and flows. Like it or not, we fill and empty every month, like the moon, the tides, and breath itself. From the time of puberty and for decades thereafter, this is a woman's bodily rhythm. It ties her to the earth, to the pulse of the universe. Then something happens. Bodies change; sometimes they even go berserk. In my own case, instead of gentle monthly menstrual cycles, I swung wildly between hot flashes which made me want to strip instantly in the most inappropriate of places, to hemorrhage-like periods, which made me fear I would bleed to death. My body and my emotions were totally out of control.

Unfortunately, Judaism has no rituals for this transition, and these troubled waters can be lonely and frightening. Needed is a ceremony, a ritual, a celebratory song of passage such as the one Miriam sang at the edge of the Red Sea. Like that song celebrating our passage through the "sea of blood," we need to acknowledge our transition—past the tide-based monthly cycles into crone, sage, wise-woman.

Readings from older women could guide and inspire us about for the future. Those assembled could share wisdom they have received from their mothers, grandmothers, and other important women in their lives. The loss of the biological cycle would be acknowledged, and each woman would have an opportunity to discuss what this passage means to her. The ceremony could end with a group blessing.

In the absence of such a ceremony, I have muddled through this period on my own. My musings have raised many questions: What is my task as I move into this later stage of my life? How do I balance my duties to myself, my family, and the world? Looking back, in twenty-five years, will I have accomplished all that I had hoped to do? How can I remain anchored to my past self and activities, yet take advantage of this next phase so I can ripen and continue to grow?

NEW LIMITS, NEW FRONTIERS

As I've grown older, as my body changes, I have become increasingly aware of my limitations, both physical and temporal, and my priorities have started to shift. I have less patience for meaningless tasks and a greater urgency to express the more creative, artistic, and spiritual parts of myself and to make space in my life for contemplation. I feel an increased need for beauty and quiet. I can spend hours arranging flowers, their delicate scents and sensuous beauty bringing pleasure to the senses and peace to the soul. Small things give me pleasure and wonder, and they bring me closer to an awareness of the Divine Presence. Such was my encounter with a tiny translucent snail that was tickling my leg as it made its passage across a stream running through our property. Instead of impatiently brushing it off, I picked it up on my finger and was rewarded by the sight of an amazing creature no more than a quarter of an inch long but perfectly formed, with minuscule feeler horns, which retracted when I gently touched them with my finger. We looked at each other for a few minutes and I then deposited it on the bank of the stream, feeling as though I had received a gift of God's manifestation, present all around us but seldom noticed in our busyness.

Nature has always been my primary path to the Divine Presence. Planting a corn seed and watching it turn first into a tiny seedling and soon sprout into a six-foot sturdy corn stalk is a constant source of wonder. Scuba diving, which opens up a colorful, fanciful, awesome world would make a true believer of almost any confirmed atheist. Traversing the stark plateaus of Tibet at 18,000 feet, surrounded by mountains and glaciers and stunning turquoise lakes, or simply wandering in the woods of western Massachusetts, where we summer, fills me with the awareness that some force beyond the human or beyond chance has created all this. This awareness is not new, but it is more powerful at this time in my life, I believe, because of the paradox of simultaneously having both more and less time to appreciate the world and its beauties.

As I wander in God's wonder-filled world, I see evidence of my own internal rhythms and of the cycling and recycling of all creation. I, too, will soon become the humus from which will spring new life. This may seem trite, but such awareness urges me to make the most of my remaining time on earth and connects me to the larger cycles and to the oneness of all. If I can stay open to this awareness, I will be less afraid of death and, like my friend and mentor Helen Nearing, be quite ready to die when it is time.

Family life, which has always been important to me, has taken on new dimensions as ours both shrinks and grows. My parents and my husband's parents have all died, and he and I are now the older generation. But our family has also grown with the addition of our new son-in-law and his family. Some day, God willing, there will be grandchildren. Cycling and recycling. How deeply satisfying this is.

And yet, I also want to remain active in the world, to

make a difference, at least in small ways. I have been a practicing psychotherapist for twenty-five years. I am at the peak of my professional powers. Will I find a way to use these professional skills while taking advantage of the new flexibility in my life?

The amazing experiences of the past two Chanukahs have directed me toward new paths. In 1994, an international, interfaith group of 200 men, women and children gathered at Auschwitz/Birkenau to commemorate the fiftieth anniversary of the end of World War II and to inaugurate a peace march to Hiroshima. The first night, which was also the eighth night of Chanukah, we came together beneath the fearsome sign *"Arbeit Macht Frei,"* "Work Makes Free." There we lit candles and prayed together, the light of our candles and faiths joining to bring a tiny bit of light to this place of the darkest night of other Jewish people. Among those present were children of Holocaust survivors and children of Nazis. Reaching across the gulf of hate, they found in each other more commonality and understanding than anywhere else. Their example has inspired me to think about searching out ways to help people bridge the gulfs of hatred and to heal such searing splits. If children of Nazis and Jews can come together, why not Palestinians and Jews? *Tikkun ha-olam.* Healing the world is the work I wish to still do.

Chanukah 1995 was spent in Dharamsala, India, the present home of the Dalai Lama and the center of the Tibetan community-in-exile. On the first night, the light from our candles merged with that of the Tibetans, who, coincidentally, were commemorating what Jews would have called the *yahrzeit* of the founder of the yellow hat sect of Tibetan Buddhism. Aside from the mingling of our candlelight, we were struck by the connections that exist between our two peoples: the Roman destruction of the Temple in Jerusalem in 70 c.e. and the Chinese destruction of Tibetan monasteries; the exile of the Jews from their homeland and the Tibetans' exile from theirs; the deeply spiritual base of both cultures. The next day, we lit a Chanukah *menorah* with the Dalai Lama and then discussed with him the sense of hope and dignity that emerges when people take forceful but nonviolent action to free themselves from oppression. As we did this, I realized that I might have a role to play in helping this happen. Joint prayer and nonviolent action—embodying the spirit of Chanukah as expressed by Zechariah in the Haftarah: "Not by might, not by power, but by My Spirit."

INTEGRATING THE PAST
WITH THE FUTURE

Tikkun ha-olam. How can I use my therapeutic skills and training to foster healing? I feel that I am now being directed to new paths, onto which I might never have ventured had I not loosened myself from former ties and commitments.

But are these really new paths? Or are they parts of myself—"lost children"—which had wandered off and which I am finally beginning to reclaim? Am I not simply cycling back to my old passion for social justice expressed three decades ago when I marched for civil rights and later against the war in Vietnam? Was not my work at a community mental health center for the poor simply a way to act upon my favorite article of faith—*tsedek, tsedek, tirdoff:* "justice, justice, shalt thou pursue"? Perhaps nothing is really new, but rather we discover new ways of giving expression to earlier voices.

Other "lost children" are also making their voices heard. I had shelved my passion for photography when I returned to school for my doctorate in psychology in 1980. But now, I find myself pulled back to the darkroom, entranced as images emerge from the murky, smelly liquid in the photo trays. Photography helps me see and frame things in new ways. I love transforming my visual and emotional experiences into printed images and thereby sharing the essence of what I perceive with others. In ways I do not fully understand, photography links me to the Creator and to Creation. It is a form of meditation: The artistic expression becomes a spiritual act.

An exciting thought tickles me: Dare I assume a new identity at this stage of my life? Can I, an inveterate "do-gooder," switch from "helper" to "artist?" Does art relate to *tikkun olam?* As I feel my way, I realize that photography need not be a separate line of development for me, but rather one which ties many pieces together. As a practicing therapist, I used my photographs in treatment with my clients. Now I can use photography to make a strong social statement, as with the photo and poetry exhibits I put together after the Auschwitz convocation and the Tibet journey.

As I move into this ripening period of my life, I am the same—and I am not the same. I am aware that certain struggles and issues have remained with me. An essay I contributed to a collection of Jewish feminist writings in 1970 began with almost the same words as this essay: "I am a woman. I am a Jewish woman." The feminist movement was then in its infancy, and Jewish women were just beginning to think about inequalities in Judaism.

Though still deeply committed to feminism, I now feel more at peace with myself and my relationship to Judaism. Although much work remains to ensure full equality for women, I am less drawn to struggle and more inclined to enfold myself in those aspects of Judaism that nourish me. Participating in monthly *Rosh Chodesh* celebrations, attending egalitarian services in which women's voices are fully heard, making a yearly retreat with Jewish feminists—each of these is deeply satisfying. Where there are lapses, as in the absence of rituals to aid in life transitions, I focus on innovation. Perhaps the aging process is mellowing me, nudging me to be aware not only of difference, but also of the "oneness" of all creation.

Thus, as I move into what will hopefully be a full last quarter-century of my life, I am increasingly aware of being tied to a larger cycle of life and death, generation and regeneration, birth and rebirth. My current task is to find my place in this cycle, to cultivate and reap the spiritual seeds that lie within, to continue to reclaim and develop my gifts and talents as fully as possible so that I can better share with others whatever wisdom and ability I have.

III. INTERGENERATIONAL RELATIONSHIPS

Children's children are the crown of the old;
and the glory of children are their parents.

— Proverbs 17:6

INTERGENERATIONAL RELATIONSHIPS

In this section, we explore personal, intergenerational relationships and attempt to acknowledge the continuity of life and the legacy of love that permeates one generation's relationship with the next.[1] In "A Table with People," Marc Kaminsky offers us a rich and deep understanding of life review, the process by which we reconsider our lives, reconcile our disappointments, and bask in our pleasures. Through conversations with his grandmother, Kaminsky weaves a beautiful narrative of her life, providing insight into both the therapeutic process of reminiscence and the experiences of the immigrant as she shifts from the old world to the new. In "A Letter to My Children," Gloria Levi bequeaths a legacy of social passion and love to her children while recognizing the emotional strains and bonds of the parent-child relationship. Suzanne Hodes writes in "Imaging My Mother" about the profound presence of her mother in her life. Her words accompany images of her mother that she captured on canvas over eighteen years.

Victor Reinstein's "Even to Your Old Age" portrays the emotional journey of aging as lovingly witnessed by a grandson. Grandparents are essential resources, promising continuity and the transmission of heritage. They are a bridge between the generations, and their stories and life experiences become nourishment to Jewish youth. They play a special role in the family, bestowing invaluable (and nonmaterial) treasures on the family. These grandparents urge us to listen carefully to the sometimes subtle, sometimes profoundly unsubtle poignancies of growing old. All these pieces reflect the importance of intergenerational relationships: bringing the gifts of the elderly to the young and the gifts of the young to the elderly.

A Table with People: Storytelling As Life Review and Cultural History

Marc Kaminsky

In old age, my grandmother Esther Schwartzman set out on a round trip to the Bessarabia whose market days and holy days continued to form the rhythm of her weeks. Starting out early in the morning, she made lightning visits, surprise visits, to the undiminished *shtetl* that resided nowhere on earth except in the psyches or souls of herself and a few other old people who journeyed there in memory.

Kostitshan, her place of origin, could not be found on a map of Romania. It was now—I learned from a refusenik taxi driver—"one big Bellevue, a whole town where they lock up crazy people." When I told my grandmother what had become of her town, she sighed with appreciation. "In Yiddish," she commented, "there's a saying: Yiddish is a motherland. Not only a *mame-loshn*, a mother tongue, but a motherland. Because land we didn't have, we couldn't own, but Yiddish, and the things we could carry away with us in Yiddish, this nobody could take from us. So if I go back to my motherland now, if I go back *there*, it's to sit down in the middle of a good conversation with a few people who aren't *here*."

Marc Kaminsky is a writer and psychotherapist in Brooklyn. He has published poems and essays and has written and edited several volumes on the culture of aging and Yiddishkeit.

THE INTERIOR JOURNEY

Gerontologist Robert Butler has called this sort of interior journey a life review.[1] Spurred by a heightened sense of mortality, old people can make themselves available to dimensions of their experience they have glossed over or denied. They open old wounds for the benefits, the blessings, that may come from entering into a fearful place in memory. They examine old conflicts and reintegrate "missing pieces" of their lives, and so they may grow more whole, more complete, more abundant. They may create a personal myth that adheres and does justice to their histories: It is the construction of the self they wish to be remembered by. And this bestows poise and intensity; it allows them to live more fully as they face the knowledge of their death.

Not their death only. A double tragedy is encountered by those who were born into a culture they have outlived.[2] This is so painful as to be inadmissible. Yet they know: Their memories carry a lost world. Those who could have witnessed their growth from childhood to maturity, those who could have given independent testimony of the value of the culture that ratified their value, those who could have constituted a continuing world of origins are lost; and they are conscious of themselves as witnesses.

This life review, personal in its aims and scope, is crossed by a larger, ethical imperative: the obligation to bear witness. Here, personal emotion is informed by collective history. My grandmother Esther belongs to a particular group of emigrants who suffered survivor's guilt at one remove. Her suffering was profound precisely because she herself did not undergo the ordeal in which her parents and her sisters and her uncles and all their families—her family—perished.

This suffering grows out of a cultural strength: the highly developed sense of kinship, of identification, between family members and between oneself and Jews everywhere. The "symbiotic tie" between the Jewish mother and her children was a vitally necessary defense against the brutal and precarious world of czarist Russia: It fostered the group cohesiveness without which individual survival was not possible. Later, this pattern of Jewish familial relationships would come into conflict with American cultural values and bring bewilderment, rage, and grief to the contending generations. The children of immigrants acquired a psychological vocabulary in which words like "autonomy" and "symbiotic tie" were moral terms. Parents and children lacked a common language in which to interpret their fight to each other. For people shaped, as my grandmother was, by *shtetl* values and feelings, this bond between parents and children was central to their idea of Jewishness and carried with it certain obligations whose fulfillment made one a *mentsh,* an ethical person. This sense of kinship was a moral sense, and it informed all her social values and her sense of social justice.

This, then, is the cultural context within which the interior journey takes place. During the course of her storytelling, she reenters the dangerous terrain that she had denied during her middle years: the daring and desperation that drove her, a timid girl, to oppose her father and to rebel. She discloses but does not discover and articulate the great act of rebellion—and the hunger for freedom, for a larger life—that actually constitutes the life she has lived. The story she tells becomes, explicitly, an act of confession. She comes into contact with the ache of guilt she feels in relation to her beloved mother and father. This becomes the gate through which she can glimpse, symbolically express, and, in playful moments, move toward claiming the vital, hope-giving, risk-taking, innovative, and—not that she could know or admit this— aggressive side of her personality. Here, she offers traces of something more and other than a personal project of

liberation. It is profoundly connected with the movements of emancipation that swept through the Pale of
Settlement after the May Laws of 1882 furthered the
pauperization of all Jews.

The ideological battles among which she lived—Zion-
ism versus socialism in all its forms versus the many per-
mutations of Orthodoxy versus opposing Chassidic sects
versus polymorphous secularism—all informed her think-
ing-feeling life. She was a little of everything. Her stories
were as hospitable to the traveling wonder rebbe as they
were to the revolutionary Russian youth who taught her
dancing. The Yiddishkeit of the Yiddishist movement, simultaneously crystallized and diffuse, provided her with
a set of convictions and a sufficient body of "doctrine"—
to call it that—to stabilize herself and her household in
America. Yiddishkeit was the arena within which her cultural, social, familial, and psychological conflicts were en-
acted.

Esther returns to the past so that she may begin, once
again, the journey of breaking away from the *shtetl*, of
breaking, one by one, the traditions in which she was
raised. She arrives, again, at the crisis of the story of the
two Yom Kippurs. She tells of growing into a new sense
of personhood and radiant purity when, at the age of
thirteen, she fasted on Yom Kippur for the first time. And
she tells how she consented to go to a basement restau-
rant on New York's Bowery at the insistence of Alter, her
betrothed. There they ate a meal together on Yom Kippur. This violation of a sacred custom, a taboo, becomes,
on his side, an act of seduction; on hers, a "sexual meal"
in which she pledges herself to him and his way. In the
controversy between Alter's rebellious secularism (which
validates her half-disowned inner rebellion) and her parents' piety, she now takes lasting vows. When she speaks
of having sought "a modern way" to carry on "the Jewish
more or less tradition," she uses the word "modern" with

the same inflection and force as I would. Here, our conceptual languages converge.

All this "emerged" for me after she died, as I was constructing successive versions of the text of the story of the life she had lived, as I gradually came to see and *hear* that life, which was a far cry from the tales she had told me. Without my discovery of the figure of the rebel, I would have gone on accepting the version of herself that she constructed after she married Alter: that she was merely carrying on the old ways, perhaps with a few minor adjustments here and there. And so I would have missed comprehending what is surely the central accomplishment of her middle years. She situated herself, Alter (who resisted for years), and her children within the Yiddishist movement, specifically within the milieu of the Sholem Aleichem Folk Institute. Here, the principles of secular Jewishness both legitimated and made possible the project of cultural bricolage that was crucial for her well-being.[3] In and through her participation in the organizing, running, and sustaining of Folk Shul 45, she synthesized the rituals of her Orthodox childhood and the literary and political modernism of Yiddish culture, and she found a form of practicing Yiddishkeit that felt authentic to her. The Passover seder and Sabbath table at which I sat as a boy were her and her cultural movement's acts of creation. This table, where personal and collective history intersected and were transformed into a secular sphere of the spirit, was what she called, in talking with me, *"a tish mit mentshn."*

STORIES OF CONFLICT

The central story that my grandmother told but could not tell, and that had to be imaginatively reconstructed, concerns the tale of the two Yom Kippurs: the story of conflict between tradition and modernity, the conflict between tradition experienced as oppression versus tradition as a domain of sacred values, of modernity as development and emancipation (enlightenment) versus modernity as destruction of all that is holy. The valences of tradition and modernity slip and change places as the terms of evaluation are destabilized. This conflict—concurrently personal, cultural, and historical—is given narrative form in my grandmother's reminiscences in what I would call "tales of separation."

The life review takes shape in a process that is concurrently psychological, discursive, and cultural. In analyzing and describing this profound act of (re)constructing a self, a (lost) world, and a worldview in the communication of one's life experience, our strategies of interpretation must show the interrelation of self, discourse, and culture in order to be adequate to the complexity of the process and to the project of transcending fragmentation and of creating one complete life. Like art, like ritual, like all forms of imaginative construction, the life review mediates between what we are given—our actual lives, with so many broken threads, unfinished and unfinishable tasks and relationships—and what we desire. This desire, in which the life review is fitfully carried on, is lived through under the pressure of a double imperative: time's running out. Where there was the suffering of fragmentation, let there be wholeness.

Be that as it may, for a long time I was at a loss as to what to do with the cartons of words I had collected from my grandmother: taped words, transcribed words, words edited and shaped. How could I give all those words form? How could I render the experience that my grandmother's utterance communicated—evoked in me—accessible to others? All dialogue involves playing upon and with assumed meanings, which are registered through intonation, gesture, and the tonalities of pauses and silences.[4] My grandmother's expressive language, particularly in speaking with me of passionate or disturbing things, acquired its depth and richness not through strictly verbal means but through the subtle saturation of a limited diction and syntax with intensities and qualifications that were precisely rendered by (for instance) a lexicon of sighs that I am convinced was as much a part of the language that she acquired from her mother, Rivka, and her grandmother Yente as her Bessarabian accent. Those abrupt inhalations, those involuntary and extravagantly long, mournful releases of burdened sound haunt my memory and imagination. I can hear them vividly now. And I think now, as I felt then, while listening to my grandmother, that it took centuries of Jewish history to shape this nuanced semiology of resignation, endurance, stoicism, and suffering.

CONSTRUCTING ESTHER'S TEXT

I began to add stories (or parts of stories) to fill in aspects of Esther's world and development that she did not or could not put into words. This included her disavowal of and guilt over separation and related aspects of her life history that she denied, struggled against, and then moved toward partially claiming and integrating. And it included aspects of everyday life through which the formative impact of Jewish culture on her personal life and worldview would be represented. An instance of such an amplification is the "story" of the *eruv,* or ritual fence that encircled the small towns of Eastern Europe on the Sabbath, converting the out-of-doors to the metaphorical inside of a house, thus making it possible for observant Jews to carry things in the street. The ritual fence that transformed the outside to the inside was yet another example of the concept of *lehavdl* in Jewish life.

Lehavdl means "to differentiate." Images of differentiation, of separation—as boundary, barrier, fence, line of demarcation, river's edge, wall of shelter, imprisoning or protective horizon—recurred or were inflected in nearly all the stories my grandmother told me. In the earliest and most "regressed" instance, the memory of her grandmother's yard—of those fences within fences that do not suffice to contain her six-year-old terror—returns with profound emotional intensity and imaginative vividness, which reaccentuates and transforms her language and her storytelling performance. Her narration becomes notably dramatic, as she shows me that the calf "goes like this" and the "gentleman of the geese, . . . loose in the yard . . . goes like this." And the language, suddenly charged with all sorts of chiming sounds, is enriched by the way she spontaneously makes her description poetically mimic her childhood fear and ignorance.

This tale revealed to me a repeating motif that was evidently a crucial principle of structuration of her reminiscing, and also a symbol through which the links among the domains of the self, discourse, and culture could be represented. Esther's table talk kept reproducing the historical ghetto wall—or rather, since no literal wall separated Jews from the Gentile community in the Moldavia of her childhood and adolescence, the boundary that divided Jewish life from the social life that surrounded it.

The injunction "Don't go near the river"—with all the symbolic overtones it carries—was the regime under which my grandmother lived. How little prepared she was, psychologically and socially, to cross an ocean against the wishes of her parents! This was one of the decisive "breaks" in her experience that she was able symbolically to express and partly repair but not directly narrate.

ESTHER'S TABLE TALK

Speaking of her own grandmother, Esther says, "and she

used to cater a lot to me, I was the oldest grandchild to my Bubba. . . . She used to show me how to make things grow. And you know how the grandchildren are devoted to the bubbas." Here, Bubba Yente's oldest grandchild is speaking to her own oldest grandchild. She is identifying the two of us in a continuing generations-long relationship in which we are each privileged recipients of privileged cultural goods. Her grandmother "catered" to nature (the trees and other growing things in her garden), to humankind (the guests whom she entertained), and to Esther herself, just as Esther caters to me and to my interests by preparing a table for me, set not with jams but with stories—with the bits and pieces of her life that, over time, as years of talk passed between us, she found ways of weaving together as stories. Because I came as her listener, she became a storyteller.

My task, in reconstructing her life history, has been not simply to "salvage" her words but also to make her silences speak, as they spoke to me, in her voice; to infiltrate her voice with a second, interpreting voice that cocreates the range of meanings that were registered in our dialogue; to construct what Bakhtin has called "double-voiced discourse," to add my interpreting word alongside her spoken word, so that her utterance is "dialogized," so that it receives the meanings she communicated to me, and enters into contact with the listener, whom it sought to reach. This is to use the dialogized word to charge her metaphor of *lehavdl*—her tales of separation—with all the revelatory, critical power of their paradoxical, difficult, light-and-dark meanings, coproduced in an unceasing dialogue with her that has not stopped in me, during my days or at night, when one grows receptive to the voices of the dead: a dialogue that has continued long after her death, until this hour, and even now is not finished.[5]

Victor Hillel Reinstein is father to Noa, Yosef, and Tzvia; husband to Sue; and rabbi to the people of Congregation Emanu-El in Victoria, British Columbia. He is currently writing about Rabbi Eliyahu Guttmacher of Graiditz, Poland.

Even to Your Old Age: Reflections on Aging

Victor Hillel Reinstein

Bubbe cried into the *tallis* (prayer shawl). Even when the gates of Heaven close at Yom Kippur's end, at the hour of *Ne'ilah* (closing prayers of Yom Kippur), with the sounding of the *shofar* (ram's horn) that calls us home, the gates are still open to tears. It was during a visit with my then 94-year-old Bubbe, Rebecca Rabinovitz, who died last year at the age of 95. I found myself thinking about aging and change during that visit, and of that which is constant and unchanging. A beautiful verse from the prophet Isaiah often came to me during my time with Bubbe: "Borne by Me from birth, . . . carried from the womb: and even to your old age I am the same; and even to your old age will I carry you: I have made, and I will bear; and I will carry, and will deliver you." It is a verse of quiet encouragement. It is God's reminder: "You are not alone, I am with you, in old age as in childhood."

Visiting with Bubbe, I began to understand why this verse means so much to me. It speaks lovingly of what remains the same throughout the our lives. It is about God as the unchanging constant, the familiar, the One Who knows us from even before we were until after we have been. God's embrace spans our entire life, holding us always with the same love as when we were newborn, guiding us through times and cycles of change, present even when we are distant, welcoming us when we return across the distant reach.

During that visit to Boston, I bought a new *tallis* with money that Bubbe had given me, then I visited her at the Hebrew Rehabilitation Center for Aged. I brought her the *tallis* so she might see it and touch it. I placed it on her bed, and she bent down, put her face into the soft wool, and cried. Through that beloved garment, sanctified now by her tears, there seemed to come a moment of union, of reunion, with times and people and places of long ago and perhaps even with God. Perhaps age is freeing her to return in her own way to God, Whom she banished long ago from her life. As a child in the Ukraine, she witnessed a bloody pogrom in which her beloved rabbi, the *Bezilirer Rebbe,* who was like a father to her and her sister, was the first to be slaughtered. She screamed at her pious mother, "You say there is a God?!" The echo of that scream has stayed with her throughout her life.

Bubbe cried into the *tallis* as she sat with me, her first grandchild, the only other rabbi she has loved. She told me her stories once again. We both cried, she and I: "You say there is a God?!" Finally, in her old-age room, through her own tears, the little girl heard what might have been her mother's answer—and mine. And in that moment the *Riboyno shel Oylam,* the Master of the Universe, reached out from exile with gentle embrace and said with tears; "borne by Me from birth, . . . carried from the womb: And even to your old age I am the same; and even to your old age will I carry you."

"THE GLORY OF CHILDREN ARE THEIR PARENTS"

That visit was my first encounter with Bubbe in her new setting. There, quite removed from her airy apartment that looked out over the ocean in the town of Winthrop where I grew up, I also encountered other people of her age, all with their own stories, their own memories, their own fears and hopes. I tried to imagine who these people had been, while still trying to see and appreciate them now as they are. I encountered aging itself on that visit: of my parents, of Bubbe, of others, of myself. It was a time of reflection and of reminiscence. An era was passing. Landmarks of the familiar were fading from the emotional landscape of my life. "Borne by Me from birth, . . . carried from the womb: and even to your old age I am the same." Even as I heard these words in relation to Bubbe, the verse was a comfort to me as I considered my own life and felt God's constant presence amid life's changing seasons.

Leaving Bubbe's room, I walked past the little *shul* in the Home for the Aged. Some men were gathering for *mincha* (afternoon prayer). I joined them and found solace in their company and in the pleasure that my presence seemed to bring them. On the *bimah,* the *"sheliach tzibbur"* (prayer leader) sat in a wheelchair. His strong and melodic voice rose with feeling even when he could not rise. I looked up when he came to the blessing in the *amidah* for healing, *"Refa'enu Hashem v'ne'ra'fe, hoshi'enu v'nivashe'a . . . ,"* "Heal us God and we shall be healed, save us and we shall be saved . . . " What does this mean to him and to them, I wondered? How does this congregation of elders hear these words? Another man was sitting in a wheelchair behind the last row of benches, near where I stood. A table before him had a special stand on it for his *siddur* (prayer book) because he could not hold it. I noticed his name on the back of the wheelchair: Dr. Gottlieb. Patients once came to him, I mused; now he is in the care of the faithful Healer of Israel. The prayer continued—" . . . for You are our praise. Bring complete healing-*refua sh'layma*-for all our afflictions, for You are God, Ruler, the faithful and compassionate Healer. Blessed are You, God, Healer of the sick of Your people Israel." As we finished *davening,* I noticed a verse from the Book of Proverbs inscribed on the wall just beneath the ceiling, stretching in Hebrew and English all the way around the room, above the endless columns of *Yahrzeit* (memorial death) plaques: "Children's children are the crown of old age; And the glory of children are their parents."

The next day, after another visit with Bubbe, again at about *mincha*, I saw the *sheliach tzibbur* wheeling his way down a corridor toward the *shul*. I caught up with him and offered a *yasher koach*—"may you have strength"—on his *davening*. I also told him that he had a beautiful *yarmulke*, which is how I recognized him from behind. He laughed, and with a playful smile asked, "And what's wrong with the guy underneath it?" I thought of the Yiddish proverb, *"Lachen is gezint, doctoyrim hasen lachen,"* "Laughter is healthy, doctors prescribe laughter." People's response to infirmity and adversity varies. Fortunate is the one who can still laugh.

*"MITZVAH*S AREN'T ALWAYS FUN"

Everything about that spring visit had been wonderful, poignantly refreshing, a touching of roots. The time spent with Bubbe had been pleasant, filled with memorable interactions with her. Visiting her with my own children was not so pleasant. On that day, Boston was sweltering and Bubbe was steaming. As she and my children and I walked about the gardens of the Home, she complained, "Can you imagine, you come to see your Bubbe and I can't offer you anything?"

As Bubbe railed against her state, and took it out on us, I had a new sense of the verse, "I will bear you"—even when you are unbearable. There are times of pain and suffering at every stage of life. There are times when we are called upon to bear the unbearable. My daughter, Noa, acknowledged that it was a difficult visit and not much fun. "You're right," I acknowledged. "It wasn't fun. It was a *mitzvah* and *mitzvah*s aren't always fun."

One day, I drove Bubbe to our house to join us for supper. It was a hot, humid day, so I wore shorts and sandals. Bubbe was mortified. "You're a rabbi," she snapped. "You shouldn't dress that way. I told everyone my grandson, the rabbi, is coming. No one's going to believe me. They'll talk about you. I know what they're like!"

"I'm sorry, Bubbe. Come, let's go to the car. We'll talk on the way to Winthrop." In the car Bubbe talked and talked, carrying on a monologue, a diatribe, ignoring anything I said. "But you're a rabbi," she cried, in tears now, having raised the issue of my attire to the day's *cause celebre*.

She had never before cared what people wore. She had never been concerned about externals. "Bubbe, you've spent the whole ride talking about my shorts. Isn't it enough?" Then she really broke down, a sunbeam of reason breaking through the clouds of her consciousness.

"I'm so stupid, I'm so stupid," she sobbed over and over. As I tried to calm her, she saw the *tzitzis* (prayer shawl fringes) sticking out from the leg of those same shorts.

"Do you wear those all the time?" she asked.

"Yes," I said, hearing the quizzical but respectful tone of her question. Then she offered a beautiful thought about the *labtzudekel*, Yiddish for the small tallis worn under the shirt; "*A labtzudekel nemt aroys aleh tsuris*," "a *labtzudekel* takes away all worry and sorrow." Would that I could do that for you, Bubbe. Then, I chuckled with her, "It's like a sorrow-proof vest."

She was quiet now, gazing off at places she had taken me on outings when I was a child. She had been a large, strong, vital woman with strong opinions and a strong will. She was often overbearing. It all helped her get through a hard life.

"REMEMBER WHO I WAS"

We each have a past, an identity beyond the faults and frailties of a given moment of the day, of a given season in our lives. I felt a lump in my throat as I looked over at my hunched, frail, confused Bubbe. When one is as old as she, it is only God Who can remember the little girl who screamed in her *shtetl*. There is no one else left. Her friends are all gone. Even elderly children can't remember what they had heard about a parent's youth. Memories of youth are shared only between the elder and God.

It is sometimes easier to speak to God than to people. "Cast us not away when we are old, . . . Do not abandon us." Although addressed to God, these Yom Kippur words of prayer are a plea to those we love: "I know I'm difficult. I know I don't remember and that I seem ungrateful, that I say unkind things. But hear my voice. Remember who I was. Please don't abandon me." That must be the worst fear upon reaching old age.

The late months or years of a very aged parent's life can also be a time of extreme pain and conflict for their children. The relationship can become emotionally abusive as the aged parent struggles desperately against fear of abandonment and oblivion: "Why didn't you visit me today? What do you mean you're going away for the weekend? The kids are coming over? Why wasn't I invited? You're a terrible daughter. I'll never forgive you." Love becomes tested in a completely different way.

Mom died first, and Bubbe followed eight months later. She could never accept the terrible order. "It's my turn," she cried. Mom was Bubbe's link to the world, and the world ceased to be for her. She had no more will to go on. Every morning when I fold up my *tallis*, I snuggle my face into the soft wool and feel her tears.

A Letter to My Children

Gloria Levi

The other day, as I was reading the Torah portion, *Ha-azinu*, Moses' final oration to his people before his death, I thought about what might have been on his mind. He was old and knew that death was imminent. As the leadership of his people was transferred to his successor, Joshua, Moses' final task was to sing from his heart to his "children" about the wisdom of his years. He had experienced a youthful spring, the flowering of adulthood summer, and the autumn of fulfillment, of harvest time. Now, he faced winter and his return to the earth. He knew pain, frustration, disappointment, joy, love, and transcendence.

As he reflected upon his life he was able to discriminate the sacred from the profane and the essential from the superfluous. Perhaps that describes aptly the concept of wisdom.

Moses' love for his "children" Israel was accompanied by his fear for their physical and spiritual well-being. Thus, he warned of the dire consequences and suffering that accompanies those who stray from righteousness. He encouraged and urged them to love God and each other. Moses profoundly understood that the moral order of our

Gloria Levi has been a gerontologist for the past twenty-eight years. She wrote Dealing With Memory Changes As You Grow Older *and a series of six short books,* Challenges of Later Life. *She lives in Vancouver, British Columbia.*

universe consists of justice, loving-kindness, and compassion.

I would like to share with you, my children, some of the thoughts that increasingly preoccupy me as I grow older. As part of another generation, I see it is inevitable that an invisible wall must separate us. We grew up in different times. Our songs, dances, heroes, and heroines were quite different. At times, I find it very difficult to communicate these thoughts to you. In the past, I have walked in your shoes, but you have not yet walked in mine. However, I feel a great need to bridge the chasm between your perceptions and mine. This letter is such an attempt.

With increasing age, my appreciation of "time" has become more elastic, stretching back into the past and forward into the future. Time no longer feels like a renewable resource but rather finite, limited, and therefore more precious. At the same time, I know—and am in awe of the fact—that I am a link in the chain of generations. Looking back, I see the world of my grandmothers and parents; looking forward, I see the world of my children and grandchildren.

My grandmother knew only the cycles of the Jewish calendar. She lived in the rhythms of Jewish time. I remember sitting at the dinner table Friday night as she read to me by candlelight in Yiddish the story of Joseph. On a Friday evening, when I see my son read the weekly Torah portion with his children in English before the Sabbath candles, I think about how much has changed—and how much is the same.

My grandmother had enormous survival skills. She never lost her equanimity. She accepted what she could not change, while directing great energy and drive to improving her lot. She lived for others, yet never lost her sense of self. She lived in a world in which responsibility to the family and the community were considered more important than individual fulfillment. She had no angst about her identity.

SEEKING A BETTER BALANCE BETWEEN
SELF AND COMMUNITY

As a parent, my father was a shadowy figure. Although revered as a *talmud chocham*, a scholar, he was not considered a successful breadwinner. It was my mother who had the street smarts, as had her mother before her. This was a common role for women of the *shtetl*. My mother was impetuous, intelligent, and passionate, and she held deeply ingrained community values. Although she was a very dedicated and devoted parent, she was often blind to the emotional needs of her children. Emotion was not part of her parental repertoire. She believed that the essentials of good parenting consisted primarily of cleanliness, good food, and educational opportunities for her children.

I absorbed much of my mother's temperament. However, unlike her, I was determined to be more sensitive to the emotional needs of my children and to foster and nurture their self-fulfillment.

As I observe all of you, my children, so deeply involved with assuring your own children's emotional well-being and striving to provide opportunities for their self-fulfillment, I wonder whether we've gone too far in maximizing our self-realization and minimizing our responsibility to extended families and to community. And I wonder whether we need a better balance between these inner and outer worlds.

When I grew up, in spite of the Depression, there was an optimism that things could get better and that an individual could make a difference. Inspired by the Jewish prophets, I was filled with passion for social justice. I marched in May Day parades in New York led by Paul Robeson and was active in civil rights and peace issues. I supported the union struggles and considered a picket line sacrosanct. Heroes and villains were sharply delineated. It may have been simplistic, but it was also very comforting.

Raising children, providing economic security, and attending to the thousand mundane tasks that filled my life gave me little time for self-reflection and contemplation. Nurturing and being nurtured came from my family. My work was challenging and gratifying, and I was constantly balancing the demands of family life, career, and community involvement.

It was a rich and exciting life. As you, my children, grew into adulthood, each major change in your lives caused a reciprocal change in mine. You moved away and I dealt with the empty nest. You married and I became an in-law. You became parents and I became a grandparent. Each change brought a new understanding and closeness to our relationship.

Recently, I've spent hours trying to find a new meaning in my life. I've examined compromised dreams and confronted mistakes I made as a wife, mother, friend, and citizen. I have learned to accept my life as something that had to be and, given the circumstances, that could not have been otherwise.

HEALING OUR PAIN

When you were younger, some of my human failings caused you pain. For this, I ask for your forgiveness. If you can try to see me as a whole person, with my virtues and my flaws, it might help ease some of your pain. I earnestly request that my approval or disapproval does not continue to be a conscious or unconscious measuring rod for your self-worth.

When I see you teaching your children the same humanistic values that I imbued in you, my heart swells with pride. I've watched you adapt new models for parenting, express concerns for the environment in your life styles, show loyalty and generosity to friends. I feel humble. Whereas I expressed much of my values through the political process, your values are expressed daily through your living. You have taught me a great deal.

I am confronted constantly by intimations of my own mortality, and this gives me pause. I resent that I need to pay more attention to maintaining my body. My new aches and pains make me feel vulnerable, and I fear a time when I will be helpless and dependent. I have a deeper, more intimate familiarity with death. In this time of taking stock, I ask myself: Have I made a difference in this world? Does my life have meaning?

This interior journey has forced me to face my fear of rejection, of being too ego-involved. I am learning how to forgive myself and others, to give and receive love, and to cherish myself and others. I have made peace with most of my hurts, struggles, and profound losses, and I feel truly blessed for the joys, delights, and loves that I have known.

I often think of Rabbi Abraham Joshua Heschel's statement: "Just as the grandeur of the sun or an oak tree is not reducible to the functions it fulfills . . . so a human being must be regarded as significant and valuable in himself or herself."[1] Instead of assessing others by their accomplishments, I try to appreciate a warm smile, a ready wit, a sense of compassion, or simply an ability to celebrate life.

My ability to celebrate life has deepened. I am more aware of those sacred moments when the sheer joy of being alive fills me with wonder and delight, when I can sense that I am an integral part of the entire cosmos. This is truly a wonderful time of my life. I pray that "God may teach us to use all of our days that we may attain a heart of wisdom."[2]

Imaging My Mother

Suzanne Hodes

INTRODUCTION

For over eighteen years, I have made drawings and paintings of my mother, Helen Hodes. Her character and strength, her sense of place and rootedness, and her final frailty have been a major theme in my art. My mother was always a major presence in my life. She has encouraged and inspired me by her strength, her wide intellectual interests, her sense of humor, and her embrace of all that is noble and beautiful in life.

For many people, art may express what is not easily said in words. Drawing was one of my ways of communicating with my mother and being part of her life. Rather than just trying to get the hair or mouth "right," I hoped to embody in my drawings and paintings some of my deep feelings for her. To create a moving portrait, one must identify with the subject. Certainly, I have tried to hold onto my mother through my art. My mother and I had a very special way of communing and communicating. It was this unspoken connection between us that I hope these drawings capture.

Suzanne Hodes received a B.A. from Brandeis and an M.F.A. from Columbia. She cofounded Artists West Studios, an artists' community in Waltham, Massachusetts. Her artwork, which has been widely exhibited in galleries and collections, reflects her commitment to peace and the dignity of human life. She and her husband live in Waltham.

"My Mother" © *1977 charcoal, 42" × 30"*

"My Mother Three Times" © 1989 charcoal, pastel triptych 50" × 92"

"Reverie" © *1989 charcoal, pastel 44" x 30"*

"Mother Reading" © 1994 charcoal, pastel 30" × 44"

"My Mother Questions Life" © 1995 charcoal, pastel 30" × 44"

In "My Mother," she is seated on our porch in Waltham, Massachusetts, looking forward with a resolute expression. She came to our home for holidays and during the summer. Many of my works show her in the New York apartment where she lived for thirty years after my father died. There, she continued to enjoy the cultural life of the city and the company of longtime friends. Most of her friends were Jewish teachers, like herself, from the New York public school system. My mother had an intellectual curiosity. Her approach to art and literature was scholarly and analytical. She was always learning, and she often read while I sketched her.

"My Mother Three Times" shows my mother in her small New York kitchen at the age of eighty, cooking breakfast. In this work, I'm using the traditional triptych format that I admire in early religious painting, a design that often includes several images in the life of a saint or other religious figure—in this instance, to narrate my mother's day. She would place pears on the windowsill to ripen, something I often do today. In honor of her eightieth birthday, I held an exhibit of paintings, drawings, and prints that featured her as subject. Many of my friends and fellow artists came with their mothers to the exhibit, as did my mother's cousins. She liked the paintings I did of her, and she enjoyed being the guest of honor at this show.

In "Reverie," my mother is in her kitchen, reading and thinking with a faraway, dreamy expression on her face. Behind her, and beyond the kitchen window, one senses the city. The clock and calendar suggest the passage of time. My mother was a great reader of world literature and took classes at the New School and at the Institute of Retired Professionals until her last years.

I drew, painted, and photographed her into her mideighties, when she began to physically decline. Although I was with her often during this difficult period, I did not want to depict the ravages of her age and illness. I felt it would be voyeuristic to show her pain. I wanted to honor the strong woman she had been.

I drew "Mother Reading" during her eighty-fifth year. She is looking down, trying to focus on reading, which became very difficult for her. The physical and mental effort required to do things was becoming much harder.

"My Mother Questions Life" shows her during the last year of her life. She began to withdraw from the world, to stop eating, and to sleep a great deal. This was very painful to see. Although she was declining, she still had fierce moments of energy. On her eighty-sixth birthday, her spirit still seemed strong.

IV. Women and Aging

In the matter of honor due to one's parents, the father is mentioned first. However, in the matter of reverence, the mother is mentioned first. From this we infer that both are to be equally honored and revered.

—Maimonides Mishna Torah
Book of Judges Mamrim 6:2

WOMEN AND AGING

The youth-oriented culture of North America is neither generous nor kind toward physical aging. Frantic worry about skin-engraved lines and jokes about being "over the hill" degrade the elderly. They especially degrade women who have spent a lifetime following society's dictates about beauty.[1]

Discriminating against the elderly and viewing old age as a social problem are ways younger people distance themselves from the aged and from their own aging. Women's experiences of aging are tied to the cultural status of women. Not only are they less visible as older people, but many women feel a sense of social erasure because they are old. This section explores some of the issues women confront as they age.

Sheva Medjuck's chapter, "Behind the Rhetoric of 'My Yiddishe Mama,'" points out that women are particularly affected by society's loathing of growing old and its quest for eternal youth and beauty. Many stereotypical images of old women are negative: the overly doting mama, the complaining *kvetch,* the demure, self-sacrificing widow. How can an old woman give voice to her experiences if she is continuously given the message to grow old silently, that complaining only burdens others and isolates her? Growing old should at least allow a woman to live as she chooses, according to her own rhythms and preferences.

Speaking to the silence that envelops the aged,

Margaret Moers Wenig's provocative chapter, "God Is a Woman and She Is Growing Older," imagines God as an old woman. Based on the litugy of Yom Kippur, Wenig's essay transports us to God's heavenly table, where we are invited to open our hearts and search our souls.

Rosie Rosenzweig's "Honoring Motherhood" analyzes ageism as it affects women in general and mothers in particular. She writes that "blaming mother"—a form of sexism and ageism—must be abandoned for a more mutual understanding and appreciation of the mother-child dynamic. In "My Mother and I," Micky Teicher shares a poignant piece of her life as an older woman who is also the primary caregiver for her mother. Although Teicher's mother was dependent on her for many services, their lives became interdependent and mutually satisfying because of the love and satisfaction Teicher reaped from her ever-evolving relationship with her mother. "Mothers never retire from mothering," writes Norma Baumel Joseph in "Commencement Beyond Fifty," a story of persevering to finally earn a doctorate despite efforts to make her feel guilty because she had a family and a life outside of the academic world. Reflecting on *Pirkei Avot*'s stages of Jewish development, Norma Joseph asks, "What is the age for women to learn?"

As evidenced throughout this anthology, aging is not a monolithic experience. Cultural anthropologist Barbara Myerhoff, who studied elderly Jews in Venice, California, in the 1970s, found that "wisdom, humor and some slowly acquired skills were natural rewards of aging" for some women she met. Myerhoff found that in contrast to men, many women "expanded with time." They became more jovial, content, and emotionally expressive. The women she studied, immigrants from European *shtetlach*, adapted to their new environments more easily than did men. Myerhoff concluded that the qualities developed by being *balebostes*, "custodians of the mundane," were especially durable and imparted resourcefulness, strength, competence, and autonomy, which buttressed them during their aged years.[2]

Given the increase in life expectancy, women, like men, may experience life roles and transitions different from those of years past. Older women often become caregivers and widows. Whether working or volunteering, they are often grandmothers with profound roles to play, offering unconditional love and support to families in difficult times. Fundamentally, they are who young women will become.

Behind the Rhetoric
of "My Yiddishe Mama":
The Status of Older Jewish Women

Sheva Medjuck

For some Jews, reflecting about mothers conjures up a comforting image of the *Yiddishe Mama*. Although some women fear and resist the expectation to "become their mothers," others are pleasantly surprised to find themselves exhibiting traits associated with their mothers and grandmothers. The bond between mothers and daughters is often romanticized with the passing of time. In reality, the position of older Jewish women is often far from that warm nostalgia.

Older Jewish women experience many of the same problems of ageism and sexism shared by all older women. Unfortunately, feminist analysis has typically ignored the older woman and done little to address ageism. In addition, the Jewish community has generally failed to recognize the damage caused by the negative stereotypes of Jewish women, and Jewish women's experiences with ageism and sexism may be compounded by anti-Semitism.

Sheva Medjuck is director of research and professor of sociology/anthropology at Mount Saint Vincent University in Halifax, Nova Scotia. She has published extensively on feminism and ethnicity and on small Jewish communities in Canada.

Until the late 1970s, older people in North America were generally regarded with compassion, although they were stereotyped as dependent, poor, needy, and frail. The 1980s and 1990s saw a reversal of this stereotype. The elderly were now "selfish, politically powerful, and potentially dangerous."[1] In February 1988, for example, the cover of *Time* magazine featured an older couple on their way to the tennis courts and the caption: "And now for the fun years! Americans are living longer and enjoying it more—but who will foot the bill?"[2] Several years later, a *New Republic* cover referred to older people as "greedy geezers."[3]

Both these caricatures of elderly people reflect ageism, and both regard all elderly as a problem. This changing stereotype is not necessarily based on changes in the actual situation of the elderly. Rather, it reflects larger political and ideological shifts in society. Treating the elderly as a group, either poor and dependent or rich and selfish, fails to recognize that the elderly are not homogeneous but represent myriad groups and experiences.

The experiences of older women and older men are also substantially different. Old-age pensions have reduced the number of older women without government-subsidized income. In Canada in 1990[4] and in the United States in 1989,[5] about 1 percent of older women had no income other than social security. Meanwhile, just under 3 percent of Canadian women and less than 1 percent of American women 65 years of age and older have incomes of $50,000 or more. Indeed, over 80 percent of Canadian women and 90 percent of American women 65 years of age and over have incomes of less than $20,000 per year. And social programs may have guaranteed some income for older individuals. Yet, the majority of older women have very modest incomes. It is difficult to ascertain how country club fees can be paid when one's income is less than $20,000.

FEMINISM AND AGING

Feminists have only recently begun to challenge ageism.[6] Germaine Greer and Betty Friedan,[7] for example, have recognized that their earlier works ignored older women and possibly even reinforced society's adoration of youth and its disparaging of the aged as lonely, ugly, sick, senile, and dependent. As these feminists celebrate their fiftieth, sixtieth and seventieth birthdays, they do not recognize themselves in these images. Friedan, for example, argues that "the problem is not how we can stay young forever, personally—or avoid facing society's problems politically by shifting them onto age. The problem is . . . how to break through the cocoon of our illusory youth and risk a new stage of life, where there are no prescribed role models to follow, no guideposts, no rigid rules or visible rewards, to step out into the true existential unknown of these new years of life now open to us, and to find our own terms for living it."[8]

Rather than approach aging with dread, Friedan writes about those who regard it as an opportunity for new adventure; Gloria Steinem calls it an "adventurous new country;" and Germaine Greer suggests that there are positive role models for the aging woman "who are not simply glittering threads, some bones, some silicone gel and hanks of hand-knotted bought hair."[9] Nevertheless, these women also recognize how difficult it is to break through the age denial—the "fountain of youth"— that is so insidiously ingrained in our culture.

The media have done much to reinforce this youth fantasy. The few images of older women in popular magazines[10] suggest that gray hair and wrinkles should be hidden at all costs. An entire industry promoting hair and skin care products, diets, and exercise thrives on the abhorrence of women's aging bodies. These attitudes may find special resonance among Jewish women, who may remember bemoaning their "Jewish" looks when they were younger. In the same way that being Jewish is acceptable as long as you do not look too Jewish, growing older can be tolerated if one does not look too old.

This denial of physical aging emanates from a loathing of growing old. For Jewish women, feminists' omission of aging from their agenda is complicated by the mainstream Jewish attitude that feminism will divide the Jewish community,[11] that it is antifamily or antivolunteerism.

As Susannah Heschel wrote, "Jewish leaders oppose feminism by popularizing the false notion that the family and particularly the self-sacrificing mother were predominantly responsible for preserving the Jewish people throughout the centuries."[12] This stance forces some women to "choose" between their identities as feminists and their identities as Jews.

IMAGES OF OLDER JEWISH WOMEN

Perhaps the most common stereotype of older Jewish women is that they are "Jewish mothers": Overprotective of their children, constantly nagging them, feeding them, and making them feel guilty about everything. (It is ironic and even tragic, that Jewish men have often perpetuated this caricature.) The classic example of this vilification is in Philip Roth's *Portnoy's Complaint*. Portnoy's mother, Sophie, is an amalgam of everything negative about Jewish middle-class suburbia in the United States in the late 1950s. She is everything that is negative about Jews, about women, and about immigrants. She is a complete stereotype—complaining, cajoling, commandeering, castrating."[13]

Certainly, this stereotype has been perpetuated not only in novels written by Jewish men but also by the larger society. But in reality, Jewish women are neither matriarchal tyrants nor self-centered princesses.[14] For example, the life stories of ten Jewish immigrant women in the book *Jewish Grandmothers* chronicle their hunger, grief and heartbreak and determination to overcome hard-ships.

According to the authors of *Jewish Grandmothers,* Sydelle Kramer and Jenny Masur, "The resemblance of the women in this book to the prevailing stereotypes is faint. They are not ignorant—they all know several languages and are well-read, besides having learned well from experience. They are not weak—they have lived through and triumphed over the traumas of immigration, culture shock, the Depression, the deaths (sometimes murders) of members of their families, poverty, anti-Semitism, and more. They are not passive. None of the women in this book was content to stay at home and do nothing; they pursued either education or a career and by doing so broke out of the ghetto of passive domesticity for women."[15]

It is difficult to understand why such stereotypes of Jewish women prevail. It is particularly difficult to understand this in the context of the Jewish community's sensitivity to anti-Semitism. Why do we recognize anti-Semitism aimed at Jewish men, but not recognize the anti-Semitism underlying attitudes toward Jewish women? One possible answer is that the common feature shared by Jewish "mother" and Jewish "princess" is an assertiveness that negatively affects Jewish men. Jewish "mother" and "princess" portrayals "suggest that men's strength is enhanced by female frailty and diminished by women's equality. Somehow, independent women are perceived as a serious threat, so these stereotypes discredit female independence and trivialize their experiences."[16]

WIDOWHOOD AND THE JEWISH COMMUNITY

In most ways, the Jewish community reflects the larger culture's attitude toward older women. The status of widows is one particularly glaring example of these attitudes.

Since women's life expectancy is greater than men's, many older Jewish women will most likely become widows. In fact, almost half of the women over 65 years of age in North America is a widow.[17] For women over 85 years old, the proportion is almost four out of five women. While the consequences of losing a spouse are difficult for most people regardless of ethnicity or age, widowhood places unique burdens on older Jewish women.

Since the Jewish community has traditionally made the family a major focus of Jewish identity, the departure of grown children, the loss of a spouse, and the transition to widowhood is especially poignant in a community that is as intensely family-focused as the Jewish community. Although some synagogues and Jewish family service agencies now offer bereavement groups for widows, it is important that issues facing older Jewish women be addressed by Jewish communal organizations.

The diversity and richness of Jewish women's lives belie the simplistic view that a woman's life is meaningless after the death of a spouse. While the lives of some Jewish widows will seem empty and roleless, others accept widowhood as an opportunity for new growth.

CAREGIVING TO
ELDERLY FAMILY MEMBERS

Traditional Jewish values also affect the caregiving responsibilities of Jewish women for older family members. North American society is undergoing major social and demographic changes. These have serious implications all women. Not only is the population aging, but also there is an increase in the number of women in the paid labor force. At the same time, the increased emphasis on keeping the elderly out of institutions raises the question of who will help the elderly who require care.

Unfortunately, the fact that more women work out of the home has done little to change their role as primary caregiver to children and aged relatives.

Traditional Jewish values compound this situation. The difficulties that women have trying to balance work and family responsibilities is exacerbated by a Jewish culture that places a high value on the family. In addition, Jews who do not live in communities with large Jewish populations may not be able to find Jewish services for the elderly nearby. In a study[18] of the needs of Jewish seniors in small Jewish communities in Canada's eastern provinces (where there are no residences for the Jewish aged), 88 percent stated that if necessary, they would live in a nursing home. But 70 percent stated that it was important or very important that the nursing home be Jewish. Unless Jewish facilities are built in such regions, many of these individuals will receive care from family members—most likely women—rather than live in non-Jewish nursing homes or leave their community so they can live in a Jewish home.

Most women care for their elderly parents or parents-in-law as a labor of love. We must ensure, however, that this physical and emotional task does not overwhelm the caregiver.

RITUALS FOR OLDER JEWISH WOMEN

Rituals help mark transitions—closing one life phase and acknowledging another. While Jewish life is rich with ritual that celebrates rites of passage, aging is rather meagerly observed. Few rituals in either the secular or the Jewish culture mark the transition to old age, indicating retirement, widowhood, or relocation to assisted living facilities as transitional moments. This absence of ritual suggests that aging is not a time to be acknowledged.

Recent ceremonies that celebrate women becoming

elders, such as "croning" or, among Jewish women, the *"simchat chochma,"* or "celebration of wisdom," provide new ways of acknowledging late-in-life passages. These ceremonies will hopefully help to dispel stereotypes of old age, while acknowledging aging as another stage of life. Jewish culture needs to adapt to and resonate with the varied experiences of older Jewish women.

Ageism, sexism, and anti-Semitism, both externally in the larger society and internally within the Jewish community, not only hurt older women but diminish us all. As a culture with a long tradition of social justice, Jews must strive to guarantee equity for all.

God Is a Woman and
She Is Growing Older

Margaret Moers Wenig

*"Turn us, O God, back to You and we shall re-
turn." Hashiveynu Adonai elecha, v'nashuva.*

Who—or what—is God? Where shall we look for God's
presence? Jewish sages and philosophers are
not unanimous in their response. But they do concur on
one matter: Who or what God truly is ultimately unknowable. God is "The Hidden One," *El Mistateyr;* the one
who conceals "His face," *Hesteyr panim;* the "Infinite, Un-
measurable One," *Eyn Sof*—unknowable, unfathomable,
indescribable.

Yet, these same sages also try to capture the Jewish
people's experience of God in images they can compre-
hend. The Kabbalists went as far as to sketch God's
form—"The Primordial Man" *Adam Kadmon*—and linked
each of God's attributes to a specific part of the human
body: head, arms, legs, torso, even male genitals.
Midrashim give us images of God weeping at the sight of

---

*Margaret Moers Wenig, the rabbi of Beth Am, the People's Tem-
ple in New York City, teaches liturgy and homiletics at Hebrew
Union College–Jewish Institute of Religion in New York City.*

Egyptians drowning in the Red Sea; God, bound in chains forced into exile with the people; and God, studying Torah with Moshe *Rabbenu,* Moses our teacher. Jewish liturgy refers to God as an immovable Rock, *Tzur Yisrael;* as a shield, *Magen Avraham;* as the commander of a host of angels, *Adonai Tzevaot;* as a shepherd, *Adonai roi.* And on the Days of Awe, the *machzor,* the holiday prayerbook, conjures images of God as Father and King, *Avinu Malkeinu.*

All these metaphors or allusions were never meant to be taken literally. Instead, they merely point us toward something we can imagine but never really see.

I invite you to imagine God along with me. I invite you to imagine God as a woman, a woman who is growing older.[1] She moves more slowly, and she cannot stand erect. Her hair is thinning. Her face is lined. Her smile is no longer innocent. Her voice is scratchy. Her eyes tire. Sometimes, She has to strain to hear.

God is a woman and She is growing older. Yet, She remembers everything. On Rosh Hashanah, the anniversary of the day on which She gave us birth, God sits down at Her kitchen table, opens the Book of Memories,[2] and begins turning the pages: And God remembers: "There, is the world when it was new and my children when they were young."

As She turns each page, She sees before her, like so many dolls in a department store window, all the beautiful colors of our skin, all the varied shapes and sizes of our bodies. She marvels at our accomplishments: the music we have written, the gardens we have planted, the skyscrapers we have built, the stories we have told, the ideas we have thought.

"They now can fly faster than the winds I send," She says to Herself, "and they sail across the waters which I gathered into seas. They even visit the moon which I set in the sky. But they rarely visit me." Pasted into the pages of Her book are all the cards we have ever sent when we did not visit Her. She notices our signatures beneath the printed words someone else has composed.[3]

Then there are the pages She would rather skip, but they stare Her in the face: Her children spoiling the home She created, brothers putting each other in chains, drivers racing down dangerous roads. She remembers Her dreams for us, dreams we never fulfilled. And She remembers the many names of all the children lost through war, famine, earthquake, disease, and suicide.[4] God remembers the times She sat by a bedside weeping because She could not halt the process She herself set into motion.[5] On *Kol Nidrei* night, God lights candles[6] for each of her children, and millions and millions of candles make the night as bright as day.[7]

God is lonely tonight, longing for her children. Her body aches for us.[8] But all that dwells on earth does perish, while God endures.[9] So She suffers the sadness of loosing all that She holds dear.

"Come home," God wants to say to us. "Come home." But She won't call. For She is afraid that we will say, "We'd love to see you but we just can't come tonight. Too much to do. Too many responsibilities to juggle."

But God knows that this is just an excuse. She knows that we avoid returning to Her because we don't want to look into Her age-worn face. She understands that it is hard for us to face a God who disappointed our childhood expectations. She did not give us everything we wanted: triumph in battle, success in business, invincibility to pain. We avoid going home to protect ourselves from our disappointment—and to protect Her. We don't want Her to see the disappointment in our eyes. Yet, God knows that it is there and She wants us come home, anyway.

If we did go home, God would usher us into Her kitchen and seat us at Her table.[10] She wants to say much to us, but we barely allow Her to get a word in edgewise, for we are afraid of what She might say. And we are equally afraid of silence, so we chatter, until She finally says, "Be still. Shhh, let Me have a good look at you."

In a single glance, She sees our birth and our death and all the years in between. She sees us as we were when we were young, when we idolized Her. She sees our middle years when our energy was unlimited and our later years when we no longer feel so needed, when chaos disrupts our bodily rhythms; when we sleep alone in a bed that once slept two.

God sees things about us we have forgotten and things we do not yet know. For naught is hidden from God's sight.

Now God says, "So tell me, how *are* you?" We are afraid to tell Her everything: whom we love, where we hurt, what we have broken or lost; what we wanted to be when we grew up. We are afraid to speak, lest we cry.

So we change the subject. "Remember the time when . . . ," we begin. "Yes, I remember," She says. Suddenly we are both talking at the same time, never completing a sentence; saying all the things the greeting cards never said.

"I'm sorry that I . . . "

"That's all right. I forgive you."

"I didn't mean to . . . "

"I know that."

"I was so angry that you hit me."

"I'm sorry that I ever hurt you. But you wouldn't listen to me."

"I know that now, but at the time I had to do it my way."

We look away now. "I never felt I could live up to your expectations," we say.

"I always believed you could do anything," She answers.

After hours of sitting and drinking tea, when there are no more words to say or to hear, God begins to hum:[11]

Ai ai ai ai ai   ai ai ai ai ai ai   ai ai ai ai   ai ai

And we are transported back to a time when our fever wouldn't break and we couldn't sleep, exhausted from crying but unable to stop. She picked us up and held us against Her bosom and supported our head in the palm of Her hand and walked with us. We could hear Her heart beating and hear the hum from Her throat:

Ah ah ba-by Ah ah ba-by   ai ai ai ai ai   ai ai ai ai ai ai   ai ai ai ai ai ai

God now touches our arm, bringing us to the present and to the future. "You will always be my child," She says, "but you are no longer a child. 'Grow old along with me. The best is yet to be, the last of life for which the first was made.'"[12]

We are growing older as God is growing older. How much like God we have become. For us, as well as for God, growing older means facing death. God will never die, but She has buried more dear ones than we shall ever love.

God holds our faces in Her two hands and whispers, "Do not be afraid,[13] I will be faithful to the promise I made to you when you were young.[14] I will be with you even to your old age. When you are gray-headed, I will hold you. I gave birth to you and I carried you and I will hold you still. Grow old along with Me."

Our fear of the future is tempered now by curiosity, since we now understand that the universe is infinite. We can greet each day with wonder: What shall I learn today? What can I create today? What will I notice that I have never seen before?

It has been a good visit, but now we are tired. Before we leave, we take a good look at Her. The face by marked time now looks wise as we understand that God knows those things that only time can teach: That one can survive the loss of a love, that one can feel secure even in the midst of an ever-changing world,[15] that there can be dignity in being alive even when every bone aches.

We now understand why we were created only to grow older: Each added day of life makes us more like God, Who is ever growing older. That must be why we are instructed to rise before an aged person and see grandeur in the faces of the old.[16] We rise as we would rise in the presence of God, and we see in the faces of the old the face of God.

Looking at Her, we are overwhelmed by awe. This aging woman looks to us now like a queen: Her chair is a throne, Her house dress is an ermine robe, and Her thinning hair[17] shines like jewels on a crown.

God wants us to come home. She is waiting patiently for us to return as She has waited every Yom Kippur. On *Kol Nidrei* night, God will not sleep. She will leave the door open and the candles burning. Perhaps on this Yom Kippur, we will be able to look into God's aging face and say, "Avinu Malkeinu, our Mother our Queen, we have come home."[18]

Honoring Motherhood:
Getting Beyond the I-It Relationship

Rosie Rosenzweig

My senior years have sensitized me to ageist attitudes. Like the chauvinist, the anti-Semite, the racist, and the homophobe, an ageist relates to people who are different as "the other." To Martin Buber, one person in this "I-It" relationship treats another as an object, a two-dimensional being with stereotypical characteristics. To the ageist, the elderly are "old folks" who have deficient psychological, physical, and intellectual functions and minimal capacity to grow or accept anything new. In short, the ageist does not see the elderly person as a person.

Mother-blaming is a form of ageism because it treats the elder as "the other." I recently heard a woman of the so-called sandwich generation—those caring for an aging parent while tending to their children—bitterly list the psychological scars that her mother had inflicted on her. I thought to myself, "Forgive and move on with your life.

Rosie Rosenzweig is a Boston poet, writer, and teacher. Her work has appeared in Sara's Daughters Sing, Lifecycles, Volume 2, Celebrating the New Moon: A Rosh Chodesh Anthology, *and* Reading Between the Lines: New Stories from the Bible. *The book editor of* Neshama Magazine, *she is writing a book about her encounters with spiritual leaders in southeast Asia.*

There isn't much time left." Until children forgive their mothers, they remain stuck in a no-growth situation.

About fifteen years ago, while my mother was recuperating from a painful cataract operation, we were walking down a hospital corridor as she blindly swung her cane and vented her anger: "What did I ever do to psychiatrists that they blame me for everything? From this they make a living?" My poignant amusement at her blunt *chutzpah,* in spite of her physical disabilities, began to reverse my belief in therapeutic mother-blaming. Eventually, I realized that my mother had done the best that she could. Role reversal in caring for one's own mother can effect a dramatic shift. It certainly influenced me.

THE PRESENT CAN REVAMP THE PAST

Being the sole caregiver to my mother (my father and two siblings had died) brought us back to an old intimacy that was now enhanced by a new spiritual aura. The past suddenly didn't seem that terrible. The childhood that I had formerly considered "deprived" seemed now to have provided the impetus for my insatiable intellectual curiosity. My present insights were revisioning the past.

If we vehemently blame our mothers for all of our character problems, we invite our children to do the same to us. A close friend's mother had become so cantankerous because of her physical suffering that she sometimes rejected her own grandchildren. Although this upset my friend, she continued to respectfully care for her mother. Frequently, she even asked her own daughter to accompany her on these expeditions as a way of teaching her to honor her grandparents.

This exemplifies Jewish *karma* and its practical workings: What you send out is what comes back. Deuteronomy 5:16 says, "Honor thy father and thy mother, as the

Lord thy God commanded thee; that thy days may be long." Revering our mothers and fathers is a path of spiritual ascension, which involves the heart, mercy, and forgiveness—something I didn't understand half a lifetime ago.

Hopefully, in addition to the honor we bestow on our parents, we will also be teaching our children a way to honor others. Such honoring is grounded in Judaism's spiritual framework.

RESPECTING OUR CHILDREN LETS THEM RESPECT US

Ageism, like chauvinism, is more than a denial of identification. It is dishonoring, since it refuses to acknowledge that we attain wisdom as we grow older.

My mother's death was additionally painful because I know that I did not fulfill my obligation as a daughter. So I have to ask myself: Will not honoring my mother 25 years before her death eventually haunt *me?* My children are now the same age that I was when I began to find serious flaws with my mother; may her memory be for a blessing. To ward off the ill effects of earlier behavior, and to assuage my guilt, I feel that my current task is to honor my own children.

I try to relate to my children, who are all adults, on their terms. Sometimes this means walking a tightrope between expressing my immediate reactions to situations and tactfully listening to their points of view. Recently, I went to Israel with my youngest daughter so I could understand her *ba'alat tshuvah,* or newly religious, world. When my son became a Buddhist and began a three-year meditation retreat, I was stunned and saddened. I could intellectually see why he chose to leave my beloved path of Judaism, but I worried that I—and the Jewish people— had lost him forever. Then his letters became increasingly loving and poetic, and he suggested that I accompany him to meet his teacher in Kathmandu. The lessons that I learned from his Tibetan meditation master now motivate my own pursuit of Jewish meditation. My son took good care of his mother, and I will always be grateful to him for this important life experience. Another of my current priorities is to be available to my grandchildren. This creates deep links between the generations.

Only time will tell whether I have ascended beyond the bad *karma* that I wrought. I may never know. I do know that my children have brought new experiences into my life that I would never have realized without them. Perhaps I will some day ascend to the wisdom that I now appreciate in my mother. Who knows, maybe the additional soul that enhances our Shabbat is that of my mother. If so, maybe she understands. I no longer find it frightening to think that I have inherited some of her wisdom. Now, contrary to my former belief, I would like to grow up to be like my mother. Like my children, I have taken some of my mother's traits and made them a part of my personality.

Commencement Beyond Fifty

Norma Baumel Joseph

I was 51 when I earned my doctorate. Officially, I was just beginning my career, although the academic world perceives anyone over 50 as edging toward early retirement. I felt strange, walking across the stage at convocation, standing side by side with youngsters, all of us formally marking our entrance into the world of professional scholarship, a realm I was entering twenty-five years "off-cycle."

Ecclesiastes says there is a season and a time for everything. To a woman, what is the season for knowledge? What is the season for developing a career? When is it appropriate to go to school, to receive instruction, to be initiated?

My story is not so unusual. Many women approach career and education when they finish raising children (although parents are never really finished raising their children). Yet, how many women who start their careers at fifty are held up as role models? Instead, the constant

---

Norma Baumel Joseph is an assistant professor in the department of religion at Concordia University, Montreal, and an associate of the chair in Quebec and Canadian Jewish Studies. She is president of the International Coalition for Agunah Rights (ICAR) and consultant to the Canadian Coalition of Jewish Women for the Get. She lives in Montreal, where she and her husband raised four children.

message is that everyone who is fifty is past their prime. If there is an acceptance of elder education, it is phrased in the language of hobby or of broadening one's perspective: a nice thing to do when you retire.

The lacunae in my career path are filled with the typical "married woman with children" excuses. I tried to continue my graduate career despite being an active mother and a rabbi's wife. Each time our family moved, progress on my doctoral thesis slowed down, although I always kept writing. Then the system—with all its sexist and ageist mechanisms—descended. I needed more time to finish. The university would not even negotiate an extension. Having children, moving, and switching my thesis topic were not sufficient excuses for tardiness.

After several years of part-time teaching, I was convinced by my colleagues to re-enroll in a doctoral program. It was not an easy process. Ageism and gender affected my passage through the system: I was often treated by faculty and fellow students as a "housewife" looking for something to fill my spare time. It took me almost twelve years to complete this second-chance degree. Deans wondered whether I would ever finish, and I wondered whether it was worth the torture. Again, I was guilty of having a growing family, of having a life.

Going back to school requires a special effort. The infantilization of the student leaves little room for dissent or for mature rejection of advice. Even graduate students must be submissive and compliant. My father, who was very proud of my academic accomplishments but worried about the time I was taking to complete my doctorate, gently asked, "Norma, do you think you will finish before I die?"

Adjustments at home were also necessary. I was writing papers at the same time my children were. I was wife, mother, teacher, student, social activist. There were too many me's for all of them to be effective. Who was I cheating? No matter what I did, I always felt that I should be doing something else: working on the dissertation, preparing a class, or cooking a meal. No one understood how foolish and incompetent I felt. When I finally earned my degree at 51, I was so embarrassed that I would not let anyone make me a party or celebrate my accomplishment.

AM I STARTING—OR ENDING— A CAREER?

I know how fortunate I am, now that I finally have a degree and a job. Although I love teaching Jewish studies at Concordia University in Montreal, I am still aware of the "age factor." Launching a career at this age is difficult, and many female scholars cannot get jobs. Universities and publishers expect "starting scholars" to be young people. Ageism is built into their blueprint. And I now have to face the publish-or-perish battle for tenure.

I am constantly aware of the need to "catch up." Will I ever feel confident or secure? In today's downsizing climate, early retirements are planned for 55-year-olds. Am I starting—or ending—a career? What chance do I have for a decent pension? Physical stamina is also a factor. I may not have the energy I had at 30, but I certainly have more experience and wisdom. Will the university recognize and reward that?

A *mishna* in *Pirkei Avot,* the *Ethics of the Fathers,* addresses aging as follows:

"At five to scripture, 10 to Mishna, 13 to religious duties, 15 to Talmud, 18 to wedding canopy, 20 to responsibility for providing for a family, 30 to fullness of strength, 40 to understanding, 50 to counsel, 60 to old age, 70 to ripe old age, 80 to remarkable strength, 90 to a bowed back, 100 is like a corpse who has already passed and gone from this world."[1]

This is an intriguing scenario. Some say it helps parents determine an appropriate educational path for their children. Others say that it merely sums up "natural" human capacities for growth and decline. But embedded in it is a sense of expanding intellectual capacities. The sages maintained that at 50, one had learned much from experience and that one's intellectual capacities were fully developed and honed. It is clear why *I* like this explanation: It contrasts sharply with current notions that one is "over the hill" at fifty. Rather than looking backward at youth, this list offers a sense of aging that is developmental and respectful.

Although this *mishna* was written for men and ignores female maturation and experience, it resonates with me. I transformed myself through study. In my fifth decade, the years of counsel, I am feel able to give advice.

WHAT IS THE
APPROPRIATENESS OF AGE?

The feminist movement may have opened new worlds to women, but will that openness render age irrelevant or appropriately relevant? Rather than discrediting those who earn their doctorates at fifty, perhaps we might expect to learn from and seek advice from such scholars.

A famous *midrash* talks about four men who sought esoteric knowledge. Each man was a sage, a pious and acknowledged teacher. The four friends were ready to experiment and enter the garden, *pardes,* of hidden knowledge together. Of the four sages, one died, one went crazy, one was destroyed, and one left in peace. There are many interpretations of this text. In one, the first man dies when he reaches a high level of knowledge, then leaps to heaven and joins God. The second man, unable to assimilate the vast knowledge, loses his mind. The third cannot accept not knowing everything and is destroyed. Only the fourth learns to accept what he can accomplish and live in this world.

Entering graduate school and an academic career at an "advanced" age is like entering that garden of knowledge. It can be frustrating rather than enlightening. Hopefully, the lives and experiences of women—both young and old—will begin to be considered when the social configuration is remapped.

I wish to enter the garden in peace. And I wish to emerge whole.

My Mother and I: A Daughter's Role in Caring for Her Aged Mother

Mickey Teicher

In 1985, when my husband retired from the University of North Carolina at Chapel Hill, we moved to Miami to be near my mother. A widow for the previous six years, she was now 86 years old. We bought a house just a few minutes' ride from her apartment. Fiercely independent, she lived alone and maintained her apartment in spotless condition. She did her own cleaning, cooking, laundry, and food shopping. My two brothers, who lived in Miami, looked after her financial needs. Both were busy with work and community activities and were less able then I to visit her regularly or provide the emotional support she needed. Neither could drive her to doctors' appointments or occasional luncheons, so my husband and I took over the chauffeuring responsibilities. I also took her shopping.

Without protest, I had simply accepted that most of the responsibility for looking after my mother fell on me—as a daughter—rather than on my brothers. There was no tension about this: We had an unspoken agreement about this division of labor.

Mickey Teicher, an art historian, has degrees from the University of North Carolina at Chapel Hill and Barry University, Miami Shores. She lives with her husband in Miami Beach.

I visited my mother almost every day. If I was tied up with my duties as director of the Judaica Museum, my husband would see her. Every Friday night, he picked her up for Shabbat dinner. At first, she was concerned about driving on Shabbat. We tried to ease her guilt by urging her to sleep over, but she insisted on returning home. I would cook more than enough for the three of us so that she would take home food for most of the week. Occasionally, Mother would attend synagogue with us on Saturday mornings, but her reluctance to ride on Shabbat made this an infrequent occurrence.

When a family celebration took place outside of Miami, I flew with her and looked after her. These occasions often involved trips to New York, where her siblings lived. Mother felt a deep bond to her brothers and sisters. She came from a large family in Poland whose members had all immigrated to the United States. She arrived in New York in 1912 after first spending a year in Buenos Aires where an aunt looked after her while her father was arranging for passage to the United States. In New York, Mother lived on the Lower East Side, where she worked in the garment industry and attended school part time. She married Morris Adler in 1920 and they had three children. Mother carefully stretched his meager earnings as a waiter to look after the family. After he retired, they moved to Florida. He died in 1979.

REVERSING THE NURTURING ROLE

My mother was a traditional "Jewish mother." Her job was to look after her children without any complaints. She was strong and feisty and took great pride in the accomplishments of her children, grandchildren, and great-grandchildren. Her interest in Israel and American politics was transmitted to all of us, as was her love of reading. Mother remembered the birthdays of her thirteen grandchildren and fourteen great grandchildren, always sending a card and a small check. When they paid her a visit, she would stay up most of the night before to bake *mandel bread,* which we affectionately called "Grandma's rocks." For several years, she busied herself knitting afghans for each female member of the family. She hoped that she could leave her children some money after she died, and she carefully husbanded her financial resources, ignoring our repeated assertions that we neither needed nor wanted her money.

The nurturing role that Mother played with her three children, especially when we were young, was reversed as she grew older. She became ever more dependent on me, although she fought hard to maintain control over her affairs. She resisted asking for help and insisted on making her own decisions. In 1990, we had a particularly difficult time when one of my brothers died. I had to try to comfort and console her as she lived through the terrible tragedy of burying a son. Her own increasing physical frailties forced her to become more dependent on me, even though she found this demeaning. She refused to let us install a medical emergency alert system in her home that would notify us if there were trouble. I respected and admired her determination to continue being independent, but it was a source of tension between us.

The routine of our life—daily visits, Friday dinners, constant chauffeuring—was rudely shattered in April 1994, when Mother fell and broke her hip. After a long hospitalization and subsequent stay in a nursing home, it became apparent that she could no longer function independently. With considerable hesitation, she finally accepted our suggestion that she move into a home for the aged. We paid rent on her apartment for two months before it became clear to her that she could not return to it. I felt guilty about her move into the home for the aged, knowing that I was unwilling to accept the alternative—

moving into my house. Mother did, however, make a reluctant adaptation to her new home.

The home was about a fifteen-minute ride from where I live, and I continued to visit her daily. If for some reason I couldn't visit, my husband would. Mother took great pride in the fact that she had more visitors than the other residents. And I felt that somehow my visits helped keep her alive. Perhaps they also helped assuage my guilt. Because of our daily visits, I was reluctant to travel, especially as she became weaker shortly before her death on July 10, 1996.

There is now an unfillable void in my life. When the time of day arrives when I was accustomed to visiting her, I feel bereft. To ease that emptiness, I feel a deep sense of desire to say *kaddish*, the mourner's prayer, for her. Instead of visiting Mother each day, I go to synagogue, where, for a few moments, I feel spiritually reunited with her.

V. JOURNEYS AND DISCOVERIES

The elderly gather wisdom and knowledge according to their experiences and the occurrences of their many days. There is no elder except one who has acquired wisdom.
—Torah Temimah on Genesis 24:1

JOURNEYS AND DISCOVERIES

Wisdom often grows with experience and can increase our satisfaction with our lives. But to fully live one's wisdom, we must meet, rather than ignore, the conditions of age. The path toward old age is a journey of many encounters. It is a biological process and an accumulation of exchanges with others and with the larger environment within which we live. Like the mysterious journey that Abraham and Sarah embarked upon in the Torah portion *Lech lecha*, growing old is a journey noted at times by well-marked signposts and at other times by confusing detours.

The following essays, all written by Jewish elders, help illuminate that path. They speak about what changes as we age and what remains the same, about how time shrinks and yet also how it expands, and about the rich, spiritual opportunities that old age may offer.

In "From Age-ing to Sage-ing," Zalman Schachter-Shalomi advises us to "grow into old age rather than be arrested by it." He suggests that "conscious aging" will help us accept the inevitability of death and open the door to spiritual eldering. Rather than ignoring our mortality, we can acknowledge death while embracing the virtues and responsibilities of being an elder. Schachter-Shalomi calls for a Senate of Elders, a place of counsel and mediation based on wisdom, inspiration, and experience. Here, "an aging ecumenism would foster a reciprocity in which older people would be inspired and revered while younger people would receive sagacity, wisdom, and counsel."

Alice Shalvi's "My Body, My Self: Waning and Waxing" describes how her age has changed her physically and spiritually: "Paradoxically, as I grow older I have both *less* time and *more* time in which to feel a growing closeness to God. . . . What I have lost in longevity, I have redeemed by profundity." In "Have You Seen Sarah?," Savina Teubal reflects on the decade since her *simchat chochma,* the "celebration of wisdom" she developed "to establish [her] presence in [her] community as an elder." During these ten years, her body may have weakened, but her spirit has remained vital.

Ben Engelman's essay, "Until God Says 'Come,' I'll Make the Best of My Life," offers us a glimpse into life as a resident at the Hebrew Rehabilitation Center for Aged in Boston. His essay acknowledges how possible and how enriching it is to retain a Jewish identity and religious practice during even the last stages of life.

Muriel Ginsberg's essay, "Participating in the Holy Burial Society," explains why she joined the *chevra kadisha,* the group that prepares the body for burial: She wished to engage more fully with the "wonders of creation and the eternal mystery of death."

As we grow nearer to death our days become ever more precious. We learn to treasure each day. Or, as my youngest daughter remarked, we learn how "to find a treasure each day." Such simple words become profound lessons for us at every age we reach.

From Age-ing to Sage-ing

Zalman Schachter-Shalomi

Just as midwives help with natural childbirth and the hospice movement helps with dying, a framework is needed to help with one's initiation into spiritual eldering. Much of the physical and custodial care for the aged has—thank God—been humanized, but to date the preparation for eldering has essentially been ignored, even though the whole spiritual discipline for becoming serene is connected with this. "Growing" older demands that we look death in the face and accept our mortality.

Looking at our mortality and accepting our death is the door through which we each must pass. The key that opens this door is in the body, the heart, the mind, and the soul. We need to use all four of these to move through the

---

The phrases "From Age-ing to Sage-ing" and "Spiritual Eldering" are registered trademarks of Rabbi Zalman Schachter-Shalomi. They are used elsewhere to entitle and describe the contents of his workshops and his writings on this topic.

Zalman Schachter-Shalomi, a rabbi and teacher, is professor emeritus at Temple University. His belief in the universality of spiritual truth has led him to study with Sufi masters, Buddhist teachers, Native American elders, Catholic monks, and humanistic and transpersonal psychologists. He is the founder of the Spiritual Eldering Institute in Philadelphia, which sponsors nondenominational workshops to help people grow into elderhood. His most recent book is From Age-ing to Sage-ing.

gate marked "fulfillment" and "completion." With inspired imagination, it opens; and with that, comes light and guidance for the next stage. As long as the fear of death is considered part of the software for the preservation of life, one cannot begin to open the door to completion.

Until now, everything that threatened my life got an automatic, knee-jerk response that pumped adrenalin, urging me to run, fight, flight: "I've got to save myself." That response, which was essential in my earlier life, now blocks my walking through the door to eldering. Because the habitual, built-in response is to save one's life, one naturally panics and does everything to avoid facing death. This blind spot also blocks conscious and deliberate spiritual eldering.

The mystic Gurdjieff taught (as have most other spiritual teachers and philosophers) that "as long as you are a machine, you can't save yourself. It's only when you stop being a machine that you come to full consciousness." Full consciousness means you are conscious about how you are conscious.

This points to recognizing what drives the "fight and flight" response: a "program" that runs in the deep background of our consciousness and repeats, "I don't want to die. I don't want to die. I don't want to look at death. I don't want to look at death." Its life-affirming function says, "At all costs, save your life." Or as *halacha*, or Jewish law, says, "A human life is worth more than even the Torah." What is halachically expressed is also part of the biological program written into our body: "Save your life at all costs."

So I can't walk through the spiritual eldering door until I can separate myself from my ego's automatic avoidance responses. As one gets older these responses, which Buddhism calls *samskaras*, become less and less energetic. This is natural and as it should be. Our energy is running low and will eventually wear out.

Part of "fight and flight" is that I don't dare look at my

death. So when my own death keeps coming up, I get anxious and distracted. I'll look in every direction to *not* face my death. But when I move beyond my fears, I begin to see a wonderful potential to complete and round out my life.

SEPTEMBER, OCTOBER, NOVEMBER

With our longer life spans, we can shape ourselves into the kind of elder we want to be. But someone who does not abandon his or her automatic response toward death does not graduate to sagehood. That person remains side-lined, stuck in the June, July, and August of life, rather than entering into the Fall and becoming an excellent September, October, November person. Part of awareness is realizing that we can't develop the September, October, November of our life if we don't look at death, and we can't develop the Fall of our life unless we look at October, November, and December. We must look from one phase into the next phase so our life's orientation is current and correct.

To perfect the knowing and becoming of a "sage," one needs to look past death. But this contemplative, philosophical, spiritual, intuitive piece of life needs to be learned. Most of us have learned how to run a computer, run a spreadsheet, write a letter, clip coupons. But we haven't learned to look at life contemplatively. Rather than displacing the condition of aging, we must meet it. We must live within the context and the condition of aging in order to maximize the parameters of our living.

A LIFETIME OF MONTHS

Asking myself, "What is eldering doing to me?" brought me to a vision of a lifetime organized into periods of seven years, with each seven years correlated to one cal-endrical month.

Imagine that from birth to age seven when our second teeth come in is January. From seven to 14 years and the onset of puberty is February. Then the time to 21 years, when we're more or less fully grown in our body, is March. April begins at that point, and ends when we reach 28 years. At 35 until 42, we set ourselves up as so-cial beings, creating new families and new careers. We're in our prime from 42 to 49, from 49 to 56, from 56 to 63. These three "months" are when we do our major work in the world. They are our July, August, and September.

To have the prime of our life between 42 and 63, we need a vision of how we want to spend our October, No-vember, and December.[1]

I am now in the October of my life. I search my soul and examine my conscience during the High Holy Days of September. When we take the year this way, Spring is when we're 21 years old and leaving Egypt. The Summer of our lives brings midlife crisis—Tisha B'Av, the destruc-tion of the Temple. In this way, the liturgical year and our lives parallel each other.

I began to wonder about and pay attention to new in-ternal processes. Earlier, my libido focused on sex, procre-ation, and acquiring material goods. My psychic energy is now concerned with preserving the distillate of my life's experiences. One day, I had a very strong insight. Moses, the Buddha, Lao Tsu and Confucius all reached a ripe old age; Jesus and Mohammed less so. Jesus was the youngest of them to die. Our North American culture, which is largely based on Christianity, doesn't have a good eldering model, perhaps because Jesus died before becoming an elder.

The Bible tells a very interesting thing. During Biblical times, everybody served in the army from age twenty to sixty. At sixty, they were free. The Levites were also in service from 20 to age 60, but from 20 to 30 they had to learn from older Levites. The active Levite years were from age 30 to age 50, when they took the Ark apart and handled the altar. From age 50 to age 60, their job was to train the 20- to 30-year-olds.

Judaism has a wonderful eldering model in Moses. When he was 120 years old, he was still active. When the time came for him to die, he consciously left his body. In China, Lao Tzu and Confucius did the same kind of thing, as did avatars in India as well as the Buddha. But America is like the young, sequestered Buddha, Siddhartha, who was unable to see old people. America isn't especially concerned with developing a model for aging.

Another experience fed my insight about growing older. During a session with my Feldenkrais trainer, I fell asleep. I hope that when it is my time to die I can slip out of my body with that ease, with everything nestled and rested. Feeling that gentle wave wash over me made me realize that spiritual work is a necessary component to the process of aging and facing death.

A SENATE OF ELDERS

We have Health Maintenance Organizations (HMO) for health. What if we created an HMO for eldering? The first level would include accountants and lawyers, who would help put our affairs in order. In the next level, a counselor would help us with relationships: "Who were your friends? Who were your lovers? What do you have to fix? How would you do that?" These counselors could help us put order to our affairs and leave the world, when the time comes, with ease.

Originally, the word "senate" referred to older people with greater wisdom and greater experience who would hear what lower courts had decided and comment on their rulings. Imagine a United Nations Senate of Elders where we would gather to meditate, hear, share, and counsel.

Several years ago, I participated in a gathering of about 150 Muslims, Sufis, Christians, Coptics, Palestinians, Israelis, Americans, Japanese, and a Native American. We gathered in the Sinai Desert and began to climb Mt. Sinai at 1:00 A.M. At sunrise we reached the summit, where we prayed and placed a stone that had been engraved with the inscription *"Dona Nobis Pacem,"* "Grant us Peace." It was an amazing moment.

Climbing up the mountain, an old Japanese man and I helped each other over the tough places. There was no need to talk because of the powerful presence of fellowship. I sat with the old Muslims, listening to them talk. What hit me was that just as the split between male and female is broader than the Sephardi-Ashkanazi split, so too is the younger-older split wider than the gulf between being Christian and Jewish. I realized that what was needed was a dialogue across the age barrier, an aging ecumenism which would foster a reciprocity in which older people would be inspired and revered while younger people would receive wisdom and counsel.

INITIATION INTO ELDERING

Staretz, in Russian, means the "old one," the "elder." Father Zosima, the *staretz* in *The Brothers Karamazov,* is a very patient, holy person. But even a *staretz* needs an initiation into eldering. Seminars I've developed to foster such a process emphasize growing old, not being old; growing into old age, but not being arrested by it. Growing old is a way to appreciate the process of aging. It is a celebration of our personal success story. We have achieved a greater maturity—and we deserve to be congratulated for that.

The seminars also teach the tools of contemplative life, such as meditation and centering prayer. We need to sit in deep silence and become mindful of the presence of God.

Another prime focus of the seminars is to teach us the basics of reviewing our lives, and observing what remains incomplete in our life. And finally, they introduce us to death and beyond. They teach us that at death, Moses received a "kiss" from God. The Kiss of Death is like the waters of *mikveh:* The finite person merges with the great All and is flooded with the Universal Mind. Death is seeing the Indwelling of God, the *shechinah,* before our last breath and melting into the White Light.

Each seminar helps prepare us for the work of being an elder and eventually dying. We create a sacred space and prepare for death and beyond. Spiritual eldering lets us accept the gifts of life and lets us give our bodies at death to the worms and our spirits to the Universal. It helps us flow into the Godstream not with the pain of an unfulfilled life but rather with a sense of appreciated completion. This model of late-life development enables older people to become spiritually radiant, physically vital, and socially responsible "Elders of the Tribe." It lets us transform the downward arc of aging into an upward arc of expanded consciousness that crowns an elder's life with meaning and purpose.

My Body, My Self:
Waning and Waxing

Alice Shalvi

The body grows old first. Now that I am past my seventieth birthday, bone shrinkage has made me even shorter than my former 5 feet, 1 inch. I can no longer reach the top shelf of my kitchen cupboard or the hangers in my wardrobe. The little finger of my left hand is slightly bent at the top joint, and it hurts when I try to straighten it. My hair, once luxuriant, wavy, and chestnut brown, has been gray for a good while already and now is also thinner. My waist, on the other hand, thickens, and I have almost given up wishfully thinking I may one day again wear some of the favorite dresses I haven't had the heart to give away.

When our first child was born, we lived in a fourth-floor walk-up. Each evening, I pulled the heavy English baby carriage up to our flat. I still go up and down stairs dozens of times a day, but I no longer run up them or even down, and when I climb the five flights to the

Alice Shalvi, born in Germany and educated in England, has lived in Jerusalem since 1949. She taught English literature at the Hebrew University for forty years; directed Pelech, an experimental high school for religious girls; and is the founding chairwoman of the Israel Women's Network. She and her husband have three sons, three daughters, and numerous grandchildren.

graphics studio where my organization prints its publications, I arrive so breathless that I pause before going in. I don't want the workers to think I am about to collapse.

Not so long ago, an old friend (that is, a friend of long standing) gave me a photo of myself taken soon after I married. Incredible. When I showed it to my daughter, she couldn't believe I ever had so narrow a waist—until she remembered trying to fit into my wedding dress and finding it too small for her.

The body grows old, though my mind—I like to think—is still alert, and I yearn to go faster than circumstances permit.

I am now a little older than my mother was when she died. Sometimes, when I pass a mirror or a shop window or involuntarily and unexpectedly encounter my reflection, I think I am seeing my mother coming toward me. Traversing long corridors at airports, carrying my always-too-heavy hand luggage, I recall her arrival for what would to be her final visit to us, the one during which she died in Jerusalem. She was, as always, bringing us food: *schmaltz*, smoked salmon, my favorite chocolate biscuits, foods the children liked—all of which were then unavailable in Israel. She looked so small and bent and tired as we watched her cross the tarmac that I wanted to pick her up and carry her in my arms.

A short while ago, my youngest grandson looked at a portrait of my mother that hangs by my bedroom door and said "Grandma, that's you, isn't it?" In a way, he was right.

INVISIBLE BONDS
BETWEEN GENERATIONS

As my body sinks toward the grave my spirits soar. Increasingly recognizing my own resemblance to a mother who, while she was alive, seemed so vastly different from myself—in background, in experience, in education and

cultural accretions, in the baggage she acquired and carried with her every day—I become aware of the invisible
bonds that link us, generation to generation.

Family takes on additional meaning as one contem-
plates and celebrates it within the context of Jewish continuity. Like the Shabbat candlesticks that once were my
mother's and are now mine and soon will belong to my
daughter, or recipes we pass from generation to generation, we also pass—consciously or unconsciously—religious traditions, although altering them at times.

Some traditions I observe with my children and
grandchildren almost exactly as I learned them from my
parents. We gather our children and grandchildren into
our home on the last night of Chanukah, and since we
each light our own eight candles, the number of *hanukiot,*
or menorahs, exuding light and warmth grows from year
to year with our growing family. We hold a family seder
every other year. This allows married children to spend
alternate years with their in-laws. We distribute *mishloah
manot,* Purim gifts, over an ever-widening geographical
range as children set up their own homes.

Other religious observances I have initiated. I celebrate Rosh Chodesh with a group of women friends. I
have been called up to the Torah to touch and kiss the
scroll, and follow the silver hand as it passes from word to
word. I have joyfully danced on Simhat Torah, bouncing
and hugging the richly-clad "bride," as I once bounced
and hugged my babies. My mother never did any of these
things; hopefully, my daughters and their daughters will.
These new observances have deepened my sense of closeness to the Divine Creator.

An emerging participation in these religious acts has
been a result of my feminist awakening. I am asserting
my rights as a descendant of those who stood at Sinai,
and I am refusing to be marginalized within my religion
any more than I would let myself be marginalized in a
secular social context. If my feminism has informed my

Judaism, my Judaism has also informed my feminism, since the most vital elements of Jewish ethics are, for me, justice and the notion of *tikkun olam*, repairing the world.

SANCTIFYING LIFE AND DEATH

A central feature of Jewish practice is the sanctification of the everyday and the commonplace by pronouncing the appropriate blessing for every act we perform, even the most mundane and trivial. So by increasing the number of activities that I personally perform, even though I am a woman, I make myself more often aware of the holiness which surrounds me and infuses my life.

Paradoxically, as I grow older I have both less time and more time in which to feel a growing closeness to God: more time because my children are grown, I am semi-retired from work, and the pressures of deadlines are diminishing; less time because the ultimate deadline—death—is approaching.

What I have lost in longevity, I have redeemed by profundity. Compelled by failing physical strength, I sit more, recline more, rest more frequently. But in those moments of physical nonaction and bodily passivity, the spirit can soar if I unleash it from everyday concerns. As I close my eyes to meditate and fold my hands in my lap in the traditional gesture of supplication, my thoughts and words reach up to God, Whose grace is always with me. David's powerful image resonates within me as it never could when I was young and all of life lay before me:

> "Though I walk through the valley of the shadow of death
> I shall fear no evil, for Thou art with me;
> Thy rod and Thy staff—they comfort me."

Like my mother before me, I have created a link in the chain of tradition. In fact, I am that link. My daughters, as well as my sons, will say *kaddish* for me. I face death with no fear.

Have You Seen Sarah?

Savina J. Teubal

The Dutch traditionally tease someone celebrating a fiftieth birthday by asking, "Have you seen Sarah?"[1] Sarah, the oldest woman recorded in the Genesis narrative, died at age 127. She was also the first of a succession of Hebrew matriarchs of whom God took note and upon whom God conferred a miracle. According to one *midrash,* Sarah regained her youth in her old age. This interpretation focuses on the miraculous conception and birth of Sarah's child long after she had stopped menstruating (Genesis 18:11). To have a baby when you are 90 years old is undoubtedly miraculous. But what I wanted to know more about were the experiences Sarah and her husband, Abraham, had over many years: It is striking that we know nothing of their lives as younger people, since nothing is recorded of that part of their lives.

Not long ago, while thinking about Sarah and Abraham, I wrote, "This story is not of a young couple going off on an exciting pilgrimage with their whole lives before them. Rather, it is a quest into the unknown in the last

Savina J. Teubal, an affiliated scholar at the University of Judaism in Los Angeles, has lectured and written extensively on women in the Hebrew Bible. She is the author of Sarah the Priestess: The First Matriarch of Genesis *and* Hagar the Egyptian: Lost Traditions of the Matriarchs. *She is the founding president of Sarah's Tent: Sheltering Creative Jewish Spirituality, which is based in southern California.*

phase of human life. Metaphorically speaking, Abraham and Sarah are embarking on a journey of the spirit, a last journey that will reunite them with the supernatural."[2] In other words, unlike the Greek gods who chose only young heroes to embark upon adventures, the Hebrew God sent an older couple on a mission.

The message seemed clear: *L'chi lach/lech l'cha* (the awesome words that set our ancestors in motion) is a divine admonition to radically change one's lifestyle, to permit one's true essence to become apparent. Becoming an elder is a time to discard the unwanted pressures left by our parents or the culture of our tribe or clan. It is truly a time when we can, when we *must,* make the effort to give to the next generation the benefits of our vision, complete with its realities and its dreams.

CREATING A *SIMCHA*

With this understanding, ten years ago I created a *simchat hochmah,*[3] a rite of passage ceremony that would establish my presence in my community as an elder, as a functional and useful human being. The occasion was my sixtieth birthday. At the time, I remember feeling that I had probably fulfilled the destiny that had been allotted me and that I should dedicate the last portion of my life-journey to helping younger people. Now I realize that I had internalized the conventional wisdom telling me that at my age (and particularly as a female), I had crossed the boundary of self-fulfillment and was now expected to assist others as well as prepare for my demise.

It took me quite a while before I understood that eldering is a many-leveled process: that one can be young and be old at the same time. I hadn't noticed, for example, that a part of me hasn't changed as I aged: I was a dreamer when I was young and I am a dreamer now. Over the years, my character has changed, but not my personality. I also realize that my vision of who I am has changed since I celebrated my sixtieth birthday. My body may be disintegrating, but my spirit is the same as when I was born. True old age is just as the wise rabbis told us: *being able to look at life as if it were just beginning.*[4]

My *simcha* ceremony was inspired by Sarah and Abraham, partly because they set out on a spiritual journey at an advanced age and partly because the path they took led them to an understanding of God and an acceptance in their lives of the guidance and power of that God. I celebrated the ritual in the month of Heshvan, in which the Torah portion *lech l'cha* is read. *Lech l'cha's* awe-inspiring call initiates the Biblical account of the first three generations of Hebrews. When she adapted the first lines of *lech l'cha* for music, songwriter Debbie Friedman feminized the first two words to *l'chi lach* to emphasize Sarah's part in the calling. Events in Sarah's life were reflected in the entire ritual: a title or change of name, a blessing, a covenant or promise, and a reconciliation with death.

Ready to embark on my own journey, I wanted my *simchat hochmah* to be a truly Jewish ritual, from specifically Jewish roots. But I also believed that I first needed to acquire the spiritual tools my religion had denied me as a woman. So I wove the ritual around participating in the Sabbath morning service: carrying the scrolls and publicly reading from the Torah on the *bima*, during which I was moved to tears. Women were never allowed to do these things in the Orthodox Syrian community in which I was raised. The intent of the *simcha* was to validate the years I had already lived and to empower me in the years I had left.

At the time I celebrated my *simcha*, my book *Sarah the Priestess* had just been published, and I was convinced that writing that book had satisfied my main mission in life: bringing Sarah back to her people. Traveling around the country, I had brought her presence to young and old, to synagogue and university. I felt fulfilled. I had realized my calling. What was left to me was to face my mortality.

Feminist scholar Rabbi Drorah Setel helped me devise the crone ceremony. At her suggestion, I left the synagogue sanctuary halfway through the service, discarded the beautiful robe I was wearing, and changed into a *kittel*, a white linen ceremonial robe traditionally worn on special religious occasions during one's lifetime and which, in death, becomes a shroud.

The symbolism of the *kittel* was sobering. The words I expressed at the time reflected my state of mind: *Today you witness, each one of you, the beginning of the cycle that reintegrates my being with the cosmos. The cycle that reaffirms my life. Like the* kittel *I wear, the ceremonial robe that unites and affirms the two aspects of the new cycle: the festive garment and the shroud.*[5]

The *simcha* left me feeling time-bound and aware of the relevance of my continued physical well-being. It also gave a new and profound dimension to "mortality," which in turn led me to a new awareness that health, not age, determines one's lifestyle.

REDISCOVERING SARAH'S WISDOM

It took me ten years after writing *Sarah the Priestess* to realize that there was an element in Sarah's story that I had failed to see. So intently had I focused on Sarah's age and the miracle of giving birth at ninety that I had completely bypassed the fact that she continued to live not as an old lady nor as a young one: *She simply continued to live her life,* making decisions, dealing with events as they happened. Sarah did not seem concerned about her age. She was 76 when she suggested that Abraham impregnate her handmaid, Hagar. Had age been the issue, Hagar could have borne a child when Sarah was younger. Nor did Sarah seem concerned about bearing a child when she was close to 90, as were Abraham[6] and God.[7] Rather, Sarah laughed at the thought of having sexual pleasure with an old man![8]

Neither Abraham nor Sarah fade into oblivion when they reach Canaan at the age of 75 and 65, respectively. According to Biblical tradition, Sarah and Abraham had sex, acquired descendants, and educated them. Their spiritual journey may have led them to a new consciousness, but it did not change their lifestyles. Ten years ago, I had failed to see that my ancient ancestors had been so active during their old age.

I was quite right to establish myself as an elder in my community. It was a meaningful, necessary milestone, which I encourage everyone to experience. However, I was wrong to think that my main mission on earth had been accomplished. Rather than fade away, my life took on an unexpected intensity. The past ten years have been even more rich and fulfilling than those of the previous decade. I wrote another book (*Hagar the Egyptian*), contributed to anthologies, produced and distributed the video of my *simcha,* and am now creating *Sarah's Tent,* an organization dedicated to the study of a new paradigm for Judaism in the twenty-first century.

I am now very aware of how I rank my priorities. The highest priority is my relationship with family and friends: I care deeply about how we enrich each others' lives and the quality of the time I spend with them. My work has also changed. I now prefer to teach in small groups where I have a friendly connection with students, where we teach each other, rather than traveling around the country lecturing to large gatherings.

Have I seen Sarah? She is the blueprint of my life. I learn from her every day. If I have an angel hovering over me, it is Sarah. The older I get, the more I identify with her, understand what she experienced, appreciate her as my ancestor and spiritual guide. Without Sarah, I could not have grown old laughing, as she did. She, too, had to learn that miracles are possible; that sexual pleasure does not evaporate with age, and that creativity is the essence of life, whether one creates a child of the body or of the intellect.

The *shechinah* blessed me with the knowledge of Sarah, and for that I am thankful and grateful. And for that I answer, Yes! I have seen Sarah!

Until God Says "Come,"
I'll Make the Best of My Life

Ben Engelman

I am ninety-one years old and have been living in the Hebrew Rehabilitation Center for Aged in Boston for the past 18 months. Two and a half years ago, I became quite ill, went into a coma, and stayed for several months in the hospital and then in another rehabilitation center. I came back to life, although I cannot see well or read, and I am in a wheelchair.

I lived most of my life in Chelsea, Massachusetts, working as a shoe salesman. I was married for over fifty years and had a good life. I don't have many complaints. My wife died eleven years ago. She was an exceptional woman. She was what she was and never pretended to be anything else. I miss her.

I have a son and a daughter. For the past two and a half years, my daughter has been responsible for helping me. She found me this Home. If you have to be confined to a facility of this nature, this place is incredible. It has many different types of therapies and doctors. On each floor is a primary doctor and several wonderful assistants. Each floor is treated like a small community, part of the larger, whole facility.

The food is marvelous (and kosher). The aides and

Ben Engelman, a retired salesman, currently lives at the Hebrew Rehabilitation Center for Aged in Roslindale, Massachusetts.

nurses that help us are so attentive and kind and maintain close communication with residents' families.

When I first came here, I worried about what I would do for twenty-four hours each day. But I am very busy. I attend art appreciation classes and the men's club in addition to physical therapy.

I love the people here. I believe in "people helping people." I've made some good friends. Ed is my best friend. By coincidence, our children and grandchildren know each other, but we didn't meet until I moved here. I'm lucky because I have a good roommate, but some people aren't so lucky. Compatibility of roommates can be a problem here: We're old and we have habits. And it's hard to adjust now to someone else's habits. Some people just aren't nice, and it's hard to have to live in a room with them. One person complained to the Residents' Council that wheelchairs take up too much room in the elevator!

I TALK TO PEOPLE, I TALK TO GOD

I talk to people all the time. Some, especially the women, are starved for conversation and I like talking to people and I don't want to be miserable. When God says, "Come," I'll come. Until then, I'm going to make the best of my life.

I go to *shul* here every day. I'm not pious, but I believe in my religion. I *daven mincha-maariv* every day. I do it without a book because I can't see and can't read. I was brought up to be very religious, but have spent most of my adult life as a Conservative Jew. I feel at home in a *shul*. On Friday afternoons, we have an adapted *Kabbalat Shabbat* service with a rabbi and a woman cantor. She finishes the service by singing "Eli Eli," which bring tears to my eyes.

I now *daven* from a wheelchair, but I participate fully

as a member of the spiritual community. I am pushed to the *bima* for an *aliyah* and manage to stand while saying the prayers over the *Torah*. Today is the *yahrzeit* for my mother, so I was called to the *Torah* and given a *m'sheberach*. The prayer for healing, *refu-ah shleima*, has always been important to me. I sit for the *amidah*, the standing prayer, and for the *aleinu*, I bend forward in my chair when others bend while standing.

Every night, I have a little talk with God and pray for the health of my children. My mother used to sing a little song to me in Yiddish: "God in His Kingdom is correct, God knows what He does." I still believe this. So I pray for my children, and then I ask God to keep my wife resting in peace. I finish with the line, *"V'ne-emar"* which says that God will always be the Ruler and His name will always be one.

I've had some downs in my life, some tragic moments. Most of my family is gone, but here I am. I say *kaddish* for my parents, my brothers, my sisters, and my wife. I believe in *kaddish*, which glorifies God. I've lived a long time, ninety-one years, and nothing would change my belief. With all the ups and downs, God has been very good to me.

I'm no different now in this Home than how I was in my own home. I am just a friendly person. Life is three words: anticipation, realization, and memories: Planning something, making the event happen, and then keeping it alive forever. Fifty years ago, I wrote a poem that was published in the *Boston Globe:*

Smile awhile and while you smile
Another smile
And soon there's miles and miles of smiles
And life's worthwhile
If you but smile.

Participating in the
Holy Burial Society

Muriel E. Ginsberg

Now, in my seventy-seventh year, I have joined our local *chevra kadisha*, the Jewish burial society, which is primarily responsible for the ritual cleansing of the body after death. Only recently did I even consider doing this. I have found that it brings me another opportunity for spiritual fulfillment.

Shortly after the recent, sudden death of his mother, our rabbi sought ways to comfort his grief. Gleaning wisdom from the three Torah portions following her death, he wrote in the synagogue bulletin, "I try to look beyond death to the holiness of life." It is exactly this "holiness of life" which motivated me to attend a *chevra kadisha* workshop, which focused on the significance and procedures of *tahara*, the ritual cleansing of the body.

At the beginning of *tahara*, we acknowledge our relationship to our God "of kindness and mercy." We then slowly turn down the sheet covering the body and wash each part of the body, gently and tenderly, with dignity and respect, to prepare it for burial. In this way, we do for the deceased what they can no longer do for themselves.

Muriel E. Ginsberg graduated from Radcliffe College and the University of Toronto School of Social Work. She lives in Victoria, British Columbia, and is active in Jewish communal organizations. She has three children and three grandchildren.

It is the only task that we perform for which we cannot be thanked by those who receive it.

In my old age, I now know that I, as well as my husband, will need this service. Someone will do it for us. In this holy community, there are only volunteers. So I join the ranks of the Jews before me. It is my way of reinforcing my commitment to the maintenance of Jewish customs and rituals.

As I grew older I began to regard death as an integral part of life, or, as Milton Steinberg wrote, "Death is the price of life." As I become more accepting of death, I become less fearful of the dead body before me. Joining the *chevra kadisha* is my way of being more open to the wonders of creation and the eternal mystery of death. Others may regard participating in the *chevra kadisha* as a communal service in which they are skilled, but I see a glimmer of God's hand directing us as we praise God in this holy work.

VI. MEETING THE CHALLENGES OF AGING

*King David was old, advanced in years; and they
covered him with clothes, but he could not become
warm.*

—1 Kings 1:1

MEETING THE
CHALLENGES OF AGING

The challenges inherent in the aging process should be neither trivialized nor minimized. Aging is often accompanied by profound losses and personal diminishment, and acknowledging and adapting to these challenges is essential.

Remaining connected to life—at all of life's stages, and certainly in assisted living facilities—is vital. In this section, "Saving Broken Tablets" by Cary Kozberg speaks about creating spiritual communities in which the elderly can come to live, not die; where they are welcomed, not abandoned. Maintaining a sense of community—where the elder still significantly contributes to society—is found on the kibbutz, as noted in Susan Berrin's chapter, "Growing Old on an Israeli Kibbutz," which is accompanied by the photographs of Aliza Auerbach.

In "Not Tired, Merely Retired," Everett Gendler reflects on retirement as a redirection of energy, an opportunity to engage his talents outside of the institutional realm where he had worked. Rachel Josefowitz Siegel's essay, "Who Will Lead the Seder, Now That I Stand Alone?" speaks courageously about widowhood, especially during Jewish holidays. Siegel notes the shift from partnerhood to being alone while creating a Passover seder. Being alone is also a significant thread in Jonathan Segol's "Consenting to Age,"which discusses Segol's grandfather's adjustment to the unexpected death of his wife.

Judith Magyar Isaacson's "Still Surviving" conveys the poignancy of life after the Holocaust. As a Holocaust survivor she faces death without dread, thankful for each day since her liberation more than half a century ago. As the number of survivors diminishes, survivors feel a greater urgency to tell their stories of survival and to speak about the life and culture of Eastern Europe which were destroyed. As Elie Wiesel once said, "As I get older, what becomes most important to me are my memories."

Saving Broken Tablets:
Planning for the Spiritual Needs
of Jews in Long-Term Care Facilities

Cary Kozberg

When Pharaoh asked Moses who among the Israelites would be leaving Egypt, Moses replied: "We will go with our young and with our old . . . for we must hold a festival unto the Lord." From the text, it seems that Moses understood what we are only now comprehending: that old people are still people. They have the same physical, social, emotional and spiritual needs as those who are younger. Indeed, they may feel these needs more keenly, given the various kinds of losses people experience as they age: loss of health, loss of status, loss of family and friends, loss of independence.

Thus, the most critical challenge for the elderly, particularly the frail elderly who resides in long-term care facilities, may be how to maintain a "sense of sameness"[1] amid the many losses that accompany advanced age. In addition to addressing the physical, social, and emotional needs of the aging in maintaining that sense of sameness, spiritual needs must be addressed as well. Many social

---

Cary Kozberg is director of rabbinical and pastoral services for Wexner Heritage Village in Columbus, Ohio, where he lives with his wife, Ellen, and their four children.

199

scientists believe that promoting spiritual well-being helps strengthen our relationship not only with God but also with self, community, and environment, thereby nurturing and sustaining personal wholeness.[2] For the frail elderly, such nurturing helps promote feelings of self-worth while also enabling reconciliation with the past and acceptance of the present.[3] As a way to enhance self-image by encouraging identification with a larger ethnic or religious group, religious rituals help affirm that life still has a meaning, one that is grounded in past traditions, is connected to the present, and offers hope for the future.

To many people, the phrase "Jewish elderly" still conjures up images of bearded *zaydes* with *yarmulkes* and of heavy-set *bubbes* wearing *babushkas*. But such images no longer accurately describe much of our aging Jewish population. Most of today's Jewish elderly were either born or at least raised in twentieth-century America. Unlike their Old World ancestors, many are college-educated, and worldly. They come from each of American Judaism's religious movements. Indeed, many are not affiliated with any religious movement and prefer to express their Jewishness in secular and cultural ways.

Also, because of a shift toward maintaining the elderly in their own residences and using support services to preserve their independence as long as possible, long-term care facilities are no longer merely "homes for the aged," and people no longer move into nursing homes just because they are "old." Instead, what was formerly called a "nursing home" is now known as a "long-term facility" because they serve adults of all ages who, because of physical and/or cognitive disabilities, need constant care.

Creating a comprehensive, sensitive program to enhance the religious and spiritual well-being of residents should be a priority in any Jewish nursing facility. Such an approach should focus on the specific needs of individual residents in Jewish nursing homes, and not on communal or denominational issues, which sometimes influence the religious component of Jewish nursing home programs.

Here are some practical suggestions to help create meaningful and stimulating religious experiences for Jews in long-term facilities.[4]

"DO NOT MAKE YOUR PRAYER A PERFUNCTORY ACT" (*PIRKEI AVOT* 2:18)

In addition to a kosher kitchen, the most familiar aspect of a Jewish nursing home's religious program is probably its regular worship services, whether on a daily or a Sabbath-and-holidays basis. Until fairly recently, worship services in most Jewish nursing homes were usually conducted in an "Orthodox" or "traditional" style. This is not surprising, for Jewish nursing homes were often established so that elderly Orthodox Jews, many of whom were immigrants, could live in an atmosphere conducive to their religious observance.

But the population in Jewish nursing homes is no longer homogenous.[5] Jews may enter them because they desire a Jewish ambiance, but they may not be familiar or comfortable with traditional worship services. Providing alternative services affirms the needs of all residents. This is important, particularly if the facility receives support from individuals and agencies representing the entire Jewish community. It also addresses the concerns of government agencies, which may be concerned with residents' rights.

Also, while long-term care residents may be frail or suffer from significant impairment, we should not assume that they cannot benefit from prayer services. On the contrary, such persons may derive substantial spiritual

and emotional benefit from such attendance and participation. Prayer can be made more edifying by

• Providing prayer books, *chumashim* and songbooks that
have large print and are easily handled.
• Using English predominantly. Hebrew is desirable for
prayers and songs that are already familiar to residents.
However, using English for responsive readings and pray-
ing in unison encourages residents to participate and helps
keep attention levels higher.
• Making sure the service can be heard and understood by
all. Residents gain little benefit from services they cannot
hear.
• Adjusting accordingly the length, content, and physical
environment of the service, particularly for those with cognitive impairment.

Many elderly have limited attention spans and cannot
sit through a Shabbat or holiday service of two or three
hours. Maximum participation by those in this population means abbreviating the service. But even if the Torah
reading is abridged, the Scroll should be taken out and
marched around the congregation, giving everyone the
opportunity to see it, touch it, and kiss it. These are important spiritual and emotional cues and can evoke
strong responses.

"FEAR NOT, FOR I AM WITH YOU" (ISAIAH 41:10)

Enriching a Jewish nursing home's religious program and
environment means responding to the challenges of entering and living in a nursing home. In addition to providing ongoing pastoral care for residents and their
families, the facility should acknowledge that "moving in"
is an important transitional life event. In most cultures

and religions, rites of passage mark transitional moments: birth, puberty, marriage, death. All have to do with symbolically saying "good-bye" to the past while trying to embrace the future. Entering a long-term care facility and coping with all that such a move means—loss of physical vitality, personal independence, approaching death—certainly is a "rite of passage" and should be marked with an appropriate "ceremony of welcoming."

Religious-oriented programs to help residents and their families spiritually cope with the progressive losses brought on by chronic disease and declining physical health are also worth considering. Such programs often take the form of healing services, which are increasingly being adopted in hospitals and synagogues throughout North America. Healing services are an important spiritual and pastoral resource to help residents and their families cope with anxiety, helplessness, and the loss of hope and purpose that often accompany physical and mental decline. Services include prayers for the body as well as for the anxious and broken spirit.

Another way to spiritually buoy the residents of a Jewish nursing home is to hold memorial services for recently deceased residents. Residents can observe the *mitzvah* of honoring the dead while acknowledging their loss.

"WITH OUR YOUNG AND WITH OUR OLD"

When Moses told Pharaoh that both the young and the old Israelites would be leaving Egypt, he understood that for a community to be a community, its youth and its aged must interact.

The Torah's commandment to us to treat the aged with respect and deference is followed by a commandment to welcome the stranger. It is common for residents of nursing homes to feel estranged from the rest of society. Our youth-focused culture usually treats the elderly in marginal, perfunctory ways. Although these are the same people who built our synagogues and developed our community institutions, they may often be treated as virtual outsiders. We need to find meaningful places for them in our community and our religious life.

One way to do this is to include them in our *simchas* and life-cycle events, other than funerals—they have enough of those. Families could hold a "dry run" of a bar/bat mitzvah ceremony in a nursing home for the benefit of a grandparent or great-grandparent who is unable to attend the ceremony itself. Inviting other residents of the facility to share in the family's joy communicates to them that they help make the celebration complete.

I can attest to how powerful such an experience can be. We celebrated my son's bar mitzvah and my daughter's bat mitzvah at Wexner Heritage House in Columbus, Ohio, where I am the rabbi. This was appropriate not only because the residents know my family but also because they are my "congregation." On both occasions, the responses were positive. To our family and friends, it was a reminder to include this segment of the Jewish community in all our celebrations. And the residents were enthusiastic about being part of the celebrations. On both occasions, my children had surrogate grandparents and great-grandparents who were beaming with *naches* as if it had been their own grandchildren or great-grandchildren.

Another way to increase interaction between young and old is for residents to "mentor" bar/bat mitzvah students. In Jewish tradition, mentoring is an ancient and sacred activity, and there is probably no more powerful way to transmit the tradition to the next generation than for elderly tutors to assist students with their preparation while sharing the memories and wisdom of their own experiences as Jews.

A hallmark of any civilized society is how it treats its elderly. The Talmud teaches that just as Moses saved the

shards of the first set of tablets and validated their sanctity by placing them in the Ark next to the second, intact
set, so we are to validate the sanctity of those who are
physically or mentally "broken." The North American
Jewish community has been exemplary in doing this by
providing facilities where the elderly can receive the care
they need and deserve, and where they can live with dignity. Indeed, we continue that tradition and build upon it
by providing for their physical, psychological, and social
needs as well as for their religious and spiritual needs.
With sensitivity and creativity, our efforts will provide a
blessing not only for the elderly, but for us as well.

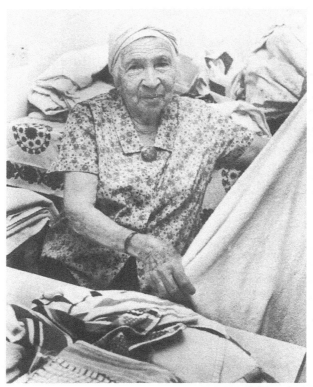

Miriam Shapris (born 1901 in Russia) at work at Kibbutz Deganiah Aleph.

Gidon Edelshtein with his grandson at Kibbutz Balfouria.

Growing Old on an Israeli Kibbutz

Susan Berrin

One of Israel's greatest treasures is its old people. Kibbutz elderly, in particular, demonstrate an enormous vitality as they live, work, and love. Kibbutz members continue to contribute to their society, feeling full membership in a community that they often helped establish. We have much to learn from the lives of old people on kibbutzim.

The kibbutz environment makes allowances for the physical needs of its elderly. Meals adhere to dietary restrictions, housing is appropriate and comfortable, and health care and leisure activities are provided. In addition, suitable "work" enhances the elders' sense of wellbeing. Without forced retirement at age 65, the older kibbutznik still works every day, although with slowly diminishing responsibilities, and lives and toils among family, neighbors, friends, and colleagues.

For a year, I had the opportunity to speak with over fifty kibbutz members from various geographic regions and political and religious movements. Spending time

Susan Berrin, the editor of A Heart of Wisdom, *was guest editor for* Sh'ma *magazine's special issue on Judaism and aging, and also edited* Celebrating the New Moon: A Rosh Chodesh Anthology. *She has a master's degree in social work from Boston University, has done research in gerontology and has produced audio-visual materials for the aged. She and her husband, Rabbi Victor Reinstein, live with their three children in Victoria, British Columbia.*

with these kibbutz elders, who were all at least 75 years old, was a privilege, and my own aging will doubtlessly be blessed by the inspirations I drew from these *chaverim,* the members of kibbutz.[1] I was consistently impressed with their stories, reflections, and insights, which convey their convictions, their often surreal histories, and the intricacies of their lives on kibbutz.

NO STIGMA FOR ACCEPTING HELP

One of the greatest advantages of being an older person on a kibbutz is the availability of health care. Unless a hospital or specialist is needed, all health services are provided on the kibbutz. The universal nature of all services reduces the stigma of accepting help. Kibbutz remains "home" from the cradle to the grave.

While each kibbutz is different, basic similarities exist. Generally, efforts are made to keep the aged person in his or her home. When they need more supervised care, they move into a twenty-four-hour supervised apartment designed specifically for the physically impaired. These apartments are equipped with kitchens and a bedroom and/or sitting room and are near the center of the kibbutz for easy access to the dining hall, factories, and services as well as for the psychological benefit of being in the middle of kibbutz activity. The location also promotes visiting by family and friends.

If needed, a member is moved into a residential facility, which provides in-house meals and services. Some aged kibbutz members who do not live in the residential facility may go there for meals. Social events, therapies, and counseling are also provided here.

Most elderly on a kibbutz are upset that they can no longer participate in the kibbutz work ethic. As one infirmed, elderly man commented, "My work was my religion. I wish that I could still work two hours in the factory, but I physically can't do it anymore. The hardest thing about reducing my work hours was that it showed I was slowing down."

The fact that adult children continue to live on the same kibbutz of their parents has advantages, but it can also create tensions. The director of one kibbutz nursing care facility said, "On the kibbutz, elderly don't have any economic problems. This is an enormous relief. But there are a lot of problems with parent-child relationships here. The children are afraid of the reversal in role—taking care of their parents—especially the children who have stayed on the kibbutz. Those children who have left a kibbutz feel easier. They can come once a week or once every two weeks and then have a clean break. It is not really normal to grow up and still live in the same 'home' as your parents—and the kibbutz is a 'home.'"

The question of parental care was echoed by a fifty-year-old: "When I was young and got sick, my parents were too busy establishing the kibbutz to care for me individually. It was the role of the nurse in the children's house, the *metapelet,* to take care of sick children. Now, it should be the role of the kibbutz elder's committee to care for the infirmed elderly, not the responsibility of individual children."

LONELINESS DESPITE A MINIMUM OF ISOLATION

Most elderly city-dwellers worry about security; many relocate so they can find a secure home. But most kibbutz elderly do not worry about their personal safety. Instead, they are concerned with the current and future status of the kibbutz. The isolation that often accompanies age, and the fear of becoming ill while alone, is absent. One widow "never" worried about her "future, even with the difficult times the kibbutz is going through. . . . The *bet kashish* [the residence for elderly] is wonderful. It provides services according to the needs of the individual. Sometimes we need the help; sometimes, we don't."

The impact of remaining within one's environs is a theme often repeated. A 78-year-old widow stated: "First of all, we are still in our own homes. We are with our *chevra*, people who have known us for years. We don't have to start over again. We *belong*, and we have a sense of belonging. Also, there are few cars, no fumes, little noise. We have a *chadar ochel* [a dining room] so we don't need to cook full time. We don't need to drive to a doctor's office or to the bank. Our doctor has known us for many years. I don't want to paint too beautiful a picture, but it is wonderful."

The original settlers of kibbutzim never dreamed of the material success that would be realized within their lifetime, and many never considered the impact of the aging process, either. As an elderly woman pointed out, "We always thought of ourselves as youthful in terms of ability and ideology. We thought our children would just continue with what we began. We never thought of putting aside money into a fund for when we got older. Twenty years ago, I wouldn't have believed that we would employ outside people to care for the elderly. Once I thought we'd never be alone—there was so much collectiveness—but now I see that some of the widows are very alone."

This woman mentions two important points. First, the kibbutz *vatikim* (the founders) lacked the foresight to create pensions for aging members, perhaps partly because they channeled all resources into the operational budget of a fledgling kibbutz, perhaps as the result of the founding group's self-image as forever youthful. Second, caregivers are employed from outside the kibbutz, which relieves family and other kibbutz members from having primary responsibility for the infirmed elderly. As the fifty-year-old head of a kibbutz health committee commented, "Taking care of elders is primarily a problem with younger members. We're just beginning to learn how to deal with this. When the kibbutz was established, there were no elderly around. There was no older generation when I and my friends grew up. We didn't have any grandparents [because of the Holocaust and immigration and settlement patterns], so we never learned how to be with older people. Now there is a problem because we lack experience with and feeling for the older people. We don't naturally know how to care for our parents as they age. So we have to hire young women from nearby towns who have grown up in three-generational homes to work here. They are very sensitive to the needs of the elderly. But this is shameful, for it is not the style of the kibbutz to hire outsiders to work with our members."

For many elderly, loneliness is a natural outcome of outliving friends and family. Yet, the deep sense of loneliness often expressed by both the elderly and the caregivers regarding the aged is more than a state of being old and alone. Loneliness on kibbutzim is exacerbated by the environment in which people live: They are physically close to others, yet don't feel connected or intimate with them. One caregiver said that "a basic problem of the elderly stems from loneliness. After all the years of living so closely together, they know each other in too many different roles. Sometimes bitterness gets in the way of friendship."

On religious kibbutzim, there is another dimension to loneliness: During the summer, when Shabbat is a very long day, many elderly without families suffer an acute aloneness. Their day feels empty without anything to preoccupy them.

Several of those I spoke with, both in and out of the religious kibbutz movement, maintained that religious kibbutzim provide an atmosphere that enhances social relations. To some on religious kibbutzim, visiting the elderly or the infirmed is a *mitzvah*, a good deed. To others, the structure of the day, which includes *tefilot*, prayers, and study sessions, provides more opportunity for social connection.

Neighbors also play an important role for the aged. Most kibbutzim organize neighborhoods by the age of their residents. This can enhance friendships and provide added security. An 80-year-old widow said, "When I return home from work at 7:00 A.M., I check to see if my neighbor's light is on. If so, I knock and say hello. She knows I come by each day." Another comments, "Every Friday at 3:30 P.M. my three neighbors come over and we drink coffee together and eat cake and catch each other up on the week, on news about our families, and discuss the latest government news."

WORK EQUALS EXISTENCE

"My father told this story: A man who was very, very old continued to work, although it was very difficult. He was a peddler and puffed and huffed as he pulled a heavy wagon of his wares up a steep hill. A younger man approached him and asked why he continued to work so hard. The older man replied, 'If I don't keep going forward, then surely I'll slip backwards.'" This story, told by a 71-year-old man who had amazing tenacity, reflects an important aspect of the kibbutz work ethic: Continuing to work is the passport to a continued existence.

The elderly work as long as they are able. Flexible work placement and schedules accommodate their physical limitations. In general, at about age 60 to 65, work hours begin to be reduced. Generally, seniors work slightly reduced hours until age 70, when their hours are again reduced. At ages 75 to 80, most elderly work about two hours daily.

Most kibbutzim also have a sheltered work environment for the elderly, usually in the form of a factory (such as plastics or furniture) subdivision. While some elderly continue to work in their former jobs, most work in factory settings that are less physically and intellectually demanding. At a kibbutz plastics factory, which was designed for the senior worker, tables are arranged so workers face each other. This promotes sociability. Tea-time with co-workers during working hours is part of the daily routine.

Since the factories open very early in the morning, the elderly can begin work by 5:00 or 6:00 A.M. Because most kibbutz elderly are early risers, this helps focus their mornings and gives them a task to be completed. If workers do not show up as scheduled, they are telephoned at home to make sure they are not ill. The fact that the elderly continue to see themselves as workers, even in a limited capacity, tends to offset their new frailty.

These comments reflect work's enormous role in the well-being of older kibbutz members:

"At 84 years old, I still feel that I am an integral part of society. They would miss me if I didn't work. It is a good feeling that I contribute to the financial success of the kibbutz."

"If I didn't have a reason to get up each morning to go to work, I wouldn't be able to start the day."

"Work is the best time of the day, not because I find the work interesting, but because I like being with the people."

For one older woman, whose husband has Alzheimer's disease, work was a part-time relief from caregiving. "Thank God, I have some time when I'm not taking care of my husband. He can manage on his own for a few hours and I then get him and take him to lunch."

CONTINUING THE
"COMMUNITY OF COMMITMENT"

A central tenet of kibbutz life is to provide a high quality life for all members. To foster such a life for their older members, kibbutzim have structures that enable aging members to still be productive and find meaning in their lives. While many services provided to the seniors are universally available to all kibbutz members (such as laundry, health care, and meals), additional services and provisions such as electric mini-carts for intra-kibbutz transportation are made for the older members.

For the now aged, pioneer kibbutznik, "work was not only a means for earning a living . . . work was a revolutionary value. Labor became a personal test for the worker and the workplace became the stage where we could demonstrate our virtue, where we could create and transmit our public image."[2]

While kibbutzim foster a society within which the elders participate in and reap the rewards of community, elders are nevertheless faced with the personal experience of aging and the issues raised by aging: "the balance between integrity and despair, the need to come to terms with a decline in strength and beauty, the need to face aloneness even in the context of community."[3] But while kibbutzim accommodate the needs of the elderly, it is unclear how much they truly value the elderly as members of their mini-society. I did not hear about any special programs to honor the aged, nor did I see any elders mentoring the next generation. Nevertheless, most elderly were extremely satisfied with the kibbutzim's commitment to providing for their care, even though many felt an aching aloneness. Perhaps this was not from lack of friendship, but the existential loneliness of coming to the end of one's life.

Who Will Lead the Seder, Now That I Stand Alone?

Rachel Josefowitz Siegel

How can I put loneliness into words? How can I convey what it's like to live alone after forty-six years of married life? How can I share what it is like to live Jewishly as a woman alone in her early seventies?

I cannot possibly enumerate the seemingly insignificant moments of daily life that I can no longer share: The things that my husband and I used to do together that I now do by myself, the things we always talked about that I now keep to myself, and the significant events that I now attend alone. At times, being alone is like a dull ache. At other times, it gives me a feeling of contentment and self-sufficiency. In some ways, I feel as if I have uncovered an inner strength that I did not fully know before. I am a little wiser, have overcome many fears and challenges, and have acquired new skills. I have made a few changes in my home that express more fully who I am, as well as doing justice to who we were together and as a family.

Rachel Josefowitz Siegel is a recently retired feminist psychotherapist. Born in Berlin and educated in Switzerland, she came to the United States in 1939. She is coeditor (with Ellen Cole) of Seen But Not Heard: Jewish Women in Therapy *and* Celebrating the Lives of Jewish Women: Patterns in a Feminist Sampler.

Some of the most profound adjustments to widowhood have been in the area of Jewish observance. When our children grew up and left home, I gradually accommodated to setting the Shabbat table for two instead of five, and celebrating the High Holidays as a couple instead of a family. But that was nothing compared to coming to terms with eating alone on Friday night or going to *shul* by myself.

When my husband Ben died five years ago, I suffered intense grief and disorientation. As a therapist I had helped others through their mourning process, and I had thought that I would be better prepared than most. But I was not prepared for the intensity of my feelings and their unpredictability. Waves of sorrow would emerge so forcefully that tears were nearly uncontrollable.

Going to *shul* without Ben was agony. His absence overshadowed whatever comfort I might have gained from the liturgy or from the presence of friends and community. Having attended *shul* together for forty-six years, we found that it had become a shared and intimate experience as much as a personal and communal one.

I wished sometimes to shriek and wail as my grandmother might have done, in the manner of some Old World widows only one or two generations removed from the white middle-class norms of North American Jews. *Shul* was a little easier when I attended with a friend or on the rare occasions when my daughter or one of my sons was in town.

Saying *kaddish*, the mourner's prayer, was acutely uncomfortable. Perhaps standing alone in my grief was so overwhelmingly emotional that I needed to protect myself from feeling anything at all. I remember one Friday night service at the National Women's Studies Conference when the women surrounded me and supported me as I wept through *kaddish*. I felt such relief.

Standing alone while saying *kaddish* felt like a metaphor for my entire life. I stood alone in my grief.

Now, I stand alone when I rejoice and when I mourn, when I plan and when I worry, when I wake up and when I go to sleep. Alone, I now take care of the many tasks previously done by Ben.

EMPTY HOUSE, EMPTY BED, EMPTY SOUL

No matter how close I may be to my friends and family, or how engaging is my work, there is always that moment when the work is done, the party is over, and I go home to an empty house and an empty bed. So many times I miss the companionship of going over the day's events together. No one else loves our children and grandchildren in quite the same way, no one else has the same history of interpreting the intricacies and contradictions of our extended family, or understands the in-jokes and the shared opinions. When I return from funerals, family gatherings, and celebrations, I especially feel Ben's absence.

During the first year of my grieving, my awareness of Ben's absence overshadowed all else. During my granddaughter Sarah's bat mitzvah, when I stood alone with her on the *bima*, her only surviving grandparent, I felt as if I had to allow physical space for Ben at my side, as if I were now carrying for both of us the *naches*, the pleasure, he would have felt and his pain at not being there. Three years later, at my granddaughter Anna's bat mitzvah, I realized that I was now more comfortable in the role of matriarch and that I could more fully appreciate the generational continuity of our family *simcha*, our celebration.

The first time that my daughter Ruth read *maftir* Jonah on Yom Kippur in her own congregation, I was again nearly overcome with that strange mixture of *naches*—and sorrow.

THE PASSOVER DILEMMA

In our family, Passover has always drawn us together more than any other holiday. Ours was a conservatively observant Jewish home that was, in many ways, egalitarian. In the last years of Ben's life, I wanted the seder to be more inclusive of women and less rigorous in *kashrut,* while Ben wanted to maintain a strictly kosher household. We compromised by simplifying the Passover preparations without giving up on *kashrut,* and we feminized the seder without giving up on tradition.

The seder has continued to express some of the most beautiful aspects of our life as a Jewish family. It has also embodied some unresolved tensions around tradition and feminism. Each year since Ben's death as Passover approaches, the question of who will lead the seder occupies my mind and soul.

My children are in their late forties, with their own homes in distant cities. Ben died about three weeks before Pesach, but we still held the family seder in our home that year. The children had made it clear that they would agree with whatever decision I made. Their loving accommodations to my needs—while they too were grieving—meant much to me and brought us closer.

After much thought about who would lead the seder, I proposed that all the children and I share the honor and responsibility. As Charles, Hyam and Ruth each led a portion of the *haggadah* with confidence and *kavannah,* spiritual intention, I was deeply aware that the promise that Ben and I had made under the *chuppah,* the marriage canopy, to build a Jewish home together had, indeed, been fulfilled.

It was a good seder. The grandchildren made their own contributions. The shared ritual, in the midst of mourning, seemed to bring out the best in each of us. It had always been Ben's seder, and I felt the legacy of his Jewish commitment as our three generations continued on without him. In subsequent years, we have varied the arrangements, but each year I face the same question: Who will lead the seder? I am building the courage to do it myself. But to do this, I would have to make time to study. Leading pieces of the service is not the same as leading it in its entirety. I can hardly imagine how I could sit at the head of the table being totally focused on the *haggadah,* while part of my mind is still on the soup and *kneidlach.* There is also the dilemma of being a feminist mother of Jewish sons: on one hand, being deeply committed to egalitarian celebrations; on the other hand, hesitant to usurp the age-old privilege from my sons.

I suspect that underlying these issues is my own struggle with traditions designed to keep a Jewish woman in the kitchen and behind the *mechitzah,* the partition. How can I presume that a woman can lead the seder when not even one daughter is mentioned among the four questioning sons? An inner voice calls this arrogant and competitive. Who am I to challenge the ancient traditions? When Ben was alive, I started to include the stories and voices of women in the seder, but I did this with his support. Now that I stand alone, can I make further changes on my own? Can I fully take charge as I have in other areas of my life? And if not now, when?

Consenting to Age

Jonathan Segol

Last year, my grandfather became old. This change came unexpectedly to me, mainly because I hadn't expected my grandmother's abrupt death. I don't think he did, either. A doctor found cancer of the pancreas and gave her a few months, and a week later it was over. Since then, my grandfather has become old.

He had always scoffed at age. Only a few years ago, a subway official stopped him at a turnstile and accused him of trying to pass for a senior citizen. This year, he will turn 90. He needs neither walkers nor pacemakers, and he reluctantly wears a hearing aid. It sits next to hair that never finished graying. Undaunted by age, he continues to work a garden in his backyard, coaxing rich tomatoes from the soil.

Gardening will be the last pastime he gives up. He grew up on a farm in the Carpathian Mountains, then located in Austria, later in Poland, still later in the Soviet Union. With his bare hands, he broke apples neatly in half. He came here when he was 18 years old. World War I had just ended. He loves knowing that America has never swept him from his home with pogroms and world wars.

Jonathan Segol studied at Oberlin and Hunter Colleges and now lives in Brooklyn, where he teaches English, writes, and performs music.

Until last year, it had always taken an effort to get him to talk about the old country. "That's all so far in the past," he would say in his thick Yiddish-Austrian accent, "there's no point in even remembering." The past had little relevance for him. Children's questions, though, could often bring out a story from his youth: "When the Cossacks came into town, we'd put up a few of them in our house, to protect us from the other ones. Once, one of them tried to steal my sister's necklace that our grandmother had given her. When he was about to leave, he was openly wearing her necklace around his neck. My mother pointed a finger at him—he was twice as big as she was—and ordered him to give back the necklace. He just laughed. Then another Cossack said, 'She's right, you know; you've got no business stealing from her.' They started shouting at each other and drew their swords. Then the first Cossack gave the necklace back to my mother."

What is the point of knowing what your family was doing eighty years ago? It wasn't only grandfather's attitude toward the past that kept him from swooping into stories. He was quiet to begin with. Grandma could carry a conversation all by herself. She was twelve years younger than he, in her seventies, and spoke with the energy of someone half her age: "We saw Allen Ginsberg read a few years ago at Brooklyn College. We stayed for 'Kaddish' because we know that's a beautiful poem. Then we left because his next poems would probably be dirty."

Then she would fill up the room with the high hearty laugh that she passed on to my mother. But besides her taste in poetry, or the fact that she was a good dancer, or that she knew what jobs would open up in the next five years, she probably expressed much of what Grandpa had to say in the course of a conversation. I can only guess what fifty-three years of marriage will do to synchronize a couple's basic opinions.

The two of them enrolled each year in courses for

senior citizens at Brooklyn College. She studied fiction. He took painting and clay sculpture. During the last several years, more and more of Grandpa's nature scenes appeared on their walls. About three or four years ago, he sculpted a self-portrait that now sits in his living room. Much of the face is accurate: the defined chin, the nose that he's passed on to me. The only significant departure was the eyes. Perhaps it was the absence of glasses or eyelashes, but the eyes appeared bigger, wider, and wearier. They made him look more like a sage.

Given the age difference between my two grandparents, it was always assumed that she would outlive him. It would have been more convenient. She balanced the checkbook, did the cooking and laundry, wrote all the letters, answered the phone, and arranged their social life. After Grandma died, my mother taught Grandpa how to run the washing machine, heat up leftovers, and keep a checkbook. He is minimally proud of having learned these chores so quickly. They all remind him of his wife. After fifty-three years of marriage, I wonder if there is anything that doesn't.

NO LONGER FEARING DEATH

A few weeks after she died, I wrote a letter to Grandpa. When he wrote back, I realized that of all the letters that had ever come to me from that house, this was the first written by him. It was like a voice I'd never heard before. In so many past conversations, he had stuck with jokes, anecdotes, and opinions but usually left the words of gravity to his wife. From now on, I would be hearing serious words from him.

Now, when I see Grandpa, he talks for hours, pausing only to serve lunch or to say he misses Grandma. Now that she's gone, he says, he no longer fears death. A few years ago, he called himself young. He wouldn't wear a hearing aid for fear of feeling old. Now, whether he lives to 95 or 100 is of no significance to him.

He goes on at length about chapters of his youth I had never heard about: when he came to America, when he worked in a factory, when he learned English, which innovations he made on the assembly line, how he got promoted, how he met Grandma. He tells his stories now without waiting to be asked, perhaps in the belief that in years to come, all that will be left of him are stories and memories.

He's stopped taking classes. There's too much work to do around the house, he says. As usual, he grew vegetables this summer, but considerably fewer: tomatoes and peppers, but no cucumbers. He is still mistaken for being twenty years younger than he is. But now those are merely incidents, not affirmations. After nine decades, he's agreed to grow old.

Not Tired, Merely Retired

Everett Gendler

Aging first directly confronted me when I was sixty-two and a half years old. Its agent was a computer printout at the private school where I taught, informing me that the normal but not mandatory retirement age where I worked would come in two and a half years, the summer I turned sixty-five. I still remember my reaction of outrage and hurt: "Hey, I'm too young to be sixty-two and a half. There must be a mistake somewhere!"

Chronologically, of course, there was no mistake. Birth certificate and family photos confirmed the calculation. Yet, in terms of health, energy, and engagement with my work, retiring at 65 seemed premature. Happily, it also seemed premature to colleagues, students, and congregants at both the school and the temple where I was a rabbi. Turning 65 became a signpost, not a stop sign.

The question, however, was merely postponed. At what point should I seek release from the still-satisfying,

Everett Gendler studied at the University of Chicago, The Jewish Theological Seminary, and Columbia University. He was rabbi at Temple Emanuel, Lowell, Massachusetts from 1971 to 1995 and Jewish chaplain and an instructor in philosophy and religious studies at Phillips Academy, Andover, Massachusetts, from 1976 to 1995. He has also been active in the peace, civil rights, Jewish renewal, and environmental movements.

still-stimulating, yet confining daily commitments at school and temple and redirect my energy more freely? It was in these terms that I considered retirement. In attempting to answer this question, I felt that societal as well as personal considerations were appropriate.

Although early retirement lets the next generation advance more quickly to more challenging work, it may also, over time, impose greater financial burdens upon the young through lengthier social security and pension payments to retirees. After learning that the standard social security retirement age would be raised to 67 in 2009, I decided to take this age as my guideline.

Yet, continuing satisfactions from my work made retirement seem, at times, unreal. So much intimacy, spirituality, and celebration at our temple Shabbat evening services; such exhilaration from ecumenical and ceremonial occasions at school; such joys from teaching. Why even think of retirement? Yet, amid these daily and weekly delights, some slight, yet significant, internal shifts signaled gentle warnings and offered subtle guidance.

I still enjoyed waking up for an 8:00 A.M. class four mornings a week, reaping pleasure from the discussions and the student papers. But every now and then, while encouraging and focusing student discussion, I would recognize a slight urge to speak myself, at greater length and complexity, and while writing comments on student papers, I occasionally felt just a slight twitch of the pen wanting to write my own essays rather than commenting on theirs.

Tutoring bar/bat mitzvah candidates at our temple, as I had done for more than twenty years, continued to be a lively and dynamic process, culminating in a celebrative service that represented a religious commitment, a rite of passage, and a communally recognized personal achievement. Yet, every now and then during the tutoring, I, the *melamed*, the teacher, would detect an internal desire to delve more deeply into Abulafia's mystical vowel combinations rather than help a student distinguish between long and short vowel sounds.

Such stirrings, although slight, seemed to me likely to grow, perhaps gradually at first but almost surely with increasing insistence as time passed. With such growth, wouldn't the blessed preponderance of satisfaction to dissatisfaction in my work decline proportionately? Needless to say, such clarity is an after-the-fact formulation, not a during-the-process description. But it was some such intuition, however dim, that inclined me toward retirement during the summer that I would turn 67.

One other personal consideration also nudged me toward this timing. If, indeed, I wanted retirement to represent a redirection of energy rather than the recognition of its demise, I would do well to retire while there was still energy to redirect, and while the question on people's lips would be "Retiring already?" rather than "Not yet retired?"

Curiously, classical Judaic texts and teachings played a lesser role in this process of deciding when to retire. I say "curiously" because most areas of my life are significantly shaped by rabbinic tradition. Why not, then, in this case? Partly, I suspect, because the practice of retirement as we have come to know it is not part of rabbinic or later Jewish tradition. Even a brief glance at an English-Hebrew dictionary makes clear that the words for retirement are not words from classical Hebraic tradition. Differences in life expectancy are probably one factor, the absence of surplus resources to sustain a public social security system another. Further, the association of age with wisdom would probably have made retirement as we know it seem an unacceptable social waste. Besides, is one ever free from the Divine demands of Torah and *mitzvot?* If not, and if one's work is so blessed as to involve them daily, why would one want to retire? For all these reasons (and surely others as well), Jewish texts and traditions offered guidance only in the most general sense of articulating basic truths about life, the universe, and our place in it.

Societal and personal considerations, coinciding with the institutional, made the decision to retire easier for me—though obviously not all that easy! Of invaluable assistance and profoundly affirming were the deeply moving farewell gatherings held for me at both school and temple. Each was a regretful yet joyous review in words and music, reflection, and revelry of many wonderful experiences through all those years. This rich harvest of memory, so abundantly gathered and generously given to me by students, colleagues, and congregants, has provided true sustenance for my spirit. I'm sure it will continue to nourish me for years to come.

A TIME FOR NEW RHYTHMS

Although retirement is still quite fresh and I continue to enjoy that generous gift of memory, I can report an intermittent anxiety: the fear that loosening the daily ties to the life of the temple and academy may sever completely my connections with the future. What can possibly substitute for the daily joys I have just relinquished? In the absence of such life-filled bonds, how—if at all—can I remain connected with life as it surges toward the future? These questions have haunted me most consistently while I was deciding when to retire and since retirement.

The answer? Again, it is tentative and highly speculative, since my new status is so recent, and the full force of the question is temporarily blunted by the current adventure of traveling in Asia during these first months of transition. Only when I return home will a realistic answer emerge. Meanwhile, even here, experiences and imaginings offer some clues to the challenge of a retirement not dictated by weariness, exhaustion, or boredom.

I am often convinced that human life is greatly assisted by well-intentioned, well-designed, well-functioning institutions. As a consequence, I invested much of my professional attention and energy in two institutions: the synagogue and the academy. Now, I need to remind myself of the obvious but sometimes forgotten truth that valuable though such channels may be, they are not the only conduits through which life flows. As we travel we meet many people, some of whom are kindred spirits. Such encounters affirm our life-spirit and our values.

One immediate example: Presently, we are in Dharamsala, India, a community of Tibetans in exile whose main temple in Lhasa has been profaned by the Chinese occupiers just as ours had been by the Greco-Syrians some 2,150 years earlier. What better place to light Chanukah candles than in the courtyard of the Namgyal Monastery, the Dalai Lama's *"shul,"* the Tibetans' primary exilic temple surrogate and the usual site for public gatherings? So we went there each night to light our candles, to sing, and to enjoy lovely interchanges with Tibetans reciting their prayers, carrying their candles, and lighting their butter lamps. We shared songs, melodies, snacks, and stories. While not an institution, our gathering was surely a blessed vessel for light—both external and internal. It was obvious, of course, that I could enjoy a challenging spiritual and intellectual life outside of the institutions that had nourished me for so many years, but at this time of disengagement from familiar institutional links, I do need reminders of this truth.

HARVESTING THE FUTURE
FROM OUR PAST

As for imaginings, let me share one image from my life that helped me make the step toward retirement. The constancy in our personal life enabled us to rear two daughters as well as raise organically grown crops on our small acreage in Andover, Massachusetts. At the same time, we enjoyed such fresh experiences as camping, travel, and extrainstitutional involvements. Some seeds from this life have borne fruit worth harvesting.

Among the courses that I taught at Phillips Academy was "Nonviolence in Theory and Practice," which focused on the work of Mahatma Gandhi and Martin Luther King, Jr. The class, which was one way to continue my earlier participation in the nonviolent movement for social change, explored both the dynamics and the philosophical and religious implications of spirit flexing its muscles. Although I no longer teach, new opportunities are already opening so I can express my long-standing beliefs as I help Tibetans apply nonviolent strategies in their political struggles.

My temple has experimented over the decades with reincorporating into its regular worship elements of nature in Judaism that were ancient, authentic, but often overlooked. Among the widely satisfying results were fresh ways to celebrate the cycles of the sun, the phases of the moon, the succession of the seasons, and the times for planting and harvesting. These fruits of our liturgical life contain, as do all fruits, seeds for further planting; in this way, life renews itself again and again. The seed is simultaneously the end of one life cycle and the beginning of the next. It symbolizes the constant renewal of life, the annual proclamation that death is indeed followed by resurrection.

If God grants me additional years of life and vigor, I imagine that I will share even more widely the seeds of this harvest through writing and occasional weekends with receptive congregations. The joyous, invigorating task of gathering these seeds, preserving them, and transmitting them to others for future plantings will connect me with life in its fullness. Harvesting will be the reassuring response to my fear of finding myself prematurely disconnected from vital life in its forward motion.

I can conceive, though not actively imagine, that further along life's path I will experience more of the decline of powers portrayed by Ecclesiastes and Shakespeare. For now, however, not tired but merely retired, I am delighted to discover that there are ways in which I can still be bound up in the bonds of life. *Ken y'hi ra-tzon.* May this be God's will. *Amen.*

Still Surviving

Judith Magyar Isaacson

A clerk in a cheese store first made me realize that I was no longer young, not even middle-aged, when he politely asked one day, "How would you like to take advantage of our senior discounts, Mrs. Isaacson?"

"No, thanks." I shook my head, blaming my white-streaked hair for betraying my age.

Nowadays, with hair more white than brown, I take it for granted that I belong to the senior bracket. I am especially grateful that I have reached this age. I call myself lucky just to have stayed alive even one day beyond July 8, 1944, the day I arrived in Auschwitz. It seems a miracle to have survived nine months in a camp that took the lives of 95 percent of those who arrived with me.

Decades later, I told another survivor of our cattle train that I had started to work on my memoirs, and she seemed surprised. "I haven't been able to deal with it," she sighed. "I am glad you are."

Understandably, many Holocaust survivors are unwilling or unable to speak about their past. They experienced worse atrocities than I, and faced further struggles upon

---

Judith Magyar Isaacson, a mathematician and former dean of students at Bates College, is the author of Seed of Sarah: Memoirs of a Survivor. *A survivor of the concentration camps Aushchwitz-Birkenau and Hessisch-Lichtenau, she has lived in Auburn, Maine, for the past fifty years with her husband. They have three children and seven grandchildren.*

returning to their native lands. Few among them have visited postwar Germany or have had opportunities to establish contact with anti-Nazi Germans.

By contrast, I was fortunate to meet my future husband, then a captain in the U.S. Army, just one month after liberation. My husband, Ike, has never let me succumb to the grief that might have overwhelmed me. We both realize that we married before knowing each other well. Now, fifty-one years later, we fully realize how lucky we were, not only with each other but also with our offspring. I, who had feared rape more than death while in the camps, am especially grateful for our three children, their mates, and our seven grandchildren.

My mother and Aunt Magda, who both survived with me, have enjoyed a surprisingly long and full life as well. Mother, at 95, and her sister Magda are very much alive. Mother never remarried, but Aunt Magda did, and we take much pleasure in our growing families.

At one time, I had given up hope to continue my education, but I returned to school in my mid-thirties and became a math teacher. I later became dean of students at Bates College in Lewiston, Maine, and worked in the profession I had dreamed of as a youth. When I turned 66 years old, my first book, *Seed of Sarah, Memoirs of a Survivor,* about my experiences before and during the Holocaust, was published. The book has since been made available in an expanded English edition as well as in German and Hungarian. The German translation and promotion of my memoir gives me hope that each subsequent generation of Germans might help to heal the festering wounds of the past—for us and for our descendants.

DEATH WITHOUT DREAD

Because of the growing interest in the Holocaust and the astonishing response my memoirs elicited, I have been kept busy as a speaker and correspondent, and I have not yet been able to finish a sequel to *Seed of Sarah* as planned. I often speak to groups about the Holocaust, not only to describe what happened, but also to introduce my audience to a way of life and a culture that has been destroyed. As we survivors age, there are fewer who can teach and share from their personal experiences.

Although my recent life sounds like a success story, when a remark to that effect came after one of my talks on the Holocaust, it shocked me. I began to ask myself, "Do I assess my life as tragic or fortunate?"

Despite the thrill I have reaped from my family, I have never stopped mourning for the family that I lost. The longer I live, the more I grieve the friends who never reached adulthood. The past has never ceased to haunt me in my dreams, even when I was a seemingly cheerful teacher or dean.

When my children were small, I had a recurring nightmare that pained me more than any horror I had experienced in life. In my dream, I cradled my infants in my arms as I leaped from rooftop to rooftop of a speeding train. Too scared to jump and too scared to stay, I was gripped by excruciating panic, unlike anything I had experienced before. Although my nightmares have changed over the years, one constant in them is a train and the urgent need to save my children.

As I grow older I feel reassured that I have learned to face death without dread. This gives me a certain freedom in my life today.

VII. Poetry and Stories

When a fig is picked at its time of ripeness, it is
good for the fig and for the tree; but if it is picked
prematurely, it is not good.

—Genesis Rabbah 62:2

POETRY AND STORIES

Poetry and stories convey life lessons through a more subtle medium than the essay. Although the journey of life is ultimately experienced alone, as several of the following pieces poignantly depict, we can sometimes make it more meaningful by recognizing its fullness with other people.

Aging—with the challenges it poses—is often a source of mystery, revelation, and acceptance, as reflected in these poems and stories. MarthaJoy Aft's poem, "40," speaks to the awakening of new roles and self-images born in midlife. Carol Rose's poem, "in my own image," recounts the physical changes of growing older and the way we adapt to them.

"Abishag Says His Hands Were Cold" is Elizabeth Anne Socolow's poem about the young girl Abishag and her desire and effort to comfort the elderly King David. "Erasures" and "Bathsheba Watches Abishag," by Ruth Daigon and Barbara Holender, respectively, speak of the memory loss, aloneness, depression, and sense of being irrelevant to others that often accompany aging. These poems describe the "blessings" and "curses" of old age.

Linda Feinberg's poem, "Dinah Goldberg, of Blessed Memory," tells of a passion for life even while one acknowledges death. When the number of days in front of us are few, each day becomes more precious.

"Ruth and Naomi" is a midrashic story, based on the love of Ruth for her mother-in-law, Naomi. Describing the deep love, compassion, and care of a young woman for her elder, dying friend, it provides a rare look at the spiritual midwifery of easing a soul out of this world. Maggie Dwyer's story, "Lot's Wife," is the touching tale of a man still loving and caring for his wife, who suffers from Alzheimer's disease. Complying to the Psalmist's injunction to God, "Do not cast me off in old age," Dwyer's protagonist, embodying determination and integrity, remains devoted to her. Although old age brings him abundant heartache, he remains deeply loving and commited to his wife, Sarah, and the spiritual quality embedded in that love helps him survive his daily visits—the "imitation of life"—with her.

While growing old remains a triumphant meeting of will and challenge to some, for others it becomes a time when their physical energies recede and when they cultivate spiritual energies that feed the inner soul more than the body.

40

MarthaJoy Aft

At Rachel's baby-naming, we examined all our friends,
for the first time aware of signs of aging.
Sprinklings of gray hair,
laugh-lines,
thickened middles,
slightly slower motions
and we realized:
It's true. One day the voyage ends.

Oh, it has a beginning—
Leslie's pink little girl,
seriously considering this world while we welcomed her.
This is the first grandchild, of a friend.
Tell me. When did it happen?
Slowly, stealthily age crept in,
first efforts unnoticed as we entered midlife.
But now, the evidence cannot be denied.
Welcome, sweet baby.
Let me hold you close, marker of mortality.

MarthaJoy Aft is a student and teacher of Jewish mysticism, a storyteller, and the editor of Neshama, *a Jewish women's spirituality periodical. She lives in Boston.*

in my own image

Carol Rose

i've been altered
by the surgeon's knife
carved in two
my womb lifted
from my body
i'm left empty

i've been altared
forced to rearrange myself
around vacant space
sacred space
like in the beginning
using the void

Carol Rose lives in Winnipeg, Manitoba, and is a writer, educator, workshop facilitator, counselor, and mother of five children. She won second prize in the 1994 Stephen Leacock International Poetry competition. Her books include Behind the Blue Gate *and* Spider Women: A Tapestry of Creativity and Healing *(forthcoming)*.

ex nihilo
i fashion the world
in my own image
call it by name
place it
in a garden
of my choosing.

Abishag Says His Hands Were Cold

Elizabeth Anne Sussman Socolow

*Now King David was old and advanced in years;
and although they covered him with clothes, he
could not get warm. Therefore his servants said to
him, "Let a young maiden be sought for my lord
the king, and let her wait upon the king, and be
his nurse; let her lie in your bosom, that my lord
the king may be warm." So they sought a beautiful maiden throughout all the territory of Israel
and found Abishag the Shunammite, and
brought her to the king. The maiden was very
beautiful; and she became the king's nurse and
ministered to him; but the king knew her not.*

(Kings 1:1–4)

I want to say
it was no torment
his hands and feet so cold,
the rest cold.

*Elizabeth Anne Sussman Socolow, a member of Detroit's T'Chiyah
Reconstructionist Congregation, is the author of a book of poems,*
Laughing at Gravity: Conversations with Isaac Newton. *As
the recipient of the 1987 Barnard Women's Poets Series Prize, she
was a guest lecturer at Barnard and Vassar Colleges.*

    The way hope opens
like a door
the wind blows closed
a moment after, leaving
the breath coming fast,
gulping the sudden air.

The spices in my grandparents' tents
were the old spices
which inhabited their robes.
Their eyes looked full
of spices and the laughter
such surprise will bring.
You can see with some old people
the distance of so many years between you
has built an arched bridge saying
walk across.

The tiles of my grandparents' baths
were the old style, hardly found now,
that green of pools of water, the color of certain
stormy summer skies.
All my life since,
I have wanted to walk toward old people.

Others imagined it was a hardship,
although he was still the king.
I wanted to tell them
when I was with him, he was scented
like the old spices, and I remembered
the first baths, the glowing warmth
climbing like sap.
When I was with him, he had that look
of amusement at so much life lived already
that the years between us made the bridge
that beckoned.

When I walked toward him, my body's eyes
grew pointed and waited for his answering tilt
that did not come. *Covers,* he would say then,
covers. I am so cold. I made myself his coverlet,
his comforter, softer than feathered quilts.
The wings of angels were not more protective
than I. I gave myself to that task as soldiers and
spies wait, covering the imagined enemy.

The dying came as an absence of spices,
a sweet syrup where pungency had been ruling.
The air and shadows seemed to stop for me too.
His death brought an absence of shadows,
as if the valley of the shadow of death
had long ago claimed
all shadow to itself.

No one can match how much he had stored
as memory, the way a room holds the spice
and the original flower before the seed,
the way wisdom reaches with arms
to embrace the world with hope.
When such a great spirit goes, you can feel
the brush of the air itself making,
from the awful vacancy, a wing.

Dinah Goldberg, of Blessed Memory

Linda H. Feinberg

Swimming up from the depths
I try to reconnect with you
but you are gone,
back to some long ago time
    in a far away world
    unknown to me
seeing family long dead
not remembering today's date
but knowing all the names
    of past generations.

The light in your eyes shines brightly
as you show me old photographs.
Then, embarrassed, you ask
if you are repeating yourself.

A moment of lucidity occurs
and tears fill your eyes
when you remember
    you are just a senile old woman.

Linda H. Feinberg's poetry and nonfiction has been published in several women's journals. A graduate of Boston University, she and her husband have three grown children.

Sadness fills me, but joy too
as I admire your courage
knowing I will one day walk this path
and hoping
    I can also keep my dignity intact.

Erasures

Ruth Daigon

1.

    I'm beginning to forget names, faces,
the day, the date, the year.
You say I'm irresponsible.
You appoint yourself my guardian.
You wear a tweed coat,
a fedora, a shoulder holster
like a secret-service man.
You carry a net to catch me when I fall,
a rope to leash me when I
move too fast or laugh too loud.
You tell me when to wake and when to sleep.
You grow a beard like a rabbi
or a judge and stroke it
while you recite my silly stories.
Soon, you'll write my poems and read them
while I sit listening in the back row.
But, you'll lie awake at night
staring into the dark—my turn to sleep.

*Ruth Daigon won the 1993 Eve of St. Agnes Award for her poem
"Negative Capability." Her latest poetry collection is* Between
One Future and the Next.

And on my last day, you'll be the one to go, leaving me
    here
living and forgetting.

2.

    There is only this house,
this room, this field and a tree
pulling away from its roots.
On one wall, a window makes a centerpiece for the eye
focused on a single ray of sun.
A trickle of water
like a thin strand of wire
drips from the tap.
In the kitchen, a fly perches
on the rim of a bowl,
wings lifting, lowering,
polishing the silence.
Outside, the road curves
away from itself.
Light spreads its slow stain
around empty coffee cups.
The quieter it is,
the slower time passes
as I listen to my breath,
the oldest sound I know.

Bathsheba Watches Abishag

Barbara D. Holender

Poor little girl,
what are you getting out of this?
David hardly knows you're in his arms
warming him. Can the old man
wake a woman even now?

When I warmed him, he warmed me back,
sang me out of my marriage bed,
bathed me in sweet sin,
set me like a jewel in his bosom—
a soldier's widow—wife to a king,
mother to a king.

Where can you go from here but down
until a stone rewards you:
"Here lies Abishag, the king's last comfort"
but no consort.

Barbara D. Holender, of Buffalo, New York, is the author of Shivah Poems: Poems of Mourning, Ladies of Genesis, Is This The Way to Athens?, *and a children's book in Hebrew,* Aineni Schmueli *(I'm Not Sam). She loves music and traveling and is presently engaged in intensive Hebrew studies.*

I watch you together
hanging on letting go.
When his time comes, I'll mourn my conqueror,
that sweet singer of Jerusalem,
The Lord's anointed ruler of Israel,
while you weep over the dust of David.

Hold him for me, child,
I can't bear to touch him.
You are too young to know
we do not love the same man.

Ruth and Naomi

Lynn Greenhough

Ruth sat quietly beside the bed. She watched the afternoon light shift across the contours of the woolen coverlet, hovering over the thin shape underneath, the sun's amber path offering no detour. The once lively and robust frame of her mother-in-law, now so frail and small, shadowed Ruth's vision. Years ago, Ruth had demanded that they look forward, walk into the unknown, find the future in an unfamiliar present. Now, the one who had walked beside her was leaving. Now, the sorrow of the present was becoming more palpable than the comfort of Ruth's memory.

Naomi stirred. Ruth offered her a little water. Then, to ease her again into rest, Ruth reached under the covers and held one of Naomi's feet in her hand. She rubbed olive oil into her arch, along the ball of her foot, down into her heel. She rubbed oil into the hard callused ridges and gently up over her swelling ankles. How many miles these feet have walked, Ruth murmured to herself, how many miles these feet have walked beside mine.

As she rubbed Naomi's yellowed feet they began to warm and pinken. She rubbed and remembered. "I will go with you and your people are my home." Naomi

---

Lynn Greenhough is a member of Congregation Emanu-El in Victoria, British Columbia, where she learns and teaches. She is partner to Holly and mother of Benjamin.

turned away from me, her body already turned west-ward. She had a sharpness, an edge that could cut like filed flint. I looked at her back, her cloak pulled tight around her against the wind, against my words. That same wind tugging at my frame seemed to fill me. I was light and wild. I was neshama, swirling, embracing, de-manding. Before the words fell from my mouth, I knew we were bound to each other. "Your people shall be my people, and your God my God." We walked many, many steps.

Ruth continued to rub the thick oil into the soles of Naomi's feet. How far we have walked together since then. My feet first following yours as we walked toward *Betlechem*, and then around the village. Our walking en-twined our lives. You gave me friendship and community. I brought you loyalty and grain. Together we found suste-nance and love and family. And we continued to walk. Daily, to the well. Seasonally, to the harvests. Soon my footstep fell alongside yours. Gradually, you slowed, your footstep fell alongside and then behind mine. And now, how still you lie, barely able to lift your head, your foot so heavy in my hand. "Where you die, I will die, and there I will be buried."

Ruth moved her stool to the middle of the bedding and took hold of Naomi's hand, "Dear God, let me hold this precious hand just a little longer." How hard our hands have worked together over the years. Naomi showed me how to bake. Her hands flew over the dough, patting out loaves perfectly round and even. Her fingers taught me to spin, to weave, to stitch. Naomi's hands rubbed my belly with fragrant oils as I grew large with child. Many afternoons we stopped our work, warmed a little water with mint, and shared a story, words seeming to roll from our tongues. Others may have called me the Moabite, but Naomi always called me Daughter.

Ruth remembered when Obed was born. Tears flushed her eyes as she thought of her tiny son, now grown broad and tall. She remembered Obed's first days. "He has had two mothers," Ruth thought, "as have I." She remembered Naomi's arms cradling her son. From Naomi's hands Ruth learned how to hold and when to release. Again she felt the swirling winds within her, the push and pull of time past and beyond. Her beloved son, her body's gift from God; her beloved Naomi returning to God.

Naomi murmured. Ruth leaned closer and stroked her cheek. It was so very creased, so very sweet. How many stories we have told each other. How many hours kneading bread, building fires, making up bedding, gathering wood, hauling water. How many chores every day were lightened by Naomi's tales. Stories within stories. Naomi wound the threads of her stories through the days as carefully and lightly as she spun threads from her spindle. By her side Ruth listened, learned, and loved.

Again her own words filled her ears. "Thus and more may God do to me if anything but death parts me from you." Naomi had been her compass, her teacher, her friend. And now, in her bed, she slowly has become a body to be bathed, limbs to be rubbed, sores to be salved. Her body, once sturdy and discreetly hidden in folds of dress and cloak, has, now in dying, become open to touch in ways unimagined.

Candlelight cast magnified shadows across the room. Naomi's breath seemed caught by the fluctuating light. Ruth was mesmerized, watching as intently as she had watched her infant son's chest rise and fall. Then, as a candle sputters in its own waxen puddle, Naomi's face tightened; she gasped, and died. Her breath finished: her soul's light was now extinguished. She, who was Naomi, was gone. Ruth sat very still. Alone.

Then the women came.

Together they washed Naomi. Three times they rinsed her, the streams of water rinsing her body's death with life itself. Together they dried her flesh and dressed

Naomi in her burial garment. Together they carried her to the burying place and placed her in the ground. Together they held each other and mourned for the woman who had been Naomi, and thanked God for the blessing of her memory.[1]

Yitgadal va-yitkadash sh'mei raba . . .

Lot's Wife

Maggie Dwyer

Bernie remembers how he nearly killed Issy Fleigl at the Y. He was down in the locker room doing a few of the stretches the therapist recommended when that shlump came up behind him.

Bernie menaced him with a few swipes of his towel.

"Don't be so touchy," Issy said. "What you need is to get more out of life. But it's not so easy at our age, is it? Cold showers are no good for the arthritis. Now we have to make do with whatever God leaves to us. *Az och un vey!*"

Clad only in a damp white sheet, Fleigl draped a damp arm around Bernie's shoulders and pulled him closer. Bernie shivered with distaste. "Listen to this, *boychik;* I've got a little story for you," Fleigl whispered.

"Jake and Becky are celebrating their fiftieth wedding anniversary. They return to the same hotel, the same room where they spent their honeymoon night. At two o'clock in the morning, Jake nudges Becky in bed and says 'Becky—*derlang mir die tzeyner, ich vill dir a beis geben.* Hand me my teeth, he tells her, so I can nibble on you.'"

Maggie Dwyer is a Winnipeg-based writer and editor whose work has appeared in Prairie Fire, Border Crossings, A Room of One's Own, *and* Necessary Fiction. *She was the guest editor for* Prairie Fire's *special issue on Canadian Jewish writing.*

Fleigl's hairy belly vibrated fitfully as he reveled in his own wit.

"You're a sick man," Bernie sighed as he pushed off the offensive arm. "At your age, isn't it time for a little dignity?"

"Life is short," countered Fleigl. "Don't lose your appetite for it. I could introduce you to a very fine woman—if you're interested."

"I am a married man," Bernie snapped and continued dressing.

"Okay, have it your way," Fleigl huffed. "If you want to miss out on Sonia Bregman, it's your funeral. Older women are very grateful, Bernie."

"Don't insult me," Bernie warned, pulling on his overcoat. "I don't want to meet anyone." He picked up his club bag and walked toward the door.

"She doesn't wear shorts and she doesn't play mah-jongg," Fleigl sang out to his departing back.

Bernie wheeled around and started back toward Fleigl. "Look here, Mr. Matchmaker, keep your beak out of my business, you," he sputtered, "you puffball." He jabbed at Fleigl's ugly mug, his finger almost scoring a hit on the nasty-looking wen that dominated the left cheek.

That encounter really soured Bernie's day. He muttered curses about Fleigl all the way to Main Street. The northbound bus was crowded with forlorn-looking young mothers with crying children and other *alta kackers* like himself. He stomped off the bus at Pritchard Avenue and dove into the moist fragrant air of the florist's shop. His order was ready: twelve luscious long-stemmed red roses like those he had given his valentine every year for the past forty-six. Every year, even the lean ones.

At the Home, Sarah was waiting for him. She was sitting with her pal, Mimi Kates, in her usual spot between the potted palms in the solarium. Ginger-haired Mimi, a former Hadassah *maven* whose meddlesome ways were a trial to many, wore as usual a ransom in gold and diamonds on her neck and liver-spotted hands.

"Look who it is, Sarah," Mimi warbles as Bernie approaches.

He bows slightly at the waist and holds the long white florist's box out to Sarah.

"My goodness," she exclaims, "Is that for me?"

Mimi hauls herself to the edge of the seat and launches her rotund body erect.

"Don't go, dear," pleads Sarah, still cradling the unopened box of flowers. "I'd like you to meet my friend." She smiles radiantly and with a delicate blush puts her white hand out to Bernie.

"Both of you are so good to me." She extends her left hand to Mimi and draws all four hands together, raising Bernie's and Mimi's to her cheeks.

Again, Bernie suffers the bitter charade of introductions to Mimi. As always, he yearns for their fine bright love, now dimmed, and for their past, now shriveled to a husk. Where did it go, he wonders, all those years Sarah and I spent *kibbitzing* behind the counter in our store? People still ask after her: "How is your darling wife?" Terrible, terrible, what can happen to a person.

Today, a flicker of recognition shows in Sarah's eyes. Though he continuously notes such signs, he no longer feels hopeful. The doctors have counseled him to be detached, not to come so often. Yet, every afternoon in their imitation of life, he sits with Sarah until twilight, bringing her news of their children and grandchildren. Stories of their older son, Nathan, who married money, living with his thin princess and their children in the palace in Tuxedo with their Filipina maid. Stories about Max, their son the lawyer turned land developer, and his barren lawyer wife, Judith, and the very important work they do. More stories about their little Rosie, the nutritionist, and the recipes she sends him. How she tries to make a cook out of him, who has never so much as boiled water for tea.

Sarah listens, but her responses are cryptic.

He tells her stories to affirm their lives, to pass the afternoons, to fill the air between them. "We've come this far," he coos and gives her hand a squeeze.

A narrow crescent of moon hovers over the North End as Bernie shivers along Polson Avenue. He loathes these mid-February twilights and the empty house he must enter. He shuffles inside, anyway, dumping the brown paper bag he is carrying on the kitchen table, and turns on the ceiling light.

Then, he goes to the cupboard, reaches in, and lifts down a bottle of rye whiskey and a shot glass. He pours himself a measure and tosses it back with a shiver. As the whiskey warms him he unbuttons his worn sheepskin coat and vigorously rubs his firm paunch.

"Now we're talking, buddy," he says to himself, and flips on the small color TV on the kitchen table. The face and voice of the pretty local anchorwoman warm up the room. Bernie pays no attention to the newscast. It's trouble everywhere; she doesn't have to tell *him*. He sets the contents of his grocery bag out on the plastic tablecloth. Three white styrofoam containers from the deli. He fetches a spoon and begins slurping up thick bean and barley soup.

Just then, the wall telephone rings. It's his youngest daughter, calling from Vancouver.

"Rosie! *Bubele,* it sounds like you're in the next room, sweetheart. How's the weather by you? Rain, that's wonderful. . . . Flowers too. You got all the luck. . . . Here? It's winter. What can we do about it?"

"Yes, sweetheart, I'm just finishing my dinner. No, you're not interrupting. Well, yes, you are interrupting, but this type of interruption, I don't mind. What am I eating? Let me tell you: a nice soup, some fish, a beautiful *kugel.* I still got lots of the food you made for me. I'm telling you, if the Queen of England drops over here, I could give her a nice dinner."

He doesn't understand why she moved away or why on earth her brother Max and his Judith endure Ottawa. The winters there are not much better. Only Nathan, his eldest, stayed in Winnipeg.

"What do you mean 'have I decided about California?' I told your brother that I'll think about it. I'm still thinking."

Nathan wanted him to leave Sarah in Winnipeg so he could spend Passover with them at a fancy resort in California. He didn't know what kind of Jew went to a spa for Pesach. Elizabeth Taylor, maybe.

"Okay, okay. I said I'll think about it. The deadline is at the end of the month. I am not shouting. I caught a little cold and I don't hear so good these last few days. I'm feeling better already, really, just talking to you.

"I saw your mother this afternoon. She's the same, lovely as always. No change.

"Thank you, sweetheart. Thank you for calling."

After saying good-bye to Rosie, Bernie went to the bedroom and took the wedding photo off the bureau and dusted the glass with the tail of his shirt. "A lot of water under the bridge, kiddo," he whispered. "A whole lot."

The first time Bernie saw Sarah was October 1, 1941. He thought he was a real *macher*, working at the scrap yards on McPhillips. Twenty years old and full of pepper. That summer Ted Williams batted .400. War was raging, and all of a sudden, scrap metal was a very important commodity. It didn't sound half bad when people asked why he wasn't enlisting to fight Hitler. Not that he didn't want to. He knew he could tear that monster apart with his bare hands.

The first time Bernie saw Sarah was at the Rosh Hashanah dance. She was dressed in pale rose silk and her blonde hair was pinned up like Betty Gable's. She was with a tall, good looking Royal Canadian Air Force sergeant in a snappy dress uniform with medals on his left breast. It was her brother Max, he found out later.

Bernie was smitten. As soon as the orchestra started playing "Don't Sit Under The Apple Tree With Anyone Else But Me," he cut in on them. He looked her right in her blue eyes and said, "This could be our song." He couldn't explain it. He told himself that the ways of fate cannot be understood. It is better to surrender than to question. They had a good life together. They enjoyed everything, even used to get pretty frisky. Just to think about it now makes him glow. They wanted to be together all the time. They were.

Now, on Friday evenings, Bernie eats dinner with his sister Rae, who is bulky and plain-speaking and dresses like her heroine, Golda Meir. At sixty-two, she's winding down a long career in teaching at a Yiddish day school.

Bernie shows her the brochures from the spa. "Look," he says, "it includes daily synagogue services, free nutritional analysis, all meals glatt kosher, and thirty minutes from the ocean. Does that sound like a *ganze metsiah* or what?"

"Maybe to Nathan's wife," Rae answers. "She only knows to shop and exercise. She wouldn't have to change a dish." Rae always found Lisa strange, with her black clothes and those two pale children with the fake names. Bree and Krystall.

After dinner, Rae gets out the cards for gin rummy. Bernie tells her about Fleigl's joke and his asinine proposition: How insulted he was and how his blood was jumping.

"Stay away from Sonia Bregman," Rae cautioned, "her dentures clack like castanets."

Bernie finally pushes his tea cup away and gets ready to struggle home. At the door, Rae presses a jar of soup into his hands and urges him to pull his hat down and his scarf up. He pretended to be impatient with her ministrations, which nourished him even more than her wholesome soup. It's the only time of the week that he didn't feel lonely.

Tonight, the seven blocks from Matheson down to Polson were free of muggers and Bernie made it back home with ease. He was sinking deep into dreamless sleep when the phone started ringing. It took him seven rings to pull on his tired robe and *shlep* out to the kitchen. On the eleventh ring, he lifted the receiver to hear the scolding voice of his son Max.

"Dad, when are you going to put an extension in your bedroom? It takes you so long to answer."

"I had to find my glasses."

"Dad, you don't need bifocals to answer the phone."

"It's after eleven o' clock here, mister. Don't argue with an old man. I know what I need."

Max asks if Bernie has made his mind up about spending Passover in California. Big shots like him and his wife need plenty of advance notice so they can arrange their complicated lives.

"Aren't you at all worried about what your mother will be doing?" Bernie demands. "Aren't you at all concerned where she is going to sit for the seder?"

"Pop, I know it's hard for you, but, we have to be realistic. It doesn't do your health any good to live the way you do. You won't be missed. Mama doesn't know who we are any more. She doesn't even know who you are."

"She doesn't even know who I am. Is that a fact? She doesn't even know who I am." The veins at his temples began to throb. "Well, let me tell you something, Mr. Know-It-All. I know who she is!"

Bernie clanged the receiver down and shuffled back to bed. For forty-five minutes, he thrashed around in his sheets. Extra blankets couldn't warm him. He didn't drift off until he laid out the spare pillows on Sarah's side and wrapped himself around them.

Then, he fell into a bottomless dream. He was in front of the house, in his shirtsleeves. All the houses in the neighborhood looked abandoned, their windows empty, their doors ajar. Wherever there had been snow was now a fine white sand. The moon's full face hung low in the south.

He gets up and strikes off toward the Home. His steps are light as floss and he follows the moon's path eagerly. At Main Street, the sand stretches toward the prairie horizon in endless undulations. The Home is entirely gone. Where it stood, a mighty golden sphinx towers on a claw legged throne beside a woman. The sand all around is covered with dry bones gleaming in the silvery light. With another look, he sees that it is Rae's doughty head on the sphinx.

"Baruch," she says, "I'm glad you're here. Give a look here to your Sarah. I've watched over her this whole night. Go close to her that you may see it is your wife." As Bernie moves toward Sarah, the sphinx unfolds its great dark wings and lifts higher with each stroke.

"Rae, don't leave me here alone."

She circles low over his head. "Next year, Bernie," she croaks. "Next year in Jerusalem."

With a sob, Bernie, his heart still turned to love, steps closer to embrace his wife. His lips touch her smooth cheek and taste salt.

"Sarah," he whispers, "I'm here, I'm here."

VIII. CEREMONIES

*Stand up before a hoary head and honor the face
of one matured in wisdom.*

—Leviticus 19:32

CEREMONIES

Ritual not only helps us acknowledge change, but also, as the anthropologist Barbara Myerhoff said, "offers an occasion of personal integration, in which one becomes aware that he/she is the same person now that he/she was long ago, despite so much change in one's body and one's world. Ritual takes up the task of allowing for an experience of continuity, for it provides the opportunities for the most basic, cherished symbols to become vivified, active and transformative."[1]

This section includes new rituals and ceremonies that address late-in-life milestones. The symbols and songs of ritual, whether traditional or innovative, wrap the elder in a prayerful shawl of acknowledgment and comfort.

There are few Jewish rituals for the years between marriage and death, yet many profound changes occur during this time. Paul Citrin's essay, "A Testament to Growing Older," outlines a program of study and celebration to acknowledge reaching the "Age of Counsel," as *Pirkei Avot* calls the fifth decade of one's life. Through the program, an individual writes a *"Tza-avat Eitza,"* a "Testament of Counsel," a statement of life's meaning and purpose which is publicly shared during Sukkot.

"An End to the Body's Silence" is Phyllis Ocean Berman's ritual that celebrates menopause. During it, in the company of friends, Berman addresses the stages of her womanhood: menstruation, sex and love, pregnancy, childbirth and child-rearing, and menopause. In

"Havdalah: A Time to Acknowledge Growing Old," Marcia Cohn Spiegel uses the ceremony of *havdalah*, which marks the separation between Shabbat's closure and the rest of the week, as the framework to ritualize and celebrate a birthday. She asks: "From what in my life do I want to separate? And what do I envision for my future?" In "A Personal 'Seder' to Celebrate Aging," Anne Tolbert uses the framework of a seder to acknowledge her sixth decade. Readings, songs, four cups of wine or juice, and a ceremonial plate of food help her share the transformative qualities of her aging.

"Let Your Heart Take Courage" is Cary Kozberg's ceremony for welcoming new residents to a long-term care facility. The transition from independent to assisted living is usually difficult. This ceremony provides a spiritual avenue for the new resident and his or her family through which to address the physical and emotional changes associated with entering such a facility. Dayle Friedman's "Older Adult Confirmation" provides inspiration and guidelines for continued Jewish education for the elderly. Its essential premise is that learning and performing *mitzvot* are lifelong experiences.

A Testament to Growing Older: The Av/Em Eitza Program

Paul Citrin

In *The Denial of Death,* anthropologist Ernest Becker reminds us of the tensions in the human heart. Fearful of our mortality, we energize ourselves to define our lives with meaning and significance. As Becker tells us, "One of the crucial projects of a person's life, of true maturity, is to resign oneself to the process of aging."[1] He suggests that we can achieve such resignation by "earning a feeling of primary value, of cosmic specialness, of ultimate usefulness to creation, of unshakable meaning."[2] Believing that a life has meaning makes us feel unique and valuable to family and community and helps ease resignation and acceptance.

By reflecting on how we have lived, what we have achieved, where we have failed, and what is yet to be accomplished, we can begin to share with others our life's meaning. At midlife, we begin to realistically face our limits and our death. Communicating what we learn as we struggle to accept our mortality can provide a legacy that reaffirms the value of our lives.[3]

Paul Citrin is senior rabbi of Main Line Reform Temple Beth Elo-him, Wynnewood, Pennsylvania. He has published several articles as well as a children's novel, Joseph's Wardrobe. *He and his wife, Susan, have four grown children.*

267

A ritual to express one's sense of meaning and understanding of life can ease the acceptance of aging and death. The following ceremony is designed to observe reaching this point in our lives. It is based on *Pirkei Avot's* calling the age of fifty the "age of counsel," *"ben chamishim le-eitza."* Several years ago, our synagogue established this observance in which someone fifty years of age or older would become a "Father of Counsel" or a "Mother of Counsel"—an *Av Eitza* or an *Em Eitza*.

An individual achieves *Av/Em Eitza* status by writing a *Tzava'at Eitza*, a Testament of Counsel. This testament addresses the important lessons he or she has learned in life—insights on human relationships, coping with hardship, and finding fulfillment—and the message one has tried to convey through life.

Unlike the classical ethical will, which was usually addressed to family members, the *Tzava'at Eitza* is presented to the synagogue community, either on the first morning of Sukkot or on the Shabbat during Sukkot. Sukkot, or the "Festival of the Ingathering" when Ecclesiastes is read, is a fitting time to share a harvest of reflections. In contrast to Ecclesiastes' laments, this program offers a time for every purpose under heaven. The individual testaments are collected in a *Sefer Eitza*, a Book of Counsel, and placed in the congregation's library.

A second factor that makes the testament different from an ethical will is its preparation. Those who wish to become an *Av/Em Eitza* study with a rabbi or teacher. This study begins with Ecclesiastes and examines classical and modern ethical wills as well as participants' lives, accomplishments, and failures. The group also explores feelings about death and dying. Participants are encouraged to keep journals, which become the basis for the *Tzava'at Eitza*.

The vehicle of becoming an *Av/Em Eitza* is new, but it is rooted in traditional study and reflection. The *Av/Em Eitza* celebration creates heroic role models, and shows us a path, as the Psalmist wrote, "to number our days so we may attain a heart of wisdom."

Following are two excerpts from Testaments of Counsel that demonstrate the wisdom gleaned through the process of becoming an *Av* or *Em Eitza*.

Live your life with an open hand, not a clenched fist. Remember what you are is God's gift to you. What you become is your gift to God. (from Marge LaZar's 1992 Testament of Counsel)

Desperate for connection, not knowing how to tap its
    source;
Needing comfort and belonging;
Brought finally forth in service in Torah.
Tikkun Olam to heal the world.
What greater joy or task could any soul desire?
Spectrum scanning, looking for my place;
At long last I've seen the rainbow whole
And pray it's not too late.

I believe that the best and most important advice that I can hand on is the necessity to keep growing, to be involved in something larger and more worthwhile than one's self, and to try to be a productive agent in the task of *tikkun olam*. (from Naomi Rosenberg's 1994 Testament of Counsel)

An End to the Body's Silence

Phyllis Ocean Berman

As the moon hovered on the edge of Chanukah, thirty-six —a magical number—of my women friends gathered to celebrate not only the Festival of Light, not only my fiftieth birthday, but also my menopause. Thirty-six women gathered to end an age-old silence. We gathered not only to speak about menopause but also to celebrate it. Just as my journey beyond menstruation would be unknown to me, so this ceremony I had just created was a journey unknown to them.

Why did I think it was so important to end the silence about menopause? Three months before my thirteenth birthday, I "got the curse" and "became a woman," to use two common euphemisms about menstruation. My mother whispered the news to her friend Selma and Mrs. Goldstein who lived next door, and thus I learned about "women's things"—and about whispering. In my seventh-grade classrooms, other girls/women were, like me,

Phyllis Ocean Berman is the program director of Elat Chayyim, a Jewish retreat center for healing, and coauthor of Tales of Tikkun: New Jewish Stories to Heal the Wounded World. *Berman founded in 1978 and now directs the Riverside Language Program, an intensive English-language school for adult immigrants and refugees from around the world. With her husband, Arthur Ocean Waskow, she lives in Philadelphia, and she shares four grown children, one son-in-law, and one daughter-in-law.*

embarrassed to talk about the changes that had or had not yet happened to them. Nothing could have been more on our minds and less on our lips.

Silence is profound. When we cannot speak about what is happening in our bodies, in our hearts, and in our souls, we draw some reasonable but damaging conclusions. We learn that what is public is limited to the world of our minds and, more likely, to the most superficial layers of our minds. We then begin making the distinction between the inner, consuming conversations we have alone or with an intimate few, and the outer disconnected ones we have with others. The disconnections are not only from others but also from ourselves: We lose the at-one-ment we could feel when we perceive ourselves whole and holy in relation to others.

For much of my adult life, I have wanted to speak about the unspeakable. I have wanted to move the body and the emotions and the spirit out of the shadows, where they appear hidden, trivial, shameful, even dirty, into the sunlight, where they are real, important, central, and acceptable. For me, the process of making an inner experience public helps me see my experience as normal, to speak my experience with passion and surety, and to feel myself integrated within and without.

SHARING TRUTHS ABOUT WOMANHOOD

In my forty-ninth year, as I began to experience the ending of my menstruations, I decided to break through the silence hovering over this passage with two circles of friends: women, ranging in age from 21 to 58, gathered from all over the country and various parts of my life, and the women and men of the *P'nai Or Havurah* and other members of the extraordinary Jewish Renewal neighborhood of Mount Airy in Philadelphia.

For the Mount Airy crowd, we held a Shabbat morning service and a Saturday night Chanukah-and-birthday party. But in the late afternoon of Shabbat, which was on the winter solstice weekend and just before Chanukah began, I gathered with my women friends to celebrate my menopause.

To these women, I had proposed that we celebrate a "seder of womanhood"—the order of the stages of womanhood as I had experienced them in my life. As with the traditional Passover seder and the increasingly familiar *Tu B'Shevat* seder, we drank four cups of beverage as we told our individual stories. We are taught in *Pirkei Avot* that 50 is the age of advice-giving; in keeping with feminist practice, rather than giving advice, we shared lessons we had learned from each stage of our woman-life.

For the first cup, I served a bright red sangria. (Cherry-apple cider was served to non–alcohol drinkers.) Sangria, the "drink" of my adolescence, represented my first stage of womanhood, menstruation. The group shared stories, some funny and some sad, about first periods and the silence around them; about later periods and their weightiness in our lives—hoping for them when we feared we might be pregnant, fearing them when we prayed we might be pregnant. We recognized ourselves again and again in each others' stories. Then we drank the first cup.

As we moved on I suggested a guideline for the remaining three cups: Since everyone in the room had already reached the stage of menstruation, we had all been able to speak from our own experiences. For the following cups, women could speak only if they had already reached that stage of life.[1]

The second cup, a sparkling champagne (sparkling apple cider for non–alcohol drinkers), was for my second stage of woman-life: the bubbly, heady introduction to sex and love. Again, we spoke about the silences that had heralded this stage of life: how little we had known about our own bodies, about our own pleasures, about the wide range of potential loving partners (women as well as men). This was not the bawdy, bragging talk of the locker-room but rather the sad, sweet talk, long overdue, of innocence and ignorance, of surprise and delight.

The third cup, milk (soy milk for non–dairy drinkers), marked my third stage: pregnancy, childbirth, nursing, child-raising. Not surprisingly, we again spoke of silences: the silence of abortion, of adoption, of not having children, of the sensuality of nursing, of the passionate protection of and connection to our children.

The fourth cup, water (mineral water for purists), represented the totally open possibilities of the fourth stage of woman-life: menopause. Only about eight in the group had reached menopause, and there was a significant difference in our sharing. What I had imagined would be the most silent of the life stages, and potentially the most depressing, now appeared quite the opposite.

HEALING OUR ALIENATION

The silence of menopause has been broken publicly. In spite of our youth-centered culture, several books about menopause have appeared, as well as a recent *Newsweek* cover focused on turning 50. Gloria Steinem, replying to the statement "You don't look 50," quipped, "*This* is what 50 looks like!" Rather than experiencing an empty nest at the end of our biologically reproductive lives, those of us who spoke felt giddy with freedom, with the chance to forge a new path of our choosing, without obligations. We were asking ourselves, some for the first time, "What do we want to do with this new opportunity?"

While the menopause ceremony suffered some of the awkwardness and embarrassment that accompanies a lifetime of silence, it was also filled with laughter, sorrow, relief, and understanding. I hope the silence that has enveloped so many other important life-turnings will, by the strength of our ceremonies and rituals, our books and our conversations, be broken. Ceremonies and rituals today, like those of old, make each life stage a time for revealing, first to ourselves, then to one another, and then to the larger human community, for breaking out of the tyranny and alienation of silence.

At the end of the ceremony, I read a Marge Piercy poem. When at last that lifelong leak of blood comes to an end, she says, "I tell you I will secretly dance and pour out a cup of wine on the earth." Now the dance need no longer be secret. Now menopause may become what the title of her poem calls it: "Something to Look Forward To."

Havdalah: A Time to Acknowledge Growing Old

Marcia Cohn Spiegel

After my fifty-fifth birthday, I felt that all I did was tend the sick and the dying, plan funerals, and arrange mourning ceremonies. I buried my parents, my husband, two sisters-in-law, a brother-in-law, my mother-in-law, aunts and uncles and cousins. I was depressed, exhausted, and confused.

In the midst of my melancholia, I attended an extraordinary ceremony, a *simchat chochmah,*[1] a celebration of wisdom, which my friend Savina Teubal had conceived for her sixtieth birthday. She celebrated her aging, her sharing of wisdom, and even her preparation for death. I shared her joy, and laughed, danced, and wept. As I did, I began to plan my own *simchat chochmah.*

Incorporating some of the design of Savina's *simchat chochmah,* I planned my "Celebration of Age" to use the framework of *havdalah,* the separation between Shabbat and the beginning of the new week. *Havdalah's* wonderful sensory symbols move us from the sacred to the ordi-

---

Marcia Cohn Spiegel, coauthor of The Jewish Women's Awareness Guide *and* Women Speak to God: The Poems and Prayers of Jewish Women, *helps adults create their own unique lifecycle rituals. Her lectures and workshops address the Jewish community's attitude toward addiction, violence and sexual abuse.*

nary: braided candle, sweet wine, exotic spices, and familiar melodies. These symbols remind us of the sweetness of Shabbat as we move into the week.

Havdalah has been a special ritual in our family. Before my daughter Linda's wedding, we celebrated it under the stars in our backyard. We observed it in my mother's garden at the end of *shiva*, the seven days of mourning. As we released her soul to God we welcomed her great-grandson, Benjamin, into the world. My cousins and I observed *havdalah* in the intensive care unit of the hospital as we gathered to bid my father good-bye on the evening of his death.

For my sixtieth birthday, I wanted to perform a special *havdalah*. But what would I be separating from? What did I want to leave behind? What did I want to become as I moved into the last part of my life? And what was my vision for the future?

I drew on several elements of Savina's service: donning a special garment, changing my name, and making a vow. I translated her ideas into my own images.

WHOLENESS AND FULFILLMENT

My ritual took place at the close of Shabbat, at *mincha*, the late afternoon service. I used the traditional afternoon service as my model, adding particular readings related to my life as a woman and as a Jew. I entered synagogue dressed in a full-length black gown as a sign of mourning. During the service, I changed into a simple white linen dress, a *kittel*. Traditionally, Jewish men receive a *kittel* when they get married; they wear it then, at Yom Kippur and Passover, and then as a shroud for their burial. My white dress became the garment that I would wear for holy days and family celebrations. As I put it on I was acknowledging the limits of my life and accepting those limits. At the same time, I was looking toward *shlemut,* wholeness and fulfillment.

In the Bible, several figures are renamed to mark transformations in their lives: Sarai becomes Sarah; Avram becomes Abraham; Jacob becomes Israel. The act of renaming creates a new spiritual identity. I chose Miriam as my new name. The Biblical Miriam, as a child, had the inspiration and courage to rescue her brother, Moses, from death; to confront Pharaoh's daughter; and even arrange for her mother to act as her brother's wet-nurse. Miriam led the Israelites in song, dance, and prayer at the shores of the Red Sea, and they acknowledged their love and respect for her when they waited for her recovery from leprosy in the wilderness. Miriam, a woman of courage, vision, and leadership, was who I wanted to be "when I grew up."

After my renaming, I invited others to come forward and rename themselves. Then, we stood under my grand-father's prayer shawl, reciting a naming blessing written by Marcia Falk: "Let us sing the soul in every name and the names of every soul."[2]

I next made a vow for the future, promising to continue confronting issues of abuse and addiction among Jews and to encourage community programs to deal with these problems. I also vowed to continue supporting my women's spiritual community. And then I planted a tree, which Jews often do at significant life moments. I chose a lemon tree. The tartness of the lemon and its sweet fragrance seemed a perfect metaphor as I moved from sorrow to joy.

CONFRONTING OUR FEARS— AND OUR FUTURE

Several friends with chronic or terminal illnesses, or who were struggling with depression, joined me in a prayer for healing. Under my grandmother's crocheted lace table-cloth, we sang "*Mi Shebeirach:* Bless those in need of healing with *r'fua sh'lei-ma,* a complete healing of body and spirit."[3] For this moment, we focused not on our suffering or pain but rather on our power to heal, to live life as fully as possible. We reflected on the fragility of our lives and praised God for our blessings.

Surrounded by my children, my close friends, and my family, I recited *kaddish,* the traditional mourner's prayer. I was encircled by those who had taught me and those whom I had taught, with whom I had shared pain and with whom I would share rejoicing.

As the synagogue darkened we crowded together to recite the blessings of *havdalah.* Together we marked this moment of transition. While the world moved from light to dark, from the holiness of the Sabbath day to the coming week, I moved from sadness and mourning to a future where I would continue to learn, to explore and to grow.[4]

This ritual is specific to neither age nor gender. For some women and men, the time to celebrate is 60; for others it might be 65 or 70. It might even be 80. The only imperative is to consider where the individual is and where the individual would like to be: to acknowledge the individual's wisdom.

As I reread my service and listen to the music, I recognize that preparing the ritual was more important than performing it. I forced myself to confront my fears and sorrows, to consider my long-range goals, and to give myself permission to move on to whatever lay ahead, unencumbered by ancient pain and open to new experiences.

A Personal "Seder"
to Celebrate Aging

Anne Tolbert

Ritual marks an important turning point in an individual's life and sanctifies it in a special Jewish context.
It provides sacred time for us to reflect on where we've been, who we are, and where we are going. As a woman who wanted support and encouragement in my spiritual growth and acknowledgment of aging, I created a ritual to celebrate my aging that would also affirm my intention to remain visible and continue to work for personal and political change: *"Biz a hundred und tvuntsik!"* "To 120!"[1]

WELCOME

Niggun: A melody is a gentle way to come together. The ceremony begins with everyone seated in a circle as they introduce themselves and indicate their relationship to the celebrant.

Anne Tolbert, a dancer and choreographer, teaches movement at the University of Massachusetts, Boston. She participates as a healer at the monthly healing service of Temple Shalom, Medford, Massachusetts, and has written alternative haggadot *for Tu B'Shevat and Passover seders.*

Reading: This selection, adapted from the writing of Albert Einstein, honors our coming together.

> Strange is our situation here on earth. Each of us comes for a short visit, not knowing why, yet sometimes seeming to divine a purpose. From the standpoint of daily life, however, here is one thing we do know: that we are here for the sake of each other, above all, for those upon whose smile and well-being our own happiness depends, and also for the countless unknown souls with whom we are connected by a bond of sympathy. Many times each day, I realize how much my own outer and inner life is built upon the labors of others, both living and dead, and how earnestly I must exert myself to give in return as much as I have received and am still receiving from others. [2]

LIGHTING THE CANDLES

B'ruchah At Shechinah, Eloheynu Ruach ha'olam, Borayt m'oray ha'aysh.
Blessed are You Shechinah, Our God Spirit of the Universe, Creator of the lights of fire.
(Each person may light a candle)

Song: *Hinay ma tov u-mah nayim, shevet achyot [sisters] gam yachad*

Reading: This poem by Rami Shapiro, which is read responsively (the leader reads one stanza, the group reads the next, etc.), challenges us to reflect and build upon our heritage.

> In each age
> we receive and transmit
> Torah.

At each moment
we are addressed by the
World.

In each age
we are challenged
by our ancient teaching.

At each moment
we stand face to face with
Truth.

In each age
we add our wisdom
to that which has gone before.

At each moment
the knowing heart
is filled with wonder.

In each age
the children of Torah
become its builders
and seek to set the world firm
on a foundation of Truth.[3]

Song: Sing Linda Hirschhorn's "Miriam's Slow Snake Dance at the Riverside"[4] while wearing a circle of colored ribbons.

THE FIRST CUP—
THE CUP OF MIRIAM: TO LIFE

We drink this cup of pure spring water to honor the prophet Miriam, who sang and danced after crossing the Sea of Reeds. Legend tells us that the well of living waters that followed Miriam throughout the wanderings in the desert provided sustenance to the Jewish people. When Miriam died, the well disappeared.

This cup of living waters, *mayim chayyim,* also resembles the promise of a fresh beginning. A baby, born from the living waters of its mother, is sustained by water, as we all are. Fresh water is our birthright, but we must protect it. This first cup celebrates birth, renewal and the promise of each new life. (Fill and lift cup)

Leader:
Zot Kos Miryam, Kos Mayim Chayyim, Chazak Chazak V'Nit-Chazayk.[5]
This is the cup of Miriam, the Cup of Living waters. Strength, strength, and may we be strengthened.
Baruch Atah Adonai, Elohaynu Melech ha-olam, shehakol ni-hiyeh b'd'varo.
Blessed are You, God, Life Source of the Universe, by Whose Word everything is created.[6]
(Drink)

THE CEREMONIAL PLATE:
FIRST SYMBOL

The orange. The seeds of this round, sweet, tart fruit represent the beginning of life, as well as life's cycle. The skin, which protects the fruit, is removed to uncover the edible fruit. This reminds us that good things are often hidden. The sections of this fruit represent the myriad possibilities that unfold as we begin life's journey.
Bruchah At Yah, Eloheynu M'kor Ha-Chayyim, Borayt pri ha-aytz.
Blessed are You, Source of Life, Creator of the fruit of the tree.
Share oranges and other fruits.

Reading: This poem, by Judy Chicago, offers a vision of the world we can work toward. (Please read respon- sively—the leader reads the first line, the group reads the next, etc.)

> And then all that has divided us will merge
> And then compassion will be wedded to power
> And then softness will come to a world that is harsh
>   and unkind
> And then both men and women will be gentle
> And then both women and men will be strong
> And then no person will be subject to another's will
> And then all will be rich and free and varied
> And then the greed of some will give way to the needs
>   of many
> And then all will share equally in the Earth's abundance
> And then all will care for the sick and the weak and the old
> And then all will nourish the young
> And then all will cherish life's creatures
> And then all will live in harmony with each other and
>   the Earth
> And then everywhere will be called Eden once again.[7]

THE SECOND CUP: TO FREEDOM

This cup of red juice (cranberry or cherry) celebrates the first stage of adolescence, the onset of puberty and men- struation, and the growing sense of one's personhood and independence. (Fill and lift cup)

B'ruchah At Shechinah, Eloheynu Malkat ha'olam, sh'hakol nihiyeh b'd'varo.

Blessed are You, Shechinah, our God, Ruler of the Uni- verse, by Whose Word everything is created. (Drink)

THE CEREMONIAL PLATE:
SECOND AND THIRD SYMBOLS

Mint. This herb, which grows wild and abundantly, reminds us of the bounty of the earth, and perhaps also of a time when we were uncultivated and wild. Before it is eaten, the mint may be dipped in vinegar or soy sauce, suggesting the freedom to experiment and the lessons we learned through experimentation.

Baruch Atah Adonai, Elohaynu Melech ha'olam, Boray pri haadamah.

Blessed are You, Our God, Ruler of the Universe, Who created the fruit of the earth.

A rose. This flower represents our personal blooming into womanhood. Thorns protect the opened rose. While we need to develop protective skills, we do not want to become too hardened. The rose that flowers into beauty, fades and withers when its season is past. (Foods made with herbs, and various sour or salty condiments are now served.)

Reading: An innovative "Ecclesiastes" (Each person reads two lines.)

> To everything there is a season
> and a time for every purpose under heaven:
> A time for tradition, and a time for change;
> A time to be alone, and a time to be together;
> A time to be young, and a time to be old;
> A time to begin monthly bleeding, and a time for it to end;
> A time to be with women, and a time to be with men;
> A time to work, and a time to play;
> A time to feel pain, and a time to feel pleasure;
> A time to be creative, and a time to rest from creativity;
> A time to experience, and a time to reflect;
> A time to be physical, and a time to be spiritual;
> A time to learn, and a time to teach;

A time to free oneself, and a time to share freedom with
   others;
A time for the sun, and a time for the moon;
A time for endings, and a time for new beginnings;
The gain is in the receiving and the giving.[8]

Stories of our adolescence, our first period, and our
first love are shared. (Use a crystal or stone to focus attention on the speaker.)

THE THIRD CUP— TO CREATIVITY

This cup represents the potential of commitment: the
choices we make while balancing relationships, meaningful work, career, marriage, and children. We are grateful
to the women who came before us and we are aware of
the sacrifices they made. This drink is a mixture: an "egg-
cream," made with chocolate syrup, milk, and seltzer. It is
my personal symbol of growing up in New York. It is the
milk of nursing made sweeter with chocolate and as
evanescent as a dancer's life. (Fill and lift cup)
*B'ruchah At Yah, Eloheynu M'kor Ha-Chayyim, shehakol ni-
hiyeh b'd'varo.*
Blessed are You God, Source of Life, by Whose Word
everything is created.
   (Drink)

THE CEREMONIAL PLATE: FOURTH AND FIFTH SYMBOLS

Nutmeg. This spice reminds us that labor is a necessary
part of life. Grating releases the spice's scent and flavor.

As with Torah study or finding one's calling, there is no reward without work.

Baruch Atah Yah, Eloheynu Ruach Ha-Olam, Boray minay b'samim.

Blessed are You our God, Whose Spirit fills creation, bringing forth spices.

(Grate and smell the nutmeg.)

Chocolate. Chocolate hardly needs explanation. It stands for the delights and rewards of life, whatever they are (love, work, children). But we pay a price for overindulgence!

B'ruchah At Yah. Eloheynu M'kor Ha-Chayyim, shehakol nihiyeh b'd'varo.

Blessed are You God, Source of Life, by Whose Word everything is created.

Share food like *kugel* flavored with nutmeg and cinnamon, spiced cheeses, etc. Then share chocolate desserts.

THE FOURTH CUP: TO COURAGE

This cup represents the problems and new opportunities we see ahead of us. (A bubbly drink such as sparking wine or flavored seltzer is offered.)

(Fill cups for those drinking wine and say)

B'ruchah At Adonai, Eloheynu Ruach Ha-Olam, Borayt pri hagafen

Holy One of Blessing, Your Spirit fills creation, forming the fruits of the vine.

(Fill cups for those drinking water and say)

Baruch Atah Adonai, Elohaynu Ruach Ha-Olam, shehakol nihiyeh b'd'varo.

Blessed are You, Spirit of the Universe, by Whose Word everything is created.

THE CEREMONIAL PLATE:
SIXTH SYMBOL

Raisins. These dried fruits are golden, sweet, and delicious. We hope that even as we wrinkle on the outside we will remain "delicious" on the inside.

B'ruchah At Yah, Eloheynu M'kor Ha-Chayyim, borayt pri ha-aytz.

Holy One of Blessing, Your Spirit fills creation, forming the fruit of the tree.

(Eat raisins and fruit compote.)

Let us discuss our expectations, fears, and hopes for this "third act" of our lives. Let us examine how our traditions can support us as we grow older. And let us strengthen the connections with our families and friends that nurture us.

Concluding reading: "After Sixty" by Marilyn Zuckerman[9]

The sixth decade is coming to an end.
Doors have opened and shut.
The great distractions are over—
passion children the long indenture of marriage.
I fold them into a chest I will not take with me when I go.

Everyone says the world is flat and finite on the other side
    of sixty.
That I will fall clear off the edge into darkness,
that no one will hear from me again
—or want to.

But I am ready for the knife slicing into the future
for the quiet that explodes inside,
to join forces with the strong old woman,
to give everything away and begin again.

Now there is time to tell the story,
—time to invent the new one,
to chain myself to a fence outside the missile base,
to throw my body before a truck loaded with phallic
    images,
to write, "Thou Shalt Not Kill" on the hull of a Trident
    submarine,
to pour my own blood on the walls of the Pentagon,
to walk a thousand miles with a begging bowl in my hand.

There are places on this planet
where women past the menopause
put on tribal robes,
smoke pipes of wisdom
—fly.

The "formal" portion of the ceremony ends with a song and/or dance. Then, with black markers, participants write a message on the colored ribbons used during Miriam's dance. This will become a decorative wall hanging or a *tallit* when the ribbons are glued or sewed on a rectangle of cloth—a ceremonial reminder of sacred time.

Let Your Heart Take Courage: A Ceremony for Entering a Nursing Home

Cary Kozberg

Gerontologists tell us that when people approach their fourth and fifth decades, they seriously begin to take stock of their lives. Rather than measure how many years they have lived, they begin to consider how many years they have left. This midlife shift consists of reviewing one's life and responding to that review with satisfaction, regret, or a mixture of the two.

As individuals approach their seventh and eighth decades, death becomes a closer reality, and the sense of loss can become overwhelming. Besides trying to cope with the loss of one's youth and the loss of job, they may also experience an accompanying loss of role and status. As contemporaries age and die, there will be the additional losses of friends and loved ones. The elderly who suffer such a loss of health and vigor that they must move to a nursing home or skilled-care facility will also feel the loss of their home and thus the loss of their independence. With so many losses with which to cope, it is

---

Cary Kozberg is director of rabbinical and pastoral services for Wexner Heritage Village in Columbus, Ohio, where he lives with his wife, Ellen, and their four children.

little wonder that many elderly enter nursing homes with the thought that nothing is left for them to do but die.

Thus, the most critical task for the very elderly person in general, and the nursing home resident in particular, is to retain a sense of identity, a "sense of sameness"[1] in the face of physical decline and the losses accompanying advanced age. Religion's role in sustaining a person's spiritual self can be significant. Religious symbols and rituals play an important part in assuring an elderly person that life will continue to hold meaning and that there will be continuity between past and present.

"Let Your Heart Take Courage" was created to communicate in a formal, liturgical way that there is life after one moves into a nursing home and that the spiritual concerns of Jews who enter nursing homes, and those of their families, must be taken seriously. The ceremony attempts to do this by

- Recognizing the need of nursing home residents to understand themselves in the context of personal losses. The ceremony also addresses the need to cope with concomitant feelings of anger, frustration, depression, and abandonment felt by residents and their families.
- Encouraging both the resident and the family members to accept the physical and/or psychological changes that have necessitated the move into a nursing facility. It also helps to prepare them for the profound changes in lifestyle that living in the facility will bring. While the ceremony is written with the idea that the resident will participate, it can be adapted to reflect residents' cognitive limitations.
- Offering hope by reminding the resident and the family members that despite feelings of abandonment and despair, there is a Source of comfort Who is always present, and that turning to this Source can bring renewed purpose and meaning. Affixing a *mezuzah* to the doorpost of the resident's room as part of the ceremony is recommended.

"Let Your Heart Take Courage" attempts to respond to feelings of loss, anger and hopelessness with the wisdom and comfort of Jewish tradition. Its message is that despite occasional visits by the Angel of Death, nursing homes can be places where life is affirmed and its sanctity celebrated. With just a bit of creativity and sensitivity, this goal can be realized.

THE CEREMONY

Leader: We gather today to consecrate a moment of transition. In the journey of life, this transition is a significant milestone. Feelings of hope and of fear, of anticipation and of anxiety, of sorrow and perhaps of relief accompany this transition. Embarking on this new phase of the journey, we reflect on the continuance of life and its progression. We contemplate the changes and the challenges yet to be faced.

With hearts full of emotion, we turn to the words of Jewish tradition, seeking faith in the midst of uncertainty and comfort in the midst of despair.

Together:
A Song of Ascents

I turn my eyes to the mountains;
from where will my help come?
My help comes from the Eternal,
maker of heaven and earth.

God will not let your foot give way;
your Guardian will not slumber.
See, the Guardian of Israel
neither slumbers nor sleeps!
The Eternal is your Guardian,

the Eternal is your Protection
at your right hand.

By day the sun will not strike you,
nor the moon by night.
The Lord will guard you from all harm;
God will guard your life.
The Lord will guard your going and coming
now and forever.[2]

Resident (or family member):
God is my light and my help;
Whom shall I fear?
The Lord is the strength of my life;
Of whom shall I be afraid?

Though armies be arrayed against me,
My heart shall not fear;
Though war should threaten,
I remain steadfast in my faith.

Hear O God, when I call with my voice,
Be gracious to me and answer me.

It is You that I seek, says my heart.
It is Your Presence that I seek, O God.

Hide not from me.
Do not cast me off, nor forsake me
O God of my salvation.
You have always been my help,
Do not abandon me.
Though my father and my mother leave me,
God will care for me.

Teach me Your way, O God;
Guide me on the right path . . .

Mine is the faith that I shall surely see
The Lord's goodness in the land of the living.

Hope in God and be strong.
Let your heart take courage,
And hope in the Eternal.[3]

Together:

שמע ישראל יי אלוהינו יי אחד

Sh'ma Yisrael Adonai Eloheynu, Adonai Echad.
Hear O Israel, Eternal our God, Eternal is one.

ברוך שם כבוד מלכותו לעולם ועד

Baruch shem kavod malchuto l'olam va-ed.
Blessed be the Name of God's glorious kingdom forever and ever.

Leader:

ואהבת את יי אלוהיך בכל לבבך ובכל נפשך
ובכל מאודך

V'ahavta et Adonai Elohecha, b'chol l'vavcha u'vchol nafshecha u'vchol m'odecha.
You shall love your God, with all your heart, with all your soul, and with all your strength.

Resident (or family member): May I respond in love and in trust to the will of the Creator of Life, with all my heart, with all of my soul, and with all of my strength.

Leader:

והיו הדברים האלה אשר אנכי מצווך היום על
לבבך

V'hayu hadvarim ha-eleh, asher Anochi metzavcha hayom al l'vavecha.
These words which I command you this day shall be upon your heart.

Resident (or family member): When my spirit darkens, may I daily take to heart the promise of the Ancient of Days: "I am with you in your distress. I will not forsake you."

Leader:

ושננתם לבניך ודברת בם בשבתך בבתיך ובלכתך בדרך ובשכבך ובקומיך

V'shinantam l'vanecha v'debarta bam, b'shivtecha bevetecha, uv'lechtecha v'derech, uv'shachb'cha uv'kumecha.

Teach them faithfully to your children, speaking of them when in your home or on a journey, when you lie down and when you arise.

Resident (or family member): Even in physical frailty, let me retain a strength of spirit. May my life maintain its sense of purpose and may I be an exemplar of courage and hope to my family and friends.

Leader:

וקשרתם לאות על ידך והיו לטטפות בין עיניך

Ukshartam l'ot al yadecha v'hayu l'totafot bein einecha.

Bind them for a sign upon your arm, and let them be a symbol between your eyes.

Resident (or family member): May Divine caring always be evident to me. May God's mercy always be present to me. May God's strength inspire me to keep my body energized and my mind active, and may The Source of Life always watch over my spirit, even when it departs this world.

Leader:

וכתבתם על מזוזות ביתך ובשעריך

Uchtavtam al mezuzot beitecha u'visharecha.

Write them upon the doorposts of your house, and upon your gates.

Resident (or family member): May the Divine Presence, symbolized by this *mezuzah*, always be felt in this room by all who enter. May that Presence continue to sustain me, as it has sustained those who came before me and as it will sustain those who will come after me. Amen.

(If appropriate, affix the *mezuzah* to the door and say:)

בָּרוּךְ אַתָּה יי אֱלוֹהֵינוּ מֶלֶךְ הָעוֹלָם אֲשֶׁר קִדְּשָׁנוּ
בְּמִצְוֹתָיו וְצִוָּנוּ לִקְבּוֹעַ מְזוּזָה.

Baruch atah Adonai, Eloheynu Melech ha-olam, asher kid-shanu b'mitzvotav, v'tzivanu likbo-ah mezuzah.

Blessed are You, Eternal our God, Ruler of the Universe, Who has sanctified us with Your commandments, and commanded us to affix the *mezuzah*.

Resident (or family member): O God, at this juncture in my life, I look back on my years with gratitude and sorrow, basking in the memories of health and vigor, of accomplishment and fulfillment. I also recall pain and loss, failure and regret. When I review my life, may I be reconciled to the happy and the sad, and may such reconciliation help bring me healing and wholeness. Thus, may I be worthy of the most precious of Your gifts—*shalom*.

O God, in my frailty, do not forsake me. If I look upon the days to come as days without pleasure or purpose, let my heart take courage. Grant my family and me the strength to let go of what can no longer be held onto and to meet the present challenge of acclimating to my new home. When fear and frustration overwhelm us, help us to have patience with those who are dedicated to assisting me. Though my circumstances have changed, let me find continued meaning and goodness in life, so that the remainder of my days will be a true crown of glory for all to behold.

Amid uncertainty, may I turn to You in hope and trust, as it is written, "Trust in God with all thy heart. . . . In all thy ways acknowledge God, and God shall direct thy paths." Amen.

Together sing or recite:

אֵלִי אֵלִי
שֶׁלֹּא יִיגָּמֵר לְעוֹלָם
הַחוֹל וְהַיָּם
רִשְׁרוּשׁ שֶׁל הַמַּיִם
בְּרַק הַשָּׁמַיִם
תְּפִלַּת הָאָדָם

Eli, Eli
she-lo yi-ga-mair le-o-lam:
ha-chol ve-ha-yam
rish-roosh shel ha-ma-yim
be-rak ha-sha-ma-yim
te-fi-lat ha-a-dam.[4]

O Lord, my God,
I pray that these things never end:
The sand and the sea,
The rush of the waters,
The crash of the heavens,
The prayer of the heart.

Staff:
On behalf of the entire staff, we want to welcome you _____ **(name of resident)** to our _____ **(name of facility)** family. We hope that the adjustment for you and your family will be an easy one, and we promise to meet your needs and concerns to the best of our ability.

As you join our family, may you be blessed and sustained by these ancient words:

Leader:

יברכך יי וישמרך

Y'va-re-khe-kha Adonai v'yish-me-re-kha
May God bless you and protect you.

יאר יי פניו אליך ויחנך

Ya-er Adonai pa-nav ay-leh-kha v'yi-khu-neh-kha
May God's face shine upon you and be gracious to you.

יאר יי פניו אליך וישם לך שלום

Ya-ir Adonai pa-nav ay-leh-kha v'ya-saym l'kha shalom
May God's face shine upon you and grant you peace.
   Amen.

Older Adult Confirmation

Dayle A. Friedman

Many older Jews, especially older Jewish women, have never had a formal Jewish education. Confirmation for older adults provides an opportunity for Jewish study and a forum where an elderly person can affirm a commitment to the Jewish tradition and the Jewish people. An adult confirmation program was initiated at the Philadelphia Geriatric Center in 1995 and 1996, the Jewish year of 5756. Twenty nursing home residents, assisted living tenants, and community-based elders met three times a month for seven months. The participants explored Jewish ethics and values by studying classic Jewish texts and reflecting on their own life experiences as they related to particular topics. Members of the group also participated in a *mitzvah* project.

Over the course of the class, members had to deal with their own frailties and such crises as receiving a terminal diagnosis, breaking a hip, and caring for a spouse who had had a stroke. Despite these challenges, they were remarkably committed to the program.

Dayle A. Friedman, a rabbi with a master's degree in social work, is director of chaplaincy services at Philadelphia Geriatric Center. She is also an adjunct faculty member of the Reconstructionist Rabbinical College and trains students from all Jewish denominational movements in the Rabbinic Education on Aging Project's clinical internship program.

For the class's *mitzvah* project, which occurred in the aftermath of Prime Minister Yitzhak Rabin's assassination, the class chose a project that brought Jewish and Arab Israelis together: the Neighborhood Home, an after-school program for Jewish and Arab children in Jaffa, Israel. The group began to raise money to purchase computers to assist the children with their studies. Each class member made a *pushke,* a *tsedakah* box, which bore information about the project.

Class members found unique ways of raising funds for their *mitzvah* projects. One gave a benefit concert in the lobby of the geriatric center and asked listeners to drop money into her *pushke.* Some nursing home residents urged fellow residents to donate quarters won at bingo. Another participant donated winnings from her bridge club. The group raised over $600 and corresponded with the children who attended the Neighborhood House. The children were thrilled that a group of elderly Jews on the other side of the world had taken such an interest in their social and academic needs.

On the second day of Shavuot, when the Ten Commandments are read in the Torah, the confirmands, whose average age was 80, proceeded into the synagogue using walkers, wheelchairs and electric carts. Wearing white robes, they conducted the service and shared their feelings about the confirmation, and a chaplain gave each a certificate.

INSPIRATION AND SATISFACTION

These confirmands provided immense inspiration to the 250 relatives and friends—representing four generations of Jews—who gathered for the ceremony. One confirmand said in her speech, "I never had a formal Jewish education, although I was raised by wonderful Jewish parents and grew up to be a proper Jewish girl. I joined the confirmation class because I wanted to learn about Jewish religion and what it means to be a Jew. I can truly say that in our discussions, I learned that there is a God. I feel wonderful that I was able to complete this course. I'm proud of myself and my fellow confirmands." In closing, a representative of the confirmands gave the chaplain a certificate that acknowledged that the group had planted a tree in her honor.

The confirmands felt a profound sense of accomplishment and affirmation. All had achieved their goal despite impairments, serious illness and loss. They knew they were models to others for lifelong Torah learning, Jewish commitment, and continued growth and renewal.

This kind of confirmation program can be conducted in a synagogue, a senior center, an assisted living center, or a nursing home. Students may need reassurance that they are not required to have any previous Jewish study. Perhaps most importantly, students need to be acknowledged for the knowledge and perspective that they bring to the study itself.

APPENDICES

And Moses came and called for the elders of the people, and set before them all the words which God had commanded him.

—Exodus 19:7

APPENDIX I:
A Guide to Jewish Textual Sources on Aging

Jewish texts—from the Bible through later rabbinic writings—abound with references to aging. The following list, gleaned from different periods of Jewish history, reflects the breadth of Jewish thought on growing old. They can be seeds for Jewish teachings and road maps for the journey of aging.[1]

TORAH

Moses said [to Pharoah], "With our young and with our old, we will go." (Exodus 10:9)

Honor your father and your mother so that your days may be long upon the soil which God, your God, has given you. (Exodus 20:12)

Stand up before a hoary head and honor the face of one matured in wisdom, and fear your God, I am God. (Leviticus 19:32)

For keeping God's commandments, statutes and ordinances, one's days are prolonged. (Deuteronomy 6:2)

One's life will be prolonged for leaving undisturbed the nest of a bird and her young. (Deuteronomy 22:7)

Remember the days of old. Consider the years of many generations: Ask thy parents, and they will recount it to thee; thy elders and they will tell thee. (Excerpted from Moses' poem of farewell.) (Deuteronomy 32:7)

And Moses was a hundred and twenty years old when he died: His eye was not dim nor his natural force abated. (As Moses died at age 120, it is often said, "May you live to be 120. *Biz a hundret und tventsik.*) (Deuteronomy 34:7)

PROPHETS AND WRITINGS

I am this day eighty-five years old. And I am as strong this day as I was in the day that Moses sent me; as my strength was then, so is my strength now. (Joshua 14:11)

Barzillai said to the King, "How long have I to live, that I should go up with the king to Jerusalem? I am this day eighty years old: And can I discern between good and evil? Can thy servant taste what I eat or drink? Can I hear any more the voice of singing men and singing women? Why then should thy servant be a further burden to my lord the King?" (2 Samuel 19:35)

Now King David was old, advanced in years; and they covered him with clothes, but he could not become warm. (1 Kings 1:1)

Old men and old women shall again dwell in the streets of Jerusalem, and each one with staff in hand. (Zachariah 8:4)

They shall be like a tree planted by the water, bringing forth fruit in its season; its leaf will not wither. (This is a blessing of vital old age for having lived a righteous life.) (Psalm 1:3)

Cast me not off in old age; forsake me not when my strength fails me. (Psalm 71:9)

Now also when I am old and gray-headed, O God, forsake me not; until I have related thy strength to this generation, and thy power to everyone that is to come. (Psalm 71:18)

The days of our years are seventy; or if reason of special strength, eighty years. (Psalm 90:10)

They shall bear fruit even in old age; they shall be ever fresh and fragrant. (Psalm 92:15)

Forget not my Torah; but let your heart keep my commandments: For length of days and long life, and peace shall they add to you. (Proverbs 3:2)

The hoary head is a crown of glory; it is found in the way of righteousness. (Proverbs 16:31)

Children's children are the crown of the old; and the glory of children are their parents. (Proverbs 17:6)

With age comes wisdom, and length of days brings understanding. (Job 12:12)

God removes the speech of the trusty, and takes away the understanding of the aged. (Job 12:20)

Days should speak, and multitudes of years should teach wisdom. But there is a spirit within; and the breath of the Creator gives them understanding. The old are not always wise; nor do the aged understand judgment. (Job 32:7–9)

Remember now the days of thy youth, before the evil days come, and the years draw near, when thou shalt say, I have no pleasure in them. (Ecclesiastes 12:1)

APOCRYPHA

It is not length of life that makes for an honorable old age . . . but rather it is wisdom which constitutes a person's silvery brow and a spotless life the true ripeness of age.[2] (Wisdom of Solomon 4:8)

If you gather not in youth, what will you find in old age? (Ben Sira 25:3)

PIRKEI AVOT—SAYINGS OF THE FATHERS

One who learns when a child, what is he like? Like ink written on fresh paper. But one who learns when old, what is he like? Like ink written on a paper of erasures. (4:25)

He who learns from the young, what is he like? Like one who eats unripe grapes and drinks wine fresh from his winepress. But he who learns from elders, what is he like? Like one who eats ripe grapes and drinks aged wine. (4:26)

TALMUD, MIDRASH, AND RABBINIC COMMENTARIES

(Talmudic sources refer to the Babylonian Talmud unless otherwise indicated.)

When the father is aged and the son takes him to his house, the son remains seated at his normal place at the head of the table, but . . . the father is nonetheless to perform the ritual washing of the hands first, to receive the first portion of food and other designations of honor at the table. (Aruch HaShulchan Yoreh De'ah 240:11)

When asked who would be honored in the world to come, Solomon answered, those that show honor to the aged. (Baba Batra 10b)

When we were young, they told us to act like adults. Now that we are old, they treat us like babies. (Bava Kama 92b)

Be careful to respect an old man who has forgotten his knowledge through no fault of his own, for it is said, "Both the whole tablets and the fragments of the tablets were placed in the Ark." (Brachot 8b)

One must rise in the presence of the elderly, but should wait until the elder is within four cubits so that they know the honor is due to them. (Chaye Adam 69:3)

It was said of Rabbi Chanina that at the age of eighty, he could still stand on one foot and remove and replace the shoe on the other foot. Rabbi Chanina said, "The warm baths and oils with which my mother rubbed me have served me well in my old age." (Chulin 24b (1:112))

Hadrian was walking along the road near Tiberias when he happened upon an old man planting trees. Hadrian asked him, "How old are you?" And the man replied, "One hundred years old." Hadrian then remarked, "Fool, do you think you shall live to eat fruit from these trees?" And the old man replied, "If I am worthy, I shall eat; if not, as my ancestors planted for me, so I am planting for my children and grandchildren." (Ecclesiastes Rabbah 2:20)

Abraham's old age was a result of his merit, he has merited both this world and the world to come as discussed by the rabbis, "And Abraham was old, *zaken*. *Zaken* means: This man has acquired two worlds. *Zaken* refers to *zeh kanah*, meaning 'he has acquired.'" (Genesis Rabbah 59:6)

One who greets an elder is as though she has greeted the face of the *shechinah*. (Genesis Rabbah 63:6)

When someone falls into sickness or old age or troubles and cannot engage in his work, he dies of hunger. But not so with Torah: For it guards him from evil while young and in old age grants him a future and hope. (Kiddushin 4:14)

Grandparents as well as parents are obligated to teach their children. (Kiddushin 30a)

Respect even the old man who has lost his learning. (Kiddushin 32a)

The ignorant think less clearly as they age; the wise more clearly as they grow older. (Kinnen 3)

One stands in the presence of a very old person, even if that person is not a sage. (Maimonides, Mishna Torah Hilchot Talmud Torah 6:9)

In the matter of honor due to one's parents, the father is mentioned first. However in the matter of reverence, the mother is mentioned first. From this, we infer that both are to be equally honored and revered. (Maimonides, Mishna Torah Book of Judges Mamrim 6:2)

An old man who has forgotten his learning [from illness], is to be treated with the same honor as the holy ark itself. (Moed Katan 3)

Even if one's father's spittle is running down his beard [i.e. from Alzheimer's disease] his child should obey him. (Seder Eliayahu Rabbah 27)

Gauge a country's prosperity by its treatment of the aged. (Sefer HaMidot, Rebbe Nachman of Breslov)

Tears in youth impair the sight in old age. (Shabbat 151b)

Youth is a crown of roses. Old age is a crown of thorns. (Shabbat 152a)

APPENDIX II:
Selected National and International Organizations Serving Jewish Elders and Their Families

Many groups serve the particular needs of Jewish elders. They provide programs and resources to elders and their families, advocacy on behalf of elderly, and support for the emotional and physical transitions of later life. Among these are the following national or international organizations.

Association of Jewish Family and Children's Agencies
"Elder Support Network"
557 Cranbury Road, Suite 2
East Brunswick, NJ 08816
(800) 634-7346, FAX (732) 432-7127
E-mail: ajfca@aol.com
Website: www.ajfca.org
AJFCA helps family members of frail elderly relatives who live in distant cities by referring them to nearby Jewish family service agencies. These agencies can then provide the relatives with such services as home-delivered meals, home aides, electric emergency monitoring systems, and transportation.

Association of Retired Rabbis (Rabbinical Assembly)
Rabbi Seymour Essrog, President
3080 Broadway
New York, NY 10027
(212) 280-6000
Provides guidance and support for retiring and retired rabbis.

Brookdale Institute of Gerontology
POB 13087, JDC Hill
Jerusalem, Israel
011-972-2-668251
A research and policy center for issues of aging in Israel.

Elderhostel
75 Federal Street
Boston, MA 02110-1941
(617) 426-7788, Fax (617) 426-8351
Website: www.elderhostel.org
Offers educational programs of Jewish interest that are
held in facilities which follow Jewish dietary laws.

National Center on Women and Aging
Brandeis University
Waltham, MA 02454-1900
(781) 736-3866
Website: www.brandeis.edu/heller/national/ind.htm
A partnership of Brandeis University, the American Society
on Aging, the Coalition of Labor Union Women, and the
National Black Women's Health Projects. Focuses on
health, gender, income security, and needs of older
women.

Association of Jewish Aging
Suite 402, 316 Pennsylvania Avenue SE
Washington, DC 20003-1175
(202) 543-7500, Fax (202) 543-4090
E-mail: ajas@ajas.org
Brings nonprofit nursing homes and housing programs together to share information, educational programs, and
legislative concerns and represent the interests of residents
in these long-term care facilities.

Spiritual Eldering Institute
7318 Germantown Avenue
Philadelphia, PA 19119
(215) 242-4074, Fax (215) 247-9703
E-mail: alephajr@aol.com
Provides resources and offers workshops on conscious aging.

Women's Institute for Continuing Jewish Education
Dr. Irene Fine, Director
4126 Executive Drive
La Jolla, CA 92037
(619) 442-2666
Offers courses and books detailing Jewish midlife and elder issues and ceremonies.

APPENDIX III:
Publications and
Audiovisual Materials

GUIDES FOR JEWISH ELDERLY

The following guides offer information and support for Jewish families, caregivers, and elderly:

The Aging Parent: A Guide for Program Planners. New York: American Jewish Committee.

Bailet, Emily. *Caring for Older Adults: A Handbook.* New York: National Council of Jewish Women. 53 West 23rd Street, New York, NY 10010.

Balter, Shlomo. *Helping Aging to Come of Age.* New York: United Synagogue of America, 1987. 155 Fifth Avenue New York, NY 10010.

Bloom, Brad. *Passages: A Newsletter Focusing on the Relationship between Aging and Reform Judaism.* New York: Union of American Hebrew Congregations.838 Fifth Avenue, New York, NY 10021-7064.

Seicol, Sam. *The Jewish Holiday: A Guide to Caregivers.* Boston: Hebrew Rehabilitation Center for Aged. 1200 Centre Street, Roslindale, MA 02131.

AUDIOVISUAL MATERIALS
FOR JEWISH ELDERLY

Aging Parents: The Family Survival Kit. Sybervision. Includes two videos and a guidebook. (800) 456-0678.

Bashert. Waltham, MA: National Center for Jewish Film. A 14-minute film about Jewish burial and mourning practices. (617) 899-7044, Fax (617) 736-2070, Email: Ncjf@logos.cc.brandeis.edu

Jewish Memories. An audiovisual slide show and program designed to stimulate reminiscence among Jewish elderly. Produced by Susan Berrin. Available from BiFolkal Productions, 911 Williamson Street, Madison, WI 53703. (608) 251-2818.

Jack M. Saul and Pauline Spiegel. *The Challenge of Aging: Jewish Identity in Later Life.* Available from the Institute for American Pluralism, American Jewish Committee, 165 East 56th Street, New York, NY 10022-2746.

BOOKS AND PERIODICALS

This extensive list of written resources on growing older has been divided into four sections: Judaism and Aging, General Aging, Women and Aging, and Intergenerational/Grandparenting Issues.

Judaism and Aging

Bergman, Shimon. *Aged in Israel: A Selected Bibliography.* Tel Aviv: Israel Gerontological Society.

Bienstock, B.G. "The Changing Image of the American Jewish Mother." In *Changing Images of the Family,* edited by V. Tufte and B. Myerhoff. New Haven: Yale University Press, 1979.

Blidstein, G. *Honor They Father and Mother: Filial Responsibility in Jewish Law.* New York: KTAV, 1975.

Borowitz, Eugene, and Kerry Olitzky. "A Jewish Perspective." In *Aging, Spirituality and Religion: A Handbook,* edited by Melvin Kimble. Minneapolis: Fortress Press, 1995.

Dorff, Elliot. "Honoring Aged Fathers and Mothers." *The Reconstructionist* (1987).

Dulin, Rachel. "The Elderly in Biblical Society." *Journal of Aging and Judaism* 1, no. 1 (1986): 49–56.

Dulin, Rachel. "He Will Renew Your Life and Sustain Your Old Age (Ruth 4:15)." *Journal of Psychology and Judaism* 20, no. 1 (1996): 99–102.

Fine, Irene. *Midlife: A Rite of Passage & The Wise Woman: A Celebration.* San Diego: Women's Institute for Continuing Jewish Education, 1988.

Guttman, David *Jewish Elderly in the English-Speaking Countries.* Westport, CT: Greenwood Press, 1988.

Harel, Zev, David Biegel, and David Guttmann, eds. *Jewish Aged in the United States and Israel: Diversity, Programs and Services.* New York: Springer Publishing, 1994.

Heschel, Abraham Joshua. "To Grow in Wisdom." In *The Insecurity of Freedom.* New York: Schocken Books, 1972.

Isenberg, Sheldon. "Aging in Judaism: Crown of Glory and Days of Sorrow." In *The Handbook of the Humanities and Aging,* edited by Thomas Cole, David Van Tassel, and Robert Kastenbaum. New York: Springer Publishing, 1992.

Kugelmass, Jack. *Miracle of Intervale Avenue.* New York: Schocken Books, 1986.

Myerhoff, Barbara. *Number Our Days.* New York: E.P. Dutton, 1978.

Myerhoff, Barbara. *Remembered Lives: The Work of Ritual, Storytelling and Growing Older,* edited by Marc Kaminsky. Ann Arbor, MI: University of Michigan Press, 1992.

Olitzky, Kerry. *Come Grow Old With Me: Aging in Judaism Is a Lifelong Process.* New York: Union of American Hebrew Congregations Press, 1983.

Olson, Tillie. *Tell Me a Riddle.* New York: Dell Publishers, 1961.

Rausch, Eduardo. *The Melton Journal, "The Art of Growing Older: Daring to Adventure Life."* New York: The Melton Center, 1994.

Reimer, Jack, and Nathaniel Stampfer, eds. *So That Your Values Live On: Ethical Wills and How to Prepare Them.* Woodstock, VT: Jewish Lights Publishing, 1991.

Schachter-Shalomi, Zalman and Ron Miller. *From Age-ing to Sage-ing: A Profound New Vision of Growing Older.* New York: Warner Books, 1995.

Schram, Peninnah. "Storytelling: A Practical Approach to Life Review." *Journal of Aging and Judaism* 2, no. 3 (1988): 187–190.

Teubal, Savina. "Simchat Hochmah." In *Four Centuries of Jewish Women's Spirituality,* edited by Ellen Umansky and Diane Ashton, 257–265. Boston: Beacon Press, 1992.

General Aging
Ardelt, Monika. "Wisdom and Life Satisfaction in Old Age." In *Journal of Gerontology* 52, no. 1 (1997): 15–27.

Booth, Wayne. *The Art of Growing Older: Writers on Living and Aging.* Chicago: University of Chicago Press, 1992.

Chinen, Allan. *In the Ever After: Fairy Tales in the Second Half of Life.* Wilmette, IL: Chiron Publishers, 1992.

Cole, Thomas, ed. *The Oxford Book of Aging.* New York: Oxford University Press, 1994.

Cole, Thomas R. *The Journey of Life: A Cultural History of Aging in America.* New York: Cambridge University Press, 1992.

Edinberg, Mark. *Talking with Your Aged Parents.* Boston: Shambhala Publications, 1996.

Erikson, Erik H., Joan M. Erikson, and Helen Q. Kivnick. *Vital Involvement in Old Age: The Experience of Old Age in Our Time.* New York: W.W. Norton, 1986.

Friedan, Betty. *The Fountain of Age.* New York: Simon and Schuster, 1993.

Goldman, Connie, and Phillip L. Berman. *The Ageless Spirit.* New York: Ballantine Books, 1992.

Hollis, James. *The Middle Passage: From Misery to Meaning in Midlife.* Toronto: Inner City Books, 1993.

Lyons, Maxine. *Elder Voices: Insights and Reflections.* Cambridge, Massachusetts: Eldercorps, 1996.

Martz, Sandra Haldeman, ed. *Grow old along with me! the best is yet to be.* Watsonville, CA: Papier-Mache Press, 1996.

Martz, Sandra Haldeman, ed. *When I Am Old I Shall Wear Purple.* Watsonville, CA: Papier-Mache Press, 1987.

Maxwell, Florida Scott. *The Measure of My Days.* New York: Alfred Knopf, 1968.

Sheehy, Gail. *New Passages.* New York: Random House, 1995.

Smith, Page. *Old Age Is Another Country: A Traveler's Guide.* Freedom, CA: The Crossing Press, 1995.

Terkel, Studs. *Coming of Age.* New York: New Press, 1995.

Thomas, William H. *Eden Alternative: Nature, Hope and Nursing Homes.* Sherbourne, NY: Eden Alternative Foundation.

Women and Aging
Brady, Maureen. *Midlife: Meditations for Women.* New York: Harper San Francisco, 1995.

Copper, Baba. "Voices: On Becoming Old Women." CALYX: *A Journal of Art and Literature by Women* 9, nos. 2 & 3 (1986): 47–57.

de Beauvoir, Simone. *A Very Easy Death.* New York: Warner Books, 1964.

Greer, Germaine. *The Change.* New York: Alfred A. Knopf, 1992.

Lifshitz, Leatrice, ed. *Only Morning in Her Shoes: Poems about Old Women.* Logan, Utah: Utah University Press, 1990.

Orenstein, Debra, ed. *Lifecycles, V. 1: Jewish Women on Life Passages and Personal Milestones.* Woodstock, VT: Jewish Lights Publishing, 1994.

Painter, Charlotte. *Gifts of Age.* San Francisco: Chronicle Books, 1988.

Safran, Rose. *Don't Go Dancing Mother.* Manchester, MA: Tide Books, 1979.

Steinem, Gloria. *Revolution from Within.* Boston: Little Brown and Co., 1992.

Thone, Ruth Raymond. *Women and Aging: Celebrating Ourselves.* Binghamton, NY: Harrington Park Press, 1992.

Zuckerman, Marilyn. *Poems of the Sixth Decade.* Cambridge, MA: Garden Street Press, 1993.

Grandparenting and Intergenerational Issues

Drucker, Malka. *Grandma's Latkes.* San Diego: Harcourt Brace, 1992.

Ganz, Yaffe. *Me and My Bubby, My Zaidy and Me.* New York: Feldheim, 1990.

Gilman, Phoebe. *Something from Nothing.* Richmond Hill, Ontario: Northwinds Press, 1992.

Horowitz, Joy. *Tessie and Pearlie.* New York: Scribner, 1996.

Kaye, L. W. "Educating Our Children about Growing Older: A Challenge to Jewish Education." *Journal of Aging and Judaism* 1, no. 1 (1986): 6–21.

Masur, Jenny, and Sydelle Kramer, eds. *Jewish Grandmothers.* Boston: Beacon Press, 1976.

Oberman, Sheldon. *The Always Prayer Shawl.* Honesdale, PA: Boyds Mills Press, 1994.

Olitzky, Kerry. *The Safe Deposit and Other Stories About Grandparents, Old Lovers and Crazy Old Men.* New York: Markus Wiener, 1989.

Ross, Lillian Hammer. *Buba Leah and the Paper Children.* Philadelphia: Jewish Publication Society, 1991.

Sendak, Philip. *In Grandpa's House.* New York: Harper and Row, 1985.

Wasserman, Selma. *The Long Distance Grandparent: How to Stay Close to Distant Grandchildren.* Vancouver, BC: Hartley and Marks, 1988.

APPENDIX IV: Glossary

Amidah (Hebrew): the standing prayer recited thrice daily

Alta kacker (Yiddish): an old, decrepit person

Av (Hebrew): father

Bima (Hebrew): the raised platform in a synagogue from which the Torah is read

Biz a hundret und tventsik (Yiddish): may you live to be 120 (a common expresion of birthday greeting, based on Moses' life of 120 years)

Bracha (Hebrew): blessing

Bubbe (Yiddish): grandmother

Chevrah Kadisha (Hebrew): holy burial society

Eitza (Hebrew): counsel/document

Em (Hebrew): mother

Gamatria (Hebrew): numerology based on Hebrew letters

Gan Eyden (Hebrew): Garden of Eden

Gemara (Hebrew): second part of the Talmud, the completion to the *Mishna*

Havdalah (Hebrew): separation (generally refers to ceremony marking the close of Shabbat or other holy days)

Hidur p'nai zaken (Hebrew): the beauty and glory of an elder's face

Kabbalah (Hebrew): Jewish mysticism

Kaddish (Hebrew): mourner's prayer

Kedusha (Hebrew): holiness, the public portion of the *amidah* prayer

Kheyrem (Hebrew): excommunication

Lehavdl (Hebrew/Yiddish): to differentiate

Maftir (Hebrew): the Prophetic portion read after the Torah reading

Masechet(ot) (Hebrew): tractate

Mazel tov (Hebrew/Yiddish): congratulations

Mentsh (Yiddish): a good person

Midrash (Hebrew): illuminating story on a text

Mincha (Hebrew): afternoon prayers

Mishna (Hebrew): the collection of Oral Laws forming the basis of the Talmud

Mitzvah (Hebrew): a good deed/commandment

Naches (Yiddish): pleasure

Naches fun der kinder (Yiddish): pleasure from the children

Niggun (Hebrew): wordless melody

Pardes (Hebrew): paradise

Pedut (Hebrew): redemption

Pirkei Avot (Hebrew): Sayings of the Fathers

Rav (Hebrew): rabbi/teacher

Rebbe (Yiddish): rabbi

Rebbitzin (Yiddish): wife of the rabbi

R'fua shleima (Hebrew): full recovery

Sayvah (Hebrew): old age, referring to the whiteness of the beard

Shechinah (Hebrew): the feminine attributes of the Divine

Sheliach tzibbur (Hebrew): the leader of Jewish communal prayer

Shivah (Hebrew): seven-day period of mourning

Shtetl (Yiddish): a small village in Eastern Europe

Shul (Yiddish): synagogue

Shvitz (Yiddish): sweat bath

Siddur (Hebrew): prayer book

Simchah (Hebrew): celebration

Simchat Chochma (Hebrew): celebration of wisdom

Tallis(it) (Yiddish/Hebrew): prayer shawl

Talmud (Hebrew): the Mishna and Gemara

Tefilah(ot) (Hebrew): prayer(s)

Tefilin (Hebrew): phylacteries

Tikkun olam (Hebrew): repair of the world

Tish mit mentshn (Yiddish): a table with people

Tsaddikim (Hebrew): spiritual masters

Tsedakah (Hebrew): acts of righteous, charity

Tshuvah (Hebrew): the inward "turning," which infers repentance

Tsitsit (Hebrew): the corner fringes on a prayer shawl

Tsuris (Yiddish): problems, worries
Yahrzeit (Yiddish): anniversary of a death
Yeshivah (Hebrew): institute of Jewish learning
Yizkor (Hebrew): memorial service
Zaken (Hebrew): an old person, also a beard
Zayde (Yiddish): grandfather
Zikna (Hebrew): old age

PERMISSIONS

I gratefully acknowledge permission to use the following materials.

"A Table with People: Storytelling as Life Review and Cultural History" by Marc Kaminsky is excerpted from a chapter by the same title in the *YIVO Annual,* Vol. 21. Reprinted with permission of the author.

"After Sixty" by Marilyn Zuckerman is reprinted from *Poems of the Sixth Decade* (Cambridge, MA: Garden City Press, 1993). Reprinted with permission of the author.

"Alternate Paths to Integrity" by Joel Rosenberg is reprinted from the *Melton Journal,* Fall, 1994. Reprinted with permission of the author.

"An End to the Body's Silence" by Phyllis Ocean Berman is adapted from "ReCreating Menopause" in *Moment Magazine,* February, 1994. Reprinted with permission of the author and publisher.

"Bathsheba Watches Abishag" is reprinted from *Ladies of Genesis* (New York: Jewish Women's Resource Center, 1991). © Barbara D. Holender. Reprinted with permission of the author.

"Dinah Goldberg, of Blessed Memory" by Linda Feinberg is reprinted from *Red Poppies and Green Clover.* Reprinted with permission of the author.

"Do Not Cast Us Away in Our Old Age" by Eliezer Diamond is reprinted from *The Melton Journal,* Fall, 1994. Reprinted with permission of the author.

"Erasures" by Ruth Daigon is reprinted from *Sarah's Daughters Sing* (New York: KTAV, 1990). Reprinted with permission of the author and publisher.

"40" by MarthaJoy Aft is reprinted from *The Journal of Reform Judaism* (Fall 1984). Reprinted with permission.

"God Is a Woman and She Is Growing Older" by Margaret Moers Wenig is adapted from a piece by the same title from *Best Sermons 5* edited by James W. Cox and Kenneth M. Cox (San Francisco: HarperCollins, 1992). Reprinted with permission of the author and publisher.

"Havdallah: A Time to Acknowledge Growing Old" by Marcia Cohn Spiegel is adapted from an earlier version which appeared in *Lilith Magazine.* Reprinted with permission of the author.

NOTES

INTRODUCTION

1. Monika Ardelt, "Wisdom & Life Satisfaction in Old Age," *Journal of Gerontology* 52:1 (1997): 16. Ardelt explains successful aging—that is, a high degree of satisfaction during one's elder years—as a result of an individual's objective conditions as well as accumulated wisdom.
2. Allan B. Chinin, *In the Ever After* (Wilmette, IL: Chiron Publications, 1992), 42.
3. This *midrash,* based on Deuteronomy 10:2, suggests that the first set of broken tablets were placed in the Ark alongside the whole tablets. Also see Rashi's commentary on BT Brachot 8b and Sanhedrin 96a.
4. Numbers 11:14–17.
5. TB Kiddushin 32b.
6. Translation from Samson Raphael Hirsch, *The Pentateuch* (New York: Judaica Press, 1986).
7. Rebbe Nachman of Breslov, *Likutei Moharan,* Section 2: daled'chet as well as *Likutei Moharan,* Section 1: samech'bet discusses the process of aging as a time of adding holiness and knowledge. It is taught that all the time that they are aging, their knowledge rests upon them (like a crown). The essence of aging is to add holiness and knowledge each day. One needs the sense of awe (*yirah*) to lengthen and magnify one's days. I would like to thank Rabbi Victor Reinstein for sharing with me his understanding of these passages.
8. Isaiah 46:3.
9. Florida Scott-Maxwell, *The Measure of My Days* (New York: Alfred Knopf, 1968), 13–14. Remaining connected to the world by investing in the future of society is a theme found in the Talmudic tale, "Honi the Circle Maker," where 70-year-old Honi explains that although he will not see the fruit of his labor, his children and grandchildren will. On this subject, General Douglas MacArthur said, "People grow old only by deserting their ideals. Years may wrinkle the skin, but to give up interest wrinkles the soul" (*New York Times,* 1984); and poet Adrienne Rich wrote, "The problem is to connect, without hysteria, the pain of one's body with the pain of the body's world." From the poem "18" in Adrienne Rich, *Your Native Land, Your Life* (New York: W.W. Norton, 1986).
10. Ingmar Bergman said, "Old age is like climbing a mountain. You climb from ledge to ledge. The higher you get, the more tired and breathless you become. But your view becomes more extensive."
11. Jane M. Thibault, "Aging as a Natural Monastery" in *Aging and Spirituality* 8:3 Fall, 1996, 8. Thibault, a clinical gerontologist, also discusses the work

of the late theologian Karl Rahner, who pioneered the concept of "every-day mysticism," in which the elderly are present in the experience of the immediate moment.

12. For a historical account of the place of the elderly, intergenerationally, in American society, see Tamara Hareven, "Historical Adulthood and Old Age" in Erik Erikson, ed. *Adulthood* (New York: W.W. Norton, 1978).
13. Rachel Dulin, "He Will Renew Your Life and Sustain Your Old Age (Ruth 4:15)," *Journal of Psychology and Judaism* 20:1 (Spring 1996): 99.
14. God instructs Avram and Sarai (who have not yet become Abraham and Sarah) in the Torah portion *Lech Lecha*, to set forth on a journey to an un-known land. This journey is often cast metaphorically as the journey into the unknown.
15. Compare *Pirkei Avot* with Confucius' life-stages:
    "At fifteen I set my heart upon learning.
    At thirty I established myself [in accordance with ritual].
    At forty I no longer had perplexities.
    At fifty I knew the Mandate of Heaven.
    At sixty I was at ease with whatever I heard.
    At seventy I could follow my heart's desire without transgressing the boundaries of right." Analects 2:4.
16. Data from the North American Jewish Data Bank based on the 1990 Jewish Population Study.
17. See Allen Glicksman and Tanya Koropeckyj-Cox, "Jewish Aged in the United States: Sociodemographic and Socioeconomic Characteristics" in *Jewish Aged in the United States and Israel* (New York: Springer Publishing, 1994).
18. "Images of Aging in America," Study report by Association of American Retired Persons (1995): 24.
19. Exodus 10:9.

TEXT STUDIES

Crown Me with Wrinkles and Gray Hair: Examining Traditional Jewish Views of Aging
1. Midrash Rabbah—Genesis 65:9.
2. Shabbat 152a.
3. Tanhuma Miketz 10.
4. Genesis 27:1.
5. 1 Kings 1:1.
6. 2 Samuel 19:35.
7. Shabbat 152a.
8. Shabbat 152a.
9. Leviticus Rabbah 8:1.
10. Shabbat 89b.

11. *Midrash Petirat Moshe,* Adolph Jellineck, ed. (Bet HaMidrash, Jerusalem: Wahrmann Books, 1967): 127.
12. Ta'anit 23a.
13. Exodus 20:12.
14. Deuteronomy 22:7.
15. Deuteronomy 25:15.
16. Deuteronomy 6:2.
17. Berakhot 8a.
18. Megillah 27b.
19. Ta'anit 20b.
20. Leviticus 19:32.
21. Generally sixty or seventy, according to Hayye Adam 69:2.
22. Tosefta Megillah 3[4].
23. Kiddushin 33a.
24. Berakhot 8b.
25. Hayye Adam 69:3.
26. Deuteronomy 32:7.
27. Job 12:12.
28. Exodus Rabbah 3:8.
29. Megillah 31b.
30. Berakhot 39a.
31. Yevamot 62b.
32. Kiddushin 82a.
33. Ecclesiastes 7:8.
34. Ruth Rabbah 7:6.
35. Kiddushin 30a.
36. Ruth 4:14.
37. Ecclesiastes Rabbah 2:20, 1-21.
38. Ta'anit 23a.
39. Abraham Joshua Heschel, "To Grow In Wisdom," in *The Insecurity of Freedom* (Philadelphia: Jewish Publication Society, 1966), 78.
40. Deuteronomy 30:11–14.
41. Orach Chaim 94:6; Mishnah Berurah 100:20.
42. Shulhan Arukh Orach Chaim 94:6 and gloss.
43. Ibid, 100a; Tur, Orach Chaim 110a.
44. Mishnah Berurah Orach Chaim 100:21.
45. Psalm 92.

"Do Not Cast Us Away in Our Old Age": Adult Children and Their Aging Parents

1. In the woman's case, there is a view specifically favoring a wife's obligations to her husband above those to her parents: "Both men and women [are obligated to honor their parents]; however, a man is capable of doing so while a [married] woman is not because others [i.e., her husband] have authority over her" (Tosefta Kiddushin 1:11 and parallels). Both the Bavli (Kiddushin 30a) and later codes (e.g. Shulhan Arukh

Yoreh De'ah 240:17) take this as a prescriptive distinction rather than a descriptive one.

2. BT Sotah 49a. See also G. Blidstein, *Honor Thy Father and Mother: Filial Responsibility in Jewish Law and Ethics* (Ktav: New York, 1975), 27–29, who points out that the rabbis considered it unnatural for a parent to neglect a child but made no similar judgment concerning neglectful children.

3. Genesis 2:24. See Blidstein, 95–97, for a representative selection of the rabbinic exegeses of this verse.

4. Maimonides' Laws of Marriage 13:14. Ra'avad and Magid Mishneh ad. loc. qualify a wife's rights to bar her in-laws from the home because she, unlike the husband, does not have proprietary rights. Maggid Mishneh's qualification is codified by Rabbi Moses Isserles in Shulhan Aruch Even Ha-Ezer 74:10.

5. See the sources cited in Blidstein, 100–108.

6. Maimonides, ibid.

7. Mishnah Ketubot 7:4.

8. See Maimonides' Laws of Gifts to the Poor 10:16: "If one sustains one's father or mother it is to be considered *tsedakah*. Moreover, it is an outstanding form of *tsedakah*, because whoever is more closely related has priority." See also Tanna de-be Eliahu Rabbah, beginning of Chapter 27.

9. Shulhan Aruch Yoreh De'ah 249:1.

10. Rabbi Moses Isserles' gloss to Shulhan Arukh Yoreh De'ah 240:5. Note that funds intended for distribution to the needy are designated for one's parents only as a last resort. As Rabbi Moses Isserles states, paraphrasing BT Kiddushin 32a, "May a curse descend upon someone [who has other funds and yet] sustains his father from *tsedakah* funds." Presumably, this is because he is diverting funding from others who are needy and because he disrespects his parent by treating him like a stranger.

11. Ketubot 49b. This ordinance was not accepted, however, as being normative. See Ra'aviah.

12. The obligations to feed, clothe, and transport one's parents are found in BT Kiddushin 31b and parallels. Tosefta Kiddushin 1:11 mentions bathing. See also the list in *Pesiqta Rabbati* 23–24 (Pesikta Rabbati, trans. W.G. Braude, vol. I [New Haven: Yale University Press, 1968], 496) and the comment of S. Lieberman, *Tosefta Ki-Feshutah,* vol. 8 (New York: Jewish Theological Seminary of America, 1973), 924, about the relationship between it and Mishnah Sanhedrin 6:6.

13. See Blidstein's cautious formulation in ibid., 64.

14. Cited in the responsa appended to Maimonides' Book of Judges, No. 15.

15. Aruch Ha-Shulhan, Yoreh De'ah, 240:21.

16. Kiddushin 32a.

17. Compare the story of Damah b. Netina (BT Kiddushin 31a and parallels). Note that, in line with this linkage, R. Joseph Karo (Erez Israel, 16th c.) rules, in Shulhan Arukh Yoreh De'ah 240:5, that although a child is not obligated to go begging door to door to raise funds for one's parents one must provide vital service even if it means that one will have to neglect one's work and eventually go begging for oneself.

18. JT Kiddushin 1:7, 61b, and parallels.
19. JT Kiddushin, loc. cit.
20. R. Yehiel Michel Epstein, Arukh Ha-Shulhan, Yoreh De'ah 240:11.
21. Seder Eliyahu Rabbah, Chapter 27 (*Tanna debe Eliyahu*, trans. W.G. Braude and I.J. Kapstein [Jewish Publication Society: Philadelphia, 1981], 337).
22. Compare I Samuel 21:14, where David feigns madness, in part by allowing spittle to run down his beard.
23. Compare also Devarim Rabbah's version of the tale of Dama b. Netina submitting to his mother striking him in public (Devarim Rabbah 1:15; *Deuteronomy Rabbah*, trans. J. Rabinowitz [London: Soncino Press, 1961], 16) in which his mother is characterized as being mentally disturbed.
24. JT Berakhot 2:8.
25. BT Kiddushin 31b. It is this latter narrative that is generally cited as the source for Maimonides' ruling.
26. Laws of Rebels 6:10.
27. Blidstein, 207 n. 157, points out that RaBad is similarly protective of a wife who is ill.
28. See Blidstein, 118, who points out that a number of Maimonidean commentators (see the sources cited in idem., 207 n. 160, and add R. Meir Epstein, Arukh Ha-Shulhan, Yoreh De'ah 240:32) claim that the basis for Maimonides' ruling is an assumption on his part that a mentally ill parent can be treated more effectively by non-relatives.
29. See Shulhan Aruch Yoreh De'ah 240:10.
30. See, for example the novellae of Nachmanides (Spain, thirteenth century) to BT Yevamot 6a, s.v. *ma:* "Honoring a parent includes only the items mentioned in the list in Tractate Kiddushin [feeding, clothing etc.] and anything else which produces benefit for the parent. A parent asking a child to act in a way which does not benefit the parent is not, however, the honor of which the Torah spoke."
31. *She'iltot deRabi Ahai Gaon*, ed. Rabbi Naftali Berlin, no. 60.
32. See the end of n. 14 in Rabbi Berlin's commentary *He'emeq She'elah*.
33. See the balanced discussion in G.J. Lavit, "Truth Telling to Patients with a Terminal Diagnosis" *Journal of Halacha and Contemporary Society* (Spring 1988), 94–124.
34. See, for example, Mishnah Kiddushin 4:12: "A man may remain alone with his mother or with his daughter, and he may sleep with them with bodies touching. If they have become of age, however, she must sleep in her clothes and he in his."
35. See, for example, Mishnah Makkot 2:2: Abba Shaul says: "As the chopping of wood [the case used to formulate the law of unwitting murder in Deuteronomy 19:5] is an act of free choice [the law of unwitting murder applies] to every free choice; *this excludes the father that smites his son* [emphasis added], or the teacher that chastises his pupil, or the agent of the court [i.e., in these three cases the law of the unwitting murderer is not applied]."

36. The question as to which parents fall under this rubric is complex; see the views cited in Blidstein, 212 n. 55.

37. Mishnah Yevamot 2:5.

38. BT Yevamot 22b.

39. BT Yevamot, loc. cit.

40. BT Bava Kamma 94b.

41. The discussion is further complicated by a passage in BT Sanhedrin 85a-b, which seems to contradict the aforementioned passage in Yevamot by apparently forbidding a child to strike his or her sinful parent.

42. See Sanhedrin 47a s.v. *al*, Tosafot Yevamot 22b s.v. *ke-she-'asah*, and Mordechai Yevamot Ch. 1 no. 13., and Blidstein, 211 n. 46 and 21 n. 47.

43. See Hilkhot Rif to Yevamot 22b and Maimonides, Laws of Rebels 5:12.

44. Laws of Rebels 6:11. It is interesting that this ruling appears immediately after Maimonides' discussion of the mentally ill parent (mentioned above). Perhaps Maimonides regarded these as two instances of illness—one emotional and one spiritual—and was emphasizing the continuing obligation of the child in both cases.

45. See, for example, n. 20 of Rabbi Shabbetai Cohen (known as ShaKh; Poland, seventeenth century) to Shulhan Aruch Yoreh De'ah 240:18.

46. Exodus Rabbah 34 (*Exodus Rabbah,* trans. M. Lehrman [London: Soncino Press, 1961], 428).

Passages: The Commentary of Moshe ibn Yehuda HaMachiri on Pirkei Avot

1. The person, the place, and indeed the place name suggest an ancient and unique understanding of the passage in *Avot* on the human life span. The name Ein Zeitim means "the spring of the olives" and resonates with powerful kabbalistic imagery. The wells and springs of life-giving water often symbolize the nourishment provided by Torah; the olive, composed of the letters *zayin, yud* and *taf,* is often depicted as the smallest discernible unit of God's manifestation in the world. The village existed as a Jewish, Arabic-speaking community into the nineteenth century, when a series of earthquakes brought the period of Jewish settlement in Ein Zeitim to a close.

2. In his book *The Middle Passage,* James Hollis, a Jungian analyst and scholar, similarly points out the differences between two Greek words for time. Hollis refers to *chronos* as linear, sequential time and *kairos* as the aspect of time that connects us to our deepest and most existential meanings.

3. Hollis, James. *The Middle Passage: From Misery to Meaning in Midlife* (Toronto: Inner city Books, 1993), 17.

4. My parents, Elazar and Shoshana Goelman, have been my teachers and teachers to countless other students throughout their lifetime. To my parents I owe my love of the Hebrew language, stories, and song. My parents had already lived a full and generous life when, in their sixties, they made *aliyah* to Israel to begin another adventure in teaching, learn-

ing, serving, and living with the Jewish people. I dedicate this chapter to them for their love, patience, dedication, and—more than anything—for being my parents.

Alternative Paths to Integrity: On Old Age in the Hebrew Bible

1. The archaic Sumerian king list describes a similar shortening of the life span, but there the lives were measured not in hundreds of years but in tens of thousands!
2. Psalm 90:10.
3. 1 Kings 1:1–4.
4. Genesis 47:7–10.
5. Erik H. Erikson, *Childhood and Society* (New York: Norton, 1963), 168.
6. Genesis 46:30.
7. Genesis 48:7.
8. Genesis 49:27.
9. Deuteronomy 34:7.

MIDLIFE PASSAGES

"You Never Knew What Powers Lay Within You"

1. Thanks to Marc Kaminsky for sharing his deep knowledge of *Yiddishkeit* with me and for offering several ideas about Bontshe Shvayg that have been developed in this essay.

Redigging the Wells of Spirituality—Again

1. Genesis 26:18.

INTERGENERATIONAL RELATIONSHIPS

1. Thomas Cole points to the intricacies of intergenerational issues in *The Oxford Book of Aging* (New York: Oxford University Press, 1994). Describing the aging individual as a link in the chain of ancestors and descendants, Cole acknowledges the varied tensions and constructs that draw an individual into the dynamics of an intergenerational family. Intergenerational issues abound today and include relatively new concerns based on longer life spans, such as prioritizing community resources and elder parents outliving their children/caretakers.

A Table with People: Storytelling As Life Review and Cultural History

1. Robert Butler, "The Life Review: An Interpretation of Reminiscence in the Aged," *Psychiatry* 26 (1963): 65–76. See Marc Kaminsky, "The Uses of Reminiscence," in *The Uses of Reminiscence,* ed. Kaminsky (New York: Haworth Press, 1984), 137–56; also Harry Moody, "A Bibliography on Reminiscence and Life Review," ibid., 231–236.
2. Barbara Myerhoff, *Number Our Days* (New York: Simon & Schuster, 1980), 1–78.
3. See Saul Goodman, ed. *Our First Fifty Years: The Sholem Aleichem Folk Institute* (New York: Sholem Aleichem Folk Institute, 1972).
4. V.N. Volosinov, "Discourse in Life and Discourse in Art (Concerning Sociological Poetics)," in his *Freudianism: A Critical Sketch,* trans. I.R. Titunik, and edited in collaboration with Neal H. Bruss (1927: Bloomington: Indiana University Press, 1976), 93–116.
5. This essay consists of selected excerpts from a work in progress titled "A Table with People: Storytelling, Life Review, Cultural History." The book will be part of a multivolume series on "The Culture of Aging and Yiddishkeit," produced under the auspices of the Myerhoff Center at YIVO.

A Letter to My Children

1. Abraham Joshua Heschel, *The Insecurity of Freedom* (New York: Schocken Books, 1972), 75.
2. Psalm 90:12.

WOMEN AND AGING

1. It is interesting to note that in the Bible, the physical appearance of old age seems to begin with Avraham. *Midrash* teaches that God had made Yitzhak look identical to Avraham in order to prove that Avraham was Yitzhak's father. Later, in order to distinguish Avraham from Yitzhak, Avraham is given the appearance of old age. (*Torah Temima* on the verse in Genesis 24:1, *Avraham Zaken Ba Bayamim.*) It is said that old age had been described prior to Avraham, but in this verse, the double expression of aging "Avraham, old, came to his days," acknowledged that he was both old in years and old in appearance. It is taught that some people are old in appearance but not in age, and others are old in age but not in appearance.
2. Barbara Myerhoff, "Bobbes and Zeydes: Old and New Roles for Elderly Jews" in *Remembered Lives,* edited by Marc Kaminsky (Ann Arbor: University of Michigan Press, 1991), 191.

Behind the Rhetoric Of "My Yiddishe Mama": The Status of Older Jewish Women

1. Thomas R. Cole, *The Journey of Life: A Cultural History of Aging in America* (New York: Cambridge University Press, 1992), 24.
2. N.R. Gibbs, "Grays on the Go," *Time*, 131:8, 65–75.
3. H. Farlie, "Talkin' Bout My Generation," *The New Republic*, March 28, 1988, 19–22.
4. Statistics Canada, 1993.
5. Calculated from data in C. Taeuber, *Statistical Handbook on Women in America* (Phoenix, AZ: The Oryx Press,1991), 156.
6. E.R. Rosenthal, "Women and Varieties of Ageism," in *Women, Aging and Ageism*, (Binghamton, NY: The Haworth Press, 1990), 1.
7. See Betty Friedan, *The Fountain of Age* (New York: Simon and Schuster, 1993) and Germaine Greer, *The Change* (New York: Alfred Knopf, 1992).
8. Friedan, 69.
9. See Friedan, 571–612, Greer, *The Change* (New York: Alfred Knopf, 1992), 9; and Gloria Steinem, *Revolution from Within* (Boston: Little Brown and Company, 1992) 248 for accounts of "aging as adventure."
10. See Friedan, 37.
11. Sheva Medjuck, "If I Cannot Dance To It, It's Not My Revolution: Jewish Women and Feminism in Canada," in *Jews In Canada*, ed. Robert J. Brym et al. (Toronto: Oxford University Press, 1993).
12. Susannah Heschel, *On Being a Jewish Feminist* (New York: Schocken Books, 1983), 5.
13. Sheva Medjuck, "From Jewish Mother to Jewish American Princess: Is This How Far We've Come?" *Atlantis* 14:1, 91.
14. Medjuck, 1988, 91.
15. S. Kramer and J. Masur, *Jewish Grandmothers* (Boston: Beacon Press, 1976), xv.
16. Medjuck, 1988, 96.
17. See Statistics Canada 1994 as well as Taeuber, 253.
18. Sheva Medjuck, "A Survey of Jewish Seniors of Atlantic Canada" (1994, unpublished).

God Is a Woman and She Is Growing Older

1. *Anim Zmirot*, a *piyyut* included in the *musaf*, the additional service on Shabbat, describes God as a young man, a warrior, and an old man. I thank Rabbi Sharon Kleinbaum for calling this *piyyut* to my attention.
2. "*Sefer hazichronot*" from the *Unetane Tokef* prayer in the reader's repetition of the *musaf amida*, Rosh Hashanah and Yom Kippur. Also see Psalms 139:16 and 56:9.
3. "*Vechotam yad kol adam bo.*" "Thou openest the book of records and it reads itself; every man's signiture is contained in it." From Philip Birnbaum's translation of *Unetane tokef* in *High Holiday Prayerbook* (New York: Hebrew Publishing Co., 1951), 362.

4. Based on the *Unatane Tokef*, "who by fire and who by water; who by sword, who by beast; who by earthquake, who by plague . . . ".

5. According to *midrash*, the *Shechinah*, which is the feminine attribute of the Divine, sits at the bedside of an ill person.

6. S.Y. Agnon in *Days of Awe* cites Mateh Efrayim on the use of candles on Yom Kippur:

> There are two kinds of candles, "candles of health" and "candles of the soul." "Candles of health" are for those who are alive. The "candles of the soul" are for dead relatives. They must be made to burn until the close of Yom Kippur. (New York: Schocken Books, 1948), 143.

7. Some Jewish sources refer to Yom Kippur as a day without any night.

8. From the *zichronot* section of the Rosh Hashanah *musaf amidah*: "Is not Ephraim my dearest child, my playful one? I often speak of him. I remember—yes, I remember him. My heart longs for him. My womb aches (*rechem arachamenu*) for him." Jeremiah 31:19.

9. Repeatedly, the High Holiday liturgy emphasizes our mortality in contrast to God's immortality, as in *Unetane tokef*: "Man comes from dust and ends in dust. . . . But Thou art King, the everlasting God."

10. Syd Lieberman in "A Short *Amidah*" in the siddur *Kol Haneshama*, offers the image of sitting in a kitchen drinking schnapps with God (Wynecote, PA: Reconstructionist Press, 1989), 184.

11. This *niggun* begins and weaves in and out of the *Vidui zutta "Ashamnu bagadnu . . . " Zamru Lo III* (New York: Cantor's Assembly 1974), 198.

12. From Robert Browning's poem "Rabbi Ben Ezra."

13. From a prayer added to the mourners' *kaddish* during Rosh Hashanah *musaf* and *minchah*. "Be not afraid of sudden terror, nor of the storm that strikes the wicked. . . . Even to your old age I will be there. When you are grey-headed, still I will sustain you; I have made you. I will carry you; I will sustain you and rescue you." Proverbs 3:25, Isaiah 8:10, 46:4.

14. From the *zichronot* section of the Rosh Hashanah *musaf amidah*, "I will keep the promise I made to you in the days of your youth." Ezekiel 16:60.

15. Refer to Al Carmines' song, "Many Gifts One Spirit": "In the midst of changing ways, give us still the grace to praise."

16. "*Mipney sevat takum, vehadarta p'nai zaken,*" Leviticus 19:32.

17. "Grey hair is a crown of glory," Proverbs 16:31.

18. This sermon, originally written for Yom Kippur, is dedicated to the three women who raised me: Mary Moers Wenig, Anna Wenig, and Molly Lane, and for the older women of Beth Am in whose faces I have seen God's face. I am grateful to my colleagues and friends Rabbi Judy Shanks and Dr. Janet Walton for their constructive criticism of early drafts of this sermon.

Commencement Beyond Fifty

1. *Pirkei Avot* 5:21 in Jacob Neusner, *The Mishnah: A New Translation* (New Haven: Yale University Press, 1988).

JOURNEYS AND DISCOVERIES

From Age-ing to Sage-ing
1. This is built on a base of seven years. Moses' life was based on a model of ten years—and we are approaching this basis more as our life span increases. Moses' life reached 120 years, based on twelve months of ten years. I'm building my model on a shorter life span of approximately seven to ten years per month of life.

Have You Seen Sarah?
1. Abraham for a male.
2. *Learn Torah With* . . . vol. 1 no. 3, Torah Aura Productions, 1994.
3. Celebration of Wisdom.
4. *Likutey Halakhot,* Tefilin 5.6.
5. *Four Centuries of Jewish Women's Spirituality: A Sourcebook,* eds. Ellen M. Umansky and Dianne Ashton (Boston, Beacon Press, 1994), 264.
6. Genesis 17:17.
7. Genesis 18:13.
8. Genesis 18:12.

MEETING THE CHALLENGES OF AGING

Saving Broken Tablets: Planning for the Spiritual Needs of Jews in Long-Term Facilities
1. Sheldon Tobin, James W. Ellor, and Susan M. Anderson-Ray, "Aging in a Modern Society," in *Enabling the Elderly: Religious Institutions Within the Community Service System* (Albany: SUNY Press, 1986), 4.
2. This is how "spiritual well-being" has been defined by the National Interfaith Coalition on Aging.
3. Cathy Young, "Spirituality and the Chronically-Ill Christian Elderly," Geriatric Nursing 14, no. 6 (1993): 198.
4. I will not discuss maintaining *kashrut* and a schedule of activities especially designed for Shabbat and Jewish Holidays. These are already widely acknowledged to be essential in promoting a Jewish religious ambience in nursing homes. Since my focus is on group programming, I also will not discuss the need to provide high-quality pastoral care to Jewish nursing home residents and their families, which is also extremely important in *any* nursing home run under religious auspices.
5. The population profile in many nursing homes under Jewish auspices is also changing in terms of religious affiliation and identification. For various reasons, most "Jewish" nursing homes no longer cater exclusively to Jews.

MEETING THE CHALLENGES OF AGING

Growing Old on an Israeli Kibbutz

1. I am indebted to the members of the *Va'ad* (elder members' committee) who took time from their busy schedules to speak with me and provided me with current and valuable information. In specific, I would like to thank the then-director of Aging Affairs, a member of Kibbutz Jezreel, Dr. Gavrush Nechushtan, whose dedication and commitment to serving seniors is beyond measure. Dr. Nechushtan is currently chairperson of "Or," a nascent organization trying to establish hospice programs in Israel.

2. Gavrush Nechushtan, "Quality of Work for the Elderly: The Kibbutz Example," an unpublished paper presented at the International Conference of Jewish Homes and Housing for the Aging, held in Jerusalem in 1988.

3. Shulamit Reinharz, "Creating Utopia for the Elderly," *Society* (January/February 1988): 57.

POETRY AND STORIES

Ruth and Naomi

1. This *midrash* is dedicated to the memory of my dear friend, Goldie Gardner; may her memory be for a blessing.

CEREMONIES

1. Barbara Myerhoff, "Bobbes and Zeydes: Old and New Roles for Elderly Jews," in *Remembered Lives,* ed. Marc Kaminsky (Ann Arbor: University of Michigan Press, 1991), 209.

A Testament to Growing Older: The Av/Em Eitza Program

1. Ernest Becker, *The Denial of Death* (New York: The Free Press, 1975), 215.
2. Ibid., 5.
3. See Elliott Jaques, "Death and the Midlife Crisis," in *Death Interpretations,* ed. H. M. Ruitenbeek (New York: Dell Publishing Co., 1969).

An End to the Body's Silence

1. This structural suggestion comes from a brilliant ritual known as a Ceremony of Celebration and Remembrance created by Rabbi Mitch Chefitz and others at the National Havurah Institute during the summer of 1991.

Havdalah

1. Savina J. Teubal, *"Simchat Chochmah," Four Centuries of Jewish Women's Spirituality,* ed. Ellen M. Umansky and Dianne Ashton (Boston: Beacon Press, 1992), 257–265.

2. Marcia Lee Falk, *The Book of Blessings: A Feminist Jewish Reconstruction of Prayer* (San Francisco: HarperCollins, 1996).

3. *"MiShebeirach,"* lyrics by Debbie Friedman and Drorah Setel, and "Miriam's Song," lyrics by Debbie Friedman, were written for this occasion. Music ©1988 by Deborah Lynn Friedman. *And You Shall Be a Blessing.* ASCAP, SoundsWrite Productions, Inc. This recording also includes the music written for Savina Teubal's *Simchat Chochmah.*

4. I was fortunate to have brilliant Jewish women help plan my ritual: Savina Teubal created the ceremony on which it was based, Drorah Setel coordinated and facilitated the service, Marcia Falk wrote new blessings, Debbie Friedman wrote new music, Sue Levi Elwell shared in facilitating the service, and Aviva Rosenbloom added her sweet voice to the ceremony.

A Personal "Seder" to Celebrate Aging

1. A special debt of gratitude is owed to Joyce Foster for her faith in me and for her support, and to Matia Angelou for inspiration, encouragement, and suggestions for this ceremony. The ceremony was initially inspired by Phyllis Ocean Berman's "Recreating Menopause" in *Moment,* February 1994.

   A note on procedures: As this ceremony takes between four and five hours, eating and drinking at appropriate times during the seder are encouraged. If people gather in the afternoon, a light lunch might be provided while they are waiting for all guests to arrive. Similarly, for evening events, a light supper might be appropriate.

   For the four ritual cups, the host should have the following drinks available: spring water, cranberry or other red juice, milk, chocolate syrup, seltzer, and sparkling wine (optional). For the ceremonial plate, an orange, fresh mint, nutmeg (and grater), a rose, chocolate, and yellow raisins are needed. Other foods, including fresh fruit and vegetables, kugels, and desserts are optional.

   Special candles and ribbons in the celebrant's favorite colors should be provided. Prior to assembling, guests could be asked to lead readings or songs.

   Other hints: Limiting the guests to eight to twelve is advised so that each person has time to share in the ritual. Using a stone or crystal (like the Native American talking stick) is one way to focus attention on any given speaker. The object is passed to each person in turn around the circle, and no one interrupts or speaks out of turn.

   A note on the blessings: Because Hebrew is not a gender-neutral language, all references to God are traditionally in the masculine forms. This creates a difficulty if one's image of God is neither male nor female. The language in this ceremony has been adapted to include feminine forms (such as *Shechinah*) to counter the image of God as exclusively male. Nonhierarchical forms such as "Source of Life," rather than "King of the world" are also used at times along with the traditional references. Participants may adapt the blessings to suit their needs.

2. *Siddur Kol Haneshamah: Sabbath Eve* (Wynecote, PA: Reconstructionist Press, 1989), 203.
3. Ibid., 101.
4. Available on the CD and cassette *Gather Round* from Oyster Records, P.O. Box 3929, Berkeley, CA 94703.
5. Kol Isha. For more information about Kos Miriam, contact Nishmat HaNashim, P.O. Box 132, Wayland, MA 01778.
6. © Kol Isha.
7. *Kol Haneshamah*, 137.
8. Anne Tolbert, 1994.
9. Marilyn Zuckerman "After Sixty," in *Poems of the Sixth Decade* (Cambridge, MA: Garden Street Press, 1993).

Let Your Heart Take Courage: A Ceremony for Entering a Nursing Home

1. Bernice Neugarten, quoted in *Enabling the Elderly: Religious Institutions With the Community Service System* by Sheldon Tobin, James W. Ellor, and Susan M. Anderson Ray (Albany, NY: SUNY Press, 1986), 4.
2. Psalm 121.
3. From Psalm 27.
4. "Toward Caesarea" by Hannah Senesh, from *Hannah Senesh: Her Life and Diary* (New York: Schocken Books, 1972).

APPENDICES

A Guide to Jewish Textual Sources on Aging

1. This schema draws on the work of Rabbi Steven Carr Rueben in the *Journal of Psychology and Judaism* 16:3 (Fall 1992) as well as Rachel Z. Dulin, "The Elderly in Biblical Society," *The Journal of Aging and Judaism* 1:1 (Fall/Winter 1986). I would also like to thank Rabbi Danny Siegel for drawing my attention to some of this source material, particularly the Talmudic passages which he translated.
2. Translation by Sheldon Isenberg.

INDEX

About JEWISH LIGHTS Publishing

People of all faiths and backgrounds yearn for books that attract, engage, educate and spiritually inspire.

Our principal goal is to stimulate thought and help all people learn about who the Jewish People are, where they come from, and what the future can be made to hold. While people of our diverse Jewish heritage are the primary audience, our books speak to people in the Christian world as well and will broaden their understanding of Judaism and the roots of their own faith.

We bring to you authors who are at the forefront of spiritual thought and experience. While each has something different to say, they all say it in a voice that you can hear.

Our books are designed to welcome you and then to engage, stimulate and inspire. We judge our success not only by whether or not our books are beautiful and commercially successful, but by whether or not they make a difference in your life.

We at Jewish Lights take great care to produce beautiful books that present meaningful spiritual content in a form that reflects the art of making high quality books. Therefore, we want to acknowledge those who contributed to the production of this book.

EDITORIAL & PROOFREADING
Sandra Korinchak / Jennifer Goneau

PRODUCTION
Maria O'Donnell

JACKET DESIGN
Karen Savary, Deering, New Hampshire

BOOK DESIGN & TYPESETTING
Set in Meridien
Sans Serif, Saline, Michigan

INDEXING
Anna Chapman, Arlington, Vermont

CPSIA information can be obtained
at www.ICGtesting.com
Printed in the USA
LVHW112228240119
605217LV00001B/184/P

9 781580 230513